THE SECTARIAN MILIEU

THE SECTARIAN MILIEU

CONTENT AND COMPOSITION OF ISLAMIC SALVATION HISTORY

JOHN WANSBROUGH

Foreword, Translations, and Expanded Notes
by Gerald Hawting

Prometheus Books
59 John Glenn Drive
Amherst, New York 14228–2197

Published 2006 by Prometheus Books

Inquiries should be addressed to
Prometheus Books
59 John Glenn Drive
Amherst, New York 14228–2197
VOICE: 716–691–0133, ext. 207
FAX: 716–564–2711
WWW.PROMETHEUSBOOKS.COM

10 09 08 07 06   5 4 3 2 1

Library of Congress Cataloging-in-Publication Data

Wansbrough, John E., 1928–2002
The sectarian milieu : content and composition of Islamic salvation history / by John Wansbrough ; foreword, translations, and expanded notes by Gerald Hawting.
p. cm.
Includes bibliographical references and index.
Originally published: Oxford; New York: Oxford University Press, 1978, in series : London oriental series.
ISBN 1–59102–378–5 (alk. paper)
1. Islam—Doctrines—History. I. Title.

BP166.1.W26 2006
297.209'021—dc22

2005056643

Printed in the United States of America on acid-free paper

CONTENTS

FOR MY CHILDREN

FOREWORD

In this companion work to his *Quranic Studies*, which had been published a year earlier (1977), Wansbrough is concerned with Muslim literature beyond the Qur'ān and the exegetical tradition associated with it, the focus of the earlier work. Here he analyses early forms (that is, texts dating mainly from the third/ninth and fourth/tenth centuries) of traditional lives of the prophet Muhammad (*sīra* and *maghāzī* literature), of legal texts (which he referred to generically as *sunna* since they stress the importance of precedent as a source of legitimacy), of polemical and apologetic works (Muslim and non-Muslim), and of theological arguments (*kalām*). While only the first of those categories is explicitly historical in form (in the sense that it is concerned to narrate events that occurred in the past), Wansbrough examines them all under the rubric of "salvation history" since, in his analysis, they all in one way or another raise questions about the way the past was understood and used.

Salvation history or Heilsgeschichte is a term coined around the middle of the twentieth century in the study of the Bible to designate accounts of the past that present it (whether explicitly or implicitly) as directed by God towards a future end. In it human actors and groups are instruments of divine providence and all events have a significance in relation to God's plan. As literature, salvation history shares many formal characteristics with profane history, and it refers to events that actually occurred, but it is essentially concerned with the proclamation of a religious truth (kerygma) and not with accurate and objective portrayal of the past for its own sake.

It is probably his use of the term "salvation history" to refer to the accounts and understanding of the past contained in early Islamic texts of the sort discussed in *The Sectarian Milieu* that, above all, has led to a widespread view of Wansbrough as pessimistic and negative about the possibility of understanding the formation of Islam. By calling the Muslim tradition on the rise of Islam salvation history, it is felt, he diminished it as a source for the writing of "real" history. He has often been seen as the most prominent representative of the "sceptical" school of historians concerned with the early history of Islam.

Contesting the approach of Wansbrough and several other scholars understood to have been associated with or in some way influenced by him, Fred Donner has written, "the practical implications for modern historians are that we cannot use the Islamic sources to reconstruct Islamic origins, and should look elsewhere for our evidence, or quit trying altogether". In the accompanying footnote Donner suggested that Wansbrough thought that looking elsewhere is futile.[1]

Wansbrough's own words may certainly be used to reinforce that impression. In his introduction and at times during *The Sectarian Milieu* he describes his task as one of literary analysis and insists that such analysis cannot tell us "what really happened" (*wie es eigentlich gewesen*, using the expression of the nineteenth-century German historian Leopold von Ranke whose ideal Wansbrough and many other twentieth-century historians used as a foil to set off their own understanding of the writing of history). He confesses to scepticism about the possibility of describing the past in that way, and offers an understanding of history that asserts the writing of it as a form of literature. He minimises the difference between the writing of history and other forms of literature such as poetry or novels. He frequently draws attention to the lateness of the texts relative to the events they purport to be reporting or describing.

It is clear, however, that he does not thereby suggest that we abandon the attempt to understand the past or that nothing can be said about the rise of Islam. His unwillingness to attempt a detailed narrative account of the first two centuries of Islam based on Islamic texts that at first sight offer the prospect of doing so is more than compensated for by an analysis and exploitation of those texts in different ways. The result is certainly historical. Only those who wish to write all history as a narrative of events, people and places would fail to be stimulated by and learn much from his alternative approach.

Faced with historical or any other form of literature, it seems, Wansbrough's first question is to ask why it exists in the form in which it does. What can be said about its origins, purpose and functions? The literature can, naturally, contain real memories of the past, but Wansbrough insists that history is not a random or arbitrary collection of such memories. What is remembered is what is thought important by those who make the effort to remember it, and remembrance is always accompanied by a continuing process of interpretation and reinterpretation. Furthermore, the way in which memory, interpretation and reinterpretation are recorded is subject to the literary forms available (and he considers that salvation history was the only form available, given the nature of the early community, for reporting the origins of Islam). Apart perhaps from the last statement, none of that seems especially provocative or unusual in contemporary thinking about history. What is innovative, though, are the suggestions he makes about the origins and nature of the Islamic literature, and about the way we should envisage the emergence of the new religion and culture.

SM is presented as a work of literary analysis. Its subtitle tells us that it is concerned with the "content and composition of Islamic salvation history". Many pages, indeed, are devoted to close analysis of reasonably long passages from the types of

1. Donner, *Narratives of Islamic Origins*, 25 and n. 65.

early Islamic literature examined in the book, and much of the analysis is concerned with style, genre, rhetorical figures and other such literary issues. However, the book is emphatically not one of interest only to students of Arabic literature, and the reason for that is that the literary analysis is related to questions and themes that must be important for anyone attempting to understand the origins and the nature of Islam.

Among such major questions and themes are: the tension evident between the concept of salvation as an event (the revelation) and that of it as a continuing process (the history of the community); the possibility of defining the essential nature of the Islamic community, using ideal types of the sort suggested by the early-twentieth-century sociologist of religion, Max Weber; and the underlying or implied ideas concerning knowledge of and attitudes to the past. Wansbrough is quite unusual among academic scholars of Islam in addressing questions of that sort. The Austrian American Gustave von Grunebaum (d. 1972), a scholar whom Wansbrough clearly admired, is one of the few comparable who comes readily to mind. Such questions indicate the way in which Wansbrough's ideas were fertilised from outside the narrow sphere of Islamic Studies.

In each case, as might be expected, the discussions are subtle and complex, reflecting the fact that the evidence is susceptible to different interpretations, that there are various ideas competing with one another, and that ideas and institutions change over time. Wansbrough seeks to come to conclusions while doing full justice to the complexity of the material, and that involves the reader in putting an effort into following his interpretations and arguments.

The difficulty of Wansbrough's writing has been frequently commented on. As Andrew Rippin pointed out in his foreword to the republication of *Quranic Studies*, that has something to do with the fact that he was addressing fellow scholars and not a wider public. He did not, therefore, feel obliged to expand his allusions or avoid technical expressions, and since his erudition was considerably more extensive than that of most of his readers, for most of them reading him is something of a challenge.

Some seem to have felt that he adopted a deliberately obscure and difficult style in order to conceal his views from the general public, perhaps out of fear for his personal safety. I am sure that that is not the case. If one reads his other academic work—in areas less contentious than Quranic Studies and the origins of Islam—it is apparent that the written style is consistent. It seems to me that what makes him difficult, apart from his erudition and the high academic register of his language, is that he always strove to say exactly what he meant, no more and no less. His conclusions are frequently put forward with several qualifications. That makes demands on readers expecting simpler and more clear-cut results, but it does justice to complex evidence and challenging research questions. To read Wansbrough in the expectation of snappy answers and memorable facts is out of keeping with his understanding of the task of the historian.

It would be pointless and misleading to attempt here a summary of his conclusions. The discussions that lead to them (and their tentative and provisional nature are often stressed) are as valuable as the conclusions themselves, and the care with which he expresses them means that attempts to summarise risk simplification and distortion. He provides his own outline of the book's argument in his preface (pp. ix–x) and a fuller summation of them at pages 138–40.

However, the discussion of the texts and the issues that arise out of them clearly relate to an image of how Islam emerged that is not argued for or set out in any sustained way in the book. The historical model within which the literary analysis works is to some extent assumed, and to some extent alluded to at different places. It may be useful, therefore, to try to present a rather more explicit and cohesive account of it, and to contrast it with more traditional models. How far it arises from or is supported by the literary analysis, and how far it precedes and determines the analysis, is something readers may wish to consider.

The tradition, naturally, tends to equate the emergence of Islam with the career of the prophet Muhammad. Although it is accepted that the full elaboration of Muslim ritual, beliefs and institutions was only accomplished following his death, in essence they are seen as formed under divine guidance in the lifetime of Muhammad himself. Thus, for example, although the theory and content of the law only came to be set out in texts dating from the late second/eighth century at the earliest, those texts and the scholars responsible for them are regarded by traditional Muslims as largely formalising and systematising ideas and practices that had been transmitted in the community previously in a looser, mainly oral, manner. The Qur'ān itself is another example of something that the tradition presents as being fixed in a written form, and its written expression subsequently improved, after the death of the prophet, but its contents, its basic form, and above all its status as scripture established already by the time of his death. Because of that and other such postulated developments, traditional scholars would have considered it meaningful to talk of Islam as a religion and community by the time of Muhammad's demise in 632 CE and to see the conquest of the Middle East by the Arabs, beginning in the same decade, as both motivated by the desire for, and achieving, the expansion of Islam.

A concomitant of that view would be that there was a united and pristine Islamic community at the very start under prophetic guidance and that the divisions within Islam that have been known since are to be understood as deviations from that original pure state. Usually, within the tradition itself, the observer identifies his own form of Islam as the historical continuation of the original community and other forms as deviations.

Academic scholarship has, naturally, often not been willing to accept the traditional approach in all its details. Some important constituents of Islam—notably the *ḥadīth*s and the theory and content of Islamic law—have been interpreted by scholars such as Ignaz Goldziher and Joseph Schacht as developments substantially later than the time of the prophet. Many have argued that when it came out of Arabia, Islam entered a world with complex and diverse religious traditions already in existence, and that Islam as we know it is the outcome of the meeting between Arabian Islam and the older traditions of the Middle East. Nevertheless, it is frequently assumed that what came from Arabia was already substantially developed and may be referred to as Islam. The state and community that the Arabs established in the Middle East is understood as the continuation of the essentially religious community and state founded by the Prophet. Events were motivated by and intimately connected with the religion of Islam.

Wansbrough, in contrast, describes Islam as the outcome of a process that occupied at least two centuries following the Arab conquests. It is clear that he is dubious regarding the contribution of Arabia to the outcome, reading much of the literature that seems to attest to the Arabian origins of Islam as deliberately aiming to produce that image. He sees the idea that Islam originated in Arabia as of central importance in Islam's own self-image, but essentially misleading. The state that resulted from the Arab conquests (and some of the events associated with it that are traditionally read as evidence of its religious orientation), in his understanding, was essentially religiously neutral, subsequently given an Islamic colouring by the way it is portrayed in the historical tradition. To the extent that the Arab conquerors had monotheist religious ideas and practices, he did not regard them as sufficiently distinct or developed to provide an independent religious identity.

Only gradually following the conquests did the new religion of Islam become a distinct form of the monotheist tradition. That was achieved by the elaboration of practices and dogmas selected as much for their symbolic associations and their ability to stand as markers of distinctiveness as for their inherent values. Wansbrough's understanding of the origins of Islam is of the elaboration of a range of institutions and practices—scripture, the idea of a prophet, ritual, sacred language, etc.—each of which would have been required of any Middle Eastern monotheistic religion developing in the Middle East at that time. Each constituent takes some time to be developed and only when a significant number of them have evolved in a reasonably elaborate form can we talk of the existence of Islam with any real meaning. That would certainly not have been the case in the time of Muhammad.

Consistent with this is his view (influenced by Bauer's analysis of the emergence of a Christian orthodoxy) of Islamic orthodoxy as subsequent to "heterodoxy" (or early competing orthodoxies). Early Islam would be characterised thus by a diversity of forms, beliefs and practices, and what came to be widely viewed as the orthodox tradition—the Sunni Islam of the majority of Muslims—would only have later established itself as such (in the third/ninth century and later), the result of a combination of some inherent advantages over its rivals and political factors that were fortuitous.

More important than the Hijaz in the time of Muhammad in generating what was to become Islam is what Wansbrough here refers to as the sectarian milieu. He sees the seeds of Islam in arguments and polemics among monotheist groups outside the major established religious traditions of the Middle East. Those arguments and polemics generated separatist religious communities (or sects) at first hardly distinguishable from many others but over time becoming more distinct. That is a recurrent feature of sectarianism and sometimes the groups that emerge remain relatively unimportant or mere variants of bigger and more important ones. Sometimes, for a variety of possible reasons, they may eventually become major, independent versions of Middle Eastern monotheism. Islam is one such group that made that transition.

In *SM* he is not primarily concerned to identify the specific source from which what became Islam arose, but it is clear that he regards Judaeo-Christianity as of particular importance. That term can be quite ambiguous and mean different things in different contexts, but almost (if not all) instances of it in *SM* refer to the religious tradition that a number of contemporary scholars prefer to call Jewish Christianity, groups which in general maintained allegiance to the Mosaic law but accepted Jesus as a prophet and messiah. They rejected the Pauline understanding of Christianity, and had various views about the nature of Jesus, some but not all of them, it is reported, accepting his virgin birth. Wansbrough sometimes refers to them as Ebionite, apparently using that term in a very broad and general sense rather than with reference to any particular sect or sub-group among them.

To associate what became Islam with one or another pre-Islamic monotheist group is an established procedure in academic scholarship. As well as Jewish Christianity, scholars have referred to religious traditions such as Samaritanism and a hypothetical stream within Judaism connecting the group that produced the Dead Sea Scrolls around the beginning of the Christian era (the Qumran community) with Karaism, a major form of Judaism that rivalled Rabbinical Judaism in the mediaeval Muslim world. In addition, scholars have sought to link Islam with more mainstream forms of Christianity and Judaism, with Manichaeism, Zoroastrianism, and with other religious groups. It should be remembered that in the seventh and eighth centuries there was a great diversity of religion in the Middle East, monotheist and non-monotheist, and the religious situation was undoubtedly richer and more complex than is evident from the available historical evidence. Even Rabbinical Judaism was a tradition still very much in the process of formation.

Wansbrough adopts this approach, however, in a way rather different from most other scholars who have followed it. Typically, scholars have postulated the existence of one or another religious group in Arabia and suggested how Muhammad might have come into contact with it and been influenced to develop the ideas to which he gave expression as Islam. This is often put as the operation of "influences" or acceptance of "borrowings". For example, many academic scholars, concerned with the common monotheist or biblical stories and allusions that one finds in the Qurʾān, have assumed that Muhammad must have come to know them by coming into contact with Jews or Christians of various sorts, usually in Arabia but perhaps on journeys that the traditional accounts tell us he made to Syria as a young man.

Wansbrough entirely eschews the idea of influences or borrowings of this sort, which assume an already existing entity that can be influenced from outside. He does not talk of Muhammad coming into contact with sectarian circles but understands the religion that will eventually evolve into Islam as arising out of the sectarian circles themselves. There is no suggestion here of something that already exists taking on foreign characteristics, but of Islam as the further development of tendencies already there in sectarian monotheist circles. Furthermore, he does not envisage Arabia as the likely setting for this, but the regions outside Arabia where the existence of such groups is attested before Islam. In fact, explicit evidence for the survival of Jewish Christianity, whether in Arabia or elsewhere in the Middle East, is sparse if not entirely non-existent, historical attestation of it apparently ceasing in the third or fourth centuries. Those scholars who have sought to connect Islam with that tradition have had to draw inferences from such things as what they interpret as the Judaeo-Christian nature of the Christology of the Qur'ān, and the doctrine of the corruption of scripture, usually referred to in Islam under the rubric of *taḥrīf*, the subject of considerable discussion in *SM*.[1]

His suggestion, although not spelled out in detail, is that a religious elite responsible for elaborating the beginnings of Islam in the sectarian setting was able to establish a relationship with the originally religiously undefined Arab state so that gradually Islam became a symbol of association with that state and the early history of the state came to be defined as the early history of Islam. The earliest Islamic literature that has come down to us, typified by its concern with polemic and issues of authority, is a result of that process.

This conception of the way in which Islam emerged clearly owes much to Wansbrough's familiarity with scholarly literature on the early history of Christianity and developments within Judaism in the early Christian period. The discovery of the Dead Sea Scrolls in the late 1940s gave impetus and a vast amount of additional material to an already developed tradition of scholarship on forms of monotheism beyond mainstream Christianity and Judaism, and Wansbrough frequently alludes to the debates and methodological issues throughout *SM*. This is fully in keeping with his understanding of Islam as integral to the history of Middle Eastern monotheism—something that should be studied using the same methods of critical scholarship that had been applied to the Judaeo-Christian tradition and, mutatis mutandis, as likely to have developed in the same way as other forms of the tradition.

1. E.g., Shlomo Pines, "Notes on Islam and on Arabic Christianity and Judaeo-Christianity", *Jerusalem Studies in Arabic and Islam* 4 (1984), 136–52. Pines sets out to draw "significant inferences" from the material he discusses. He does, however, draw attention to an account, stemming apparently from Arculf, a bishop of Gaul who visited Jerusalem in the time of the caliph Muʿāwiya, that refers to Christian Jews (Iudaei Christiani) in Jerusalem at the time (ibid., 145–7). Wansbrough would undoubtedly have been cautious about accepting this report as historical attestation of the fact.

In *SM*, he constantly moves between the detailed analyses of early Islamic texts and more general reflections in which he cites academic scholarship on the history of Middle Eastern monotheism beyond the study of Islam. In the traditional academic study of Islam this approach is rather uncommon, and a frequent theme in criticism of Wansbrough's work is that he made comparisons that were not appropriate, or that he tried to force Islam into a mould that did not fit. Of course, that is a matter of judgment that in many cases will reflect the critic's own presuppositions. It is apparent, however, that by using only Islam's own accounts of its origins we are unlikely to generate very different alternative possibilities.

Wansbrough's unhappiness with the traditional accounts and those academic ones that he considered mere reworkings of them did not result from any feeling that they were incoherent or logically inconsistent. It is clear from what he says about the traditional accounts of the collection of the Qur'ān in *QS* that he thought that they were plausible in their own terms. Aware as he was of the state of scholarship on other areas of the history of the monotheistic religious tradition, though, he considered the tradition-based accounts of early Islam as both unsophisticated and intellectually unsatisfying.

Ultimately, early Islam, like many other areas of history, is not a field in which many things can be proven beyond doubt in a way that compels acceptance from anyone familiar with the evidence and the arguments. What is persuasive to one reader will often seem dubious to another. Much depends on the suppositions and ideas with which one begins. Wansbrough's analysis of the texts he discusses in *SM*, and the concern he finds in them with polemic and issues of authority, is consistent with his conception of the emergence of Islam from the sectarian milieu. Clearly he will not persuade all readers of the validity of his interpretations, but there will surely be few who will not be stimulated and challenged by them.

This volume also reprints "Res Ipsa Loquitur: History and Mimesis", a lecture delivered by Wansbrough to the Israel Academy of Sciences and Humanities slightly less than a decade after the publication of *SM*. In those years he had moved away from the study of early Islam to that of the ancient (fourteenth century BCE?) polity of Ugarit (Ras Shamra) on what is now the north Syrian coast. The lecture summarises and develops some of the reflections on the nature of history as a form of literature that he had expressed in *SM* but with the added interest that here he compares two apparently quite different cases: pre-Islamic Arabia, the evidence for which consists almost entirely of literary texts (produced by Muslim and academic scholars) of the sort analysed in *SM*; and Ugarit, where the evidence is almost entirely archaeological. He is not really concerned with the conclusions that scholars in each of the two fields have put forward but with their convergent conceptions and methods. This "witty and spicy" (to use a phrase he himself employed with reference to some of the polemic discussed in *SM*) piece turned out to be a summation of his thoughts about the nature of history and the historians who write it.

Gerald Hawting
School of Oriental and African Studies, London
April 2005

PREFACE

MY purpose in these chapters is not historical reconstruction, but rather, source analysis. For the several varieties of documentation produced by the early Muslim community I have selected the term 'salvation history' for a number of what seem to me fairly cogent reasons. These are derived from a comparison with literary types generated by the Biblical paradigm, a procedure which appeared, at least to me, not merely desirable but unavoidable. The analysis is, however, stylistic and not productive of strictly historical conclusions. For a literary assessment, on the other hand, questions of facticity are of rather less significance than structural features. Of these the most obvious might be designated teleological, cumulative, kerygmatic, and nomothetic. Arrangement along a linear time-span is a characteristic of most historiography, as is the tendency to plot causality as a logical and cumulative sequence. The origin of these notions and their adoption as historical techniques are matters of philosophical rather than literary interest. But salvation history is also essentially kerygmatic, and that feature deserves in this particular context some notice. The substance of proclamation is less important than the fact of assertion, that a case is being argued, evidence gathered, and proofs adduced. In the presentation of testimonia salvation history conforms to laws of its own, and it is hardly surprising to find that those descriptions of community origins associated with the monotheist confessions exhibit more similarities than differences. Now, whether the matter proclaimed is derived from reminiscence (e.g. as an element of cultic memory) or from interpretation (e.g. as an aetiological myth) is, again, less important than the mode of expression common to both, which is historicization. Lest that observation seem dismally tautological, let me add that it is in my opinion precisely this capacity for historicizing truth which makes of salvation history a distinct literary type. It is, moreover, the creation and perpetuation of that type which distinguishes the monotheist confessions from other religious communities.

To plot the position of Islamic salvation history along that literary spectrum is the aim of this study. My first chapter contains a selective analysis of historiographical styles from the *sīra–maghāzī* literature, intended to illustrate the historicizing of memory, myth, and doctrine. These materials exhibit a fairly extensive collection of the *topoi* employed in monotheist interconfessional polemic, a fact which may account for the nomothetic character of salvation history. There, the formative principle is that of history as event. In the second chapter I have undertaken an examination of the sources of confessional authority and of the types of sectarian community derived from these. It seemed to me that emphasis upon the apostolic paradigm, taken together with the exegetical bias of halakhic terminology and the vested interests of a clerical élite, indicate a community type most aptly described as ritualist. In contrast with the midrashic styles of the *sīra–maghāzī* literature, the paradigmatic character of *sunna* as well as the evidence of juridical dispute (*ikhtilāf*) and halakhic abrogation (*naskh*), suggest a notion of history as process. In my third chapter I have attempted to trace the linguistic and literary imagery of sectarian symbolism, namely that which was eventually elaborated as the Islamic doctrines of divine attributes and abrogation. Their origin in interconfessional polemic and ultimate incorporation as dogma may be described by reference to a process which I call 'terminological transfer'. Here it may be thought that the composition of salvation history was dependent upon, and limited by, the availability of linguistic and literary resources. The fourth and final chapter contains a tentative and emphatically provisional reply to the theological question of history as event or of history as process. From my proposed epistemological categories, to be regarded as strictly experimental, it seemed not unreasonable to detect in the formation of Islam an interception of the concept 'process' by that of 'event': an original notion of development seems at some point to have been truncated and replaced by a retroflective interpretation of community origins. The result was thus not history but nostalgia.

Now, the product of source analysis can in my opinion be of value only for further source analysis, not for the quite different task of describing 'what really happened'. About the possibility of achieving the latter, at least for the topic investigated in these pages, I am frankly sceptical, much as Thomas Mann was about the enthusiasm of a stenographer who remarked, upon completing the typescript of his *Joseph und seine Brüder* 'Nun weiß man doch, wie sich das alles in Wirklichkeit zugetragen hat' (Mann, *Neue Studien*, Frankfurt, 1948, p. 160). To the anticipated objection that narrative history and novel are after all quite different literary forms, I trust that the following chapters will provide my reply.

I should like finally to express my gratitude to the School of Oriental and African Studies for granting me leave of absence to complete this book, for including it in the London Oriental Series, and for meeting the expense of publication.

February 1978 J. W.

ABBREVIATIONS

BJRL	*Bulletin of the John Rylands Library*
BSOAS	*Bulletin of the School of Oriental and African Studies*
EI	*Encyclopaedia of Islam*, second edition
GAS	F. Sezgin, *Geschichte des arabischen Schrifttums*
GCAL	G. Graf, *Geschichte der christlichen arabischen Literatur*
GdQ	T. Nöldeke and F. Schwally, *Geschichte des Qorans i–ii*
GS	I. Goldziher, *Gesammelte Schriften* (*ed. J. de Somogyi*) *i–vi*
IOS	*Israel Oriental Studies*
JAOS	*Journal of the American Oriental Society*
JESHO	*Journal of economic and social history of the Orient*
JJS	*Journal of Jewish Studies*
JQR	*Jewish Quarterly Review*
JSS	*Journal of Semitic Studies*
MSOS	*Mitteilungen des Seminars für orientalische Sprachen*
MUSJ	*Mélanges de l'Université Saint-Joseph*
MW	*Muslim World*
POC	*Proche-Orient chrétien*
QS	J. Wansbrough, *Quranic Studies*
REI	*Revue des études Islamiques*
RHR	*Revue de l'Histoire des Religions*
ROC	*Revue de l'Orient chrétien*
RSO	*Rivista degli studi orientali*
ZDMG	*Zeitschrift der deutschen morgenländischen Gesellschaft*

BIBLIOGRAPHY

Abbott, N. *Qur'ānic commentary and tradition*, University of Chicago Press, 1967

Abel, A. 'Le Chapitre CI du Livre des Hérésies de Jean Damascène: son inauthenticité', *Studia Islamica* xix (1963) 5–25

—— 'Changements politiques et littérature eschatologique dans le monde musulman', ibid. ii (1954) 23–43

—— 'L'Apocalypse de Baḥīra et la notion islamique de Mahdī', *Annuaire de l'Institut de Philologie et Histoire orientale* iii (1935) 1–12

—— 'Le Chapitre sur l'imāmat dans le Tamhīd d'al-Bāqillānī', *Le Shīʿisme imāmite*, Paris, 1970, 55–67

Abū Qurra. *Mayāmir Thāudūrus Abī Qurra* (ed. C. Bāshā), Beirut, 1904

Ahrens, K. 'Christliches im Qoran', *ZDMG* lxxxiv (1930) 15–68, 148–90

Albeck, C. *Einführung in die Mischna*, Berlin, 1971

Allard, M. *Analyse conceptuelle du Coran sur cartes perforées*, Paris, 1963

Alt, A. *Kleine Schriften zur Geschichte des Volkes Israel* i–ii, München, 1953

Andrae, T. *Les Origines de l'islam et le christianisme*, Paris, 1955

—— *Die Person Muhammeds in Lehre und Glauben seiner Gemeinde*, Stockholm, 1918

Anīs, Ibrāhīm. *Mūsīqā 'l-shiʿr*, Cairo, 1952

ʿArafat, W. 'Early critics of the authenticity of the poetry of the Sīra', *BSOAS* xxi (1958) 453–63

—— 'An aspect of the forger's art in early Islamic poetry', *BSOAS* xxviii (1965) 477–82

—— 'The historical significance of later Anṣārī poetry I–II', *BSOAS* xxix (1966) 1–11, 221–32

Arkoun, M. 'Logocentrisme et vérité religieuse dans la pensée islamique', *Studia Islamica* xxxv (1972) 5–51

Aune, D. *The Cultic setting of realized eschatology in early Christianity*, Leiden, 1972

Bacher, W. *Die exegetische Terminologie der jüdischen Traditionsliteratur* i–ii, Hildesheim, 1965

Bāqillānī. *Kitāb al-Tamhīd* (ed. R. McCarthy), Beirut, 1957

Barr, J. *The semantics of Biblical language*, Oxford, 1961

Barrett, C. 'Jews and Judaizers in the Epistles of Ignatius', in *Jews, Greeks and Christians* (Festschrift W. Davies), Leiden, 1976, 220–44

Barth, C. 'Zur Bedeutung der Wüstentradition', *Vetus Testamentum*, Suppl. xv (1966) 14–23

Barthes, R. 'Historical discourse', in M. Lane (ed.), *Structuralism: a reader*, London, 1970, 145–55

Bartsch, H. *Kerygma and myth: a theological debate* i–ii, London, 1972

Bauer, W. *Rechtgläubigkeit und Ketzerei im ältesten Christentum* (2nd edn. G. Strecker), Tübingen, 1964

Baumstark, A. 'Jüdischer und christlicher Gebetstypus im Koran', *Der Islam* xvi (1927) 229–48

—— 'Das Problem eines vorislamischen christlich-kirchlichen Schrifttums in arabischer Sprache', *Islamica* iv (1931) 562–75

Becker, C. 'Christliche Polemik und islamische Dogmenbildung', *Islamstudien* i–ii, Hildesheim, 1967, i, 432–49

—— 'Der Islam als Problem', ibid. i, 1–23

—— 'Der Islam im Rahmen einer allgemeinen Kulturgeschichte', ibid. i, 24–39

Berger, P. *The social reality of religion*, London, 1973

Betz, O. *Offenbarung und Schriftforschung in der Qumransekte*, Tübingen, 1960

Bianchi, U. *Le origini dello gnosticismo*, Leiden, 1970

Bishop, E. 'The Qumran scrolls and the Qur'ān', *MW* xlviii (1958) 223–36

Blau, J. 'Sind uns Reste arabischer Bibelübersetzungen aus vorislamischer Zeit erhalten geblieben?', *Le Muséon* lxxxvi (1973) 67–72

—— *A Grammar of Christian Arabic, based mainly on South Palestinian texts from the first millennium*, CSCO Subsidia 27–9, Louvain, 1966–7

Bouyges, M. 'Nos informations sur ʿAliy . . . aṭ-Ṭabarī', *MUSJ* xxviii (1949–50) 69–114

Brandon, S. *History, time and deity*, Manchester University Press, 1965

Bravmann, M. *The spiritual background of early Islam*, Leiden, 1972

—— *Studies in Semitic philology*, Leiden, 1977

Browne, L. 'The Patriarch Timothy and the Caliph Al-Mahdī', *MW* xxi (1931) 38–45

Brunschvig, R. 'L'Argumentation d'un théologien musulman du xᵉ siècle contre le judaïsme', *Homenaje a Millas-Vallicrosa* i (Barcelona, 1954) 225–41

Buhl. F. 'Ein paar Beiträge zur Kritik der Geschichte Muhammed's', *Orientalische Studien Theodor Nöldeke . . . gewidmet*, Giessen, 1906, i, 7–22

Bukhārī, *Al-Saḥīḥ* (ed. L. Krehl), Leiden, 1868

Bultmann, R. *Theology of the New Testament* i–ii, London, 1965

Burton, J. *The collection of the Qur'ān*, Cambridge, 1977

—— 'Those are the high-flying cranes', *JSS* xv (1970) 246–65

Cahen, C. 'Note sur l'accueil des chrétiens d'Orient à l'islam', *RHR* clxvi (1964) 51–8

Caskel, W. 'Aijām al-ʿarab: Studien zur altarabischen Epik', *Islamica* iii (Suppl.) 1931

Cheikho, L. 'Al-Muḥāwara al-dīniyya . . . bayna 'l-khalīfa Al-Mahdī wa-Tīmāthāus al-jathālīq', *Al-Machriq* xix (1921) 359–74, 408–18

—— *Vingt traités théologiques (d'auteurs arabes chrétiens)*, Beirut, 1920

—— 'Un traité inédit de Honein', *Orientalische Studien Theodor Nöldeke . . . gewidmet*, Giessen, 1906, i, 283–91

Colpe, C. 'Anpassung des Manichäismus an den Islam' (Abū ʿĪsā al-Warrāq)', *ZDMG* (1959) 82–91

Corcos, D. *Studies in the history of the Jews of Morocco*, Jerusalem, 1976

Crone, P. and Cook, M. *Hagarism: the making of the Islamic world*, Cambridge, 1977

Culler, J. *Structuralist poetics: structuralism, linguistics and the study of literature*, London, 1975

Daube, D. *The New Testament and Rabbinic Judaism*, London, 1956

Davies, W. *Paul and Rabbinic Judaism*, London, 1970

Dentan, R. *The idea of history in the ancient Near East*, Yale University Press, 1955

Dick, I. 'Théodore Abū Qurra, évêque melkite de Harrān: la personne et son milieu', *POC* xii (1962) 209–23, 319–32; xiii (1963) 114–29

Eichner, W. 'Die Nachrichten über den Islam bei den Byzantinern', *Der Islam* xxiii (1936) 133–62, 197–244

Eliash, J. 'The Shīʿite Qur'ān: a reconsideration of Goldziher's interpretation', *Arabica* xvi (1969) 15–24

Engnell, I. 'Methodological aspects of Old Testament study', *Vetus Testamentum*, Suppl. vii (1960) 13–30

Ess, J. van. *Zwischen Ḥadīṯ und Theologie: Studien zum Entstehen prädestinatianischer Überlieferung*, Berlin, 1975

—— 'Ein unbekanntes Fragment des Naẓẓām', *Der Orient in der Forschung* (Festschrift für O. Spies), Wiesbaden, 1967, 170–201

—— *Das Kitāb an-Nakṯ des Naẓẓām und seine Rezeption im Kitāb al-Futyā des Ǧāḥiẓ*, Göttingen, 1972

—— 'Das *Kitāb Al-Irgā'* des Ḥasan B. Muḥammad B. Al-Ḥanafiyya', *Arabica* xxi (1974) 20–52

—— 'Maʿbad Al-Ǧuhanī', *Islamwissenschaftliche Abhandlungen* (Festschrift F. Meier), Wiesbaden, 1974, 49–77

—— 'Ḍirār b. ʿAmr und die "Cahmīya": Biographie einer vergessenen Schule', *Der Islam* xliii (1967) 241–79; xliv (1968), 1–70, 318–20

—— 'Les Qadarites et la Ġailānīya de Yazīd III', *Studia Islamica* xxxi (1970) 269–86

—— 'The beginnings of Islamic theology', *The Cultural Context of Medieval Learning*, Dordrecht, 1975, 87–111

Finkel, J. 'Jewish, Christian, and Samaritan influences on Arabia', *MacDonald Presentation Volume*, Princeton, 1933, 147–66

Fischel, H. *Rabbinic literature and Greco-Roman philosophy*, Leiden, 1973

Flusser, D. 'The Dead Sea Sect and pre-Pauline Christianity', *Scripta Hierosolymitana* iv (Jerusalem, 1965) 215–66

—— 'The four empires in the Fourth Sibyl and in the Book of Daniel', *IOS* ii (1972) 148–75

—— 'Salvation present and future', *Types of Redemption* (eds. Werblowsky–Bleeker), Leiden, 1970, 46–61

Fohrer, G. *Geschichte der israelitischen Religion*, Berlin, 1969

Fritsch, E. *Islam und Christentum im Mittelalter: Beiträge zur Geschichte der muslimischen Polemik gegen das Christentum in arabischer Sprache*, Breslau, 1930

Fück, J. 'Die Originalität des arabischen Propheten', *ZDMG* xc (1936) 509–25

García Gómez, E. 'Polémica religiosa entre Ibn Ḥazm e Ibn Al-Nagrīla', *Andalus* iv (1936–9) 1–28

Gardet, L. *La Cité musulmane: vie sociale et politique*, Paris, 1961

Gerhardsson, B. *Memory and manuscript: oral tradition and written transmission in Rabbinic Judaism and early Christianity*, Copenhagen, 1964

Gertner, M. 'The Masorah and the Levites: an essay in the history of a concept', *Vetus Testamentum* x (1960) 241–84

—— 'The terms pharisaioi, gazarenoi, hupokritai: their semantic complexity and conceptual correlation', *BSOAS* xxvi (1963) 245–68

Gibson, M. 'On the Triune nature of God', *Studia Sinaitica* vii, London, 1899

Goitein, S. *Studies in Islamic history and institutions*, Leiden, 1966

Goldin, J. 'Of change and adaptation in Judaism', *History of Religions* iv (1964–5) 269–94

Goldziher, I. *Die Richtungen der islamischen Koranauslegung*, Leiden, 1920

—— *Vorlesungen über den Islam*, Heidelberg, 1910

—— *Muhammedanische Studien* i–ii, Halle, 1889–90

—— 'Kämpfe um die Stellung des Ḥadīṯ im Islam', *GS* v, 86–98

—— 'Le Dénombrement des sectes mohametanes', *GS* ii, 406–14

—— 'Beiträge zur Literaturgeschichte der Šīʿa und der sunnitischen Polemik', *GS* i, 261–346

Gombrich, E. *In search of cultural history*, Oxford, 1974

Goodblatt, D. *Rabbinic instruction in Sasanian Babylonia*, Leiden, 1975

Graf, G. 'Disputation zwischen Muslimen und Christen', *Veröffentlichungen aus den badischen Papyrus-Sammlungen*, Heft 5, Heidelberg, 1934

—— *Geschichte der christlichen arabischen Literatur* i–v, Citta del Vaticano, 1944–53

—— *Die arabischen Schriften des Theodor Abu Qurra, Bischofs von Harran*, Forschungen zur christlichen Literatur- und Dogmengeschichte, x, 3–4, Paderborn, 1910

——'Wie ist das Wort Al-Masīḥ zu übersetzen?', *ZDMG* civ (1954) 119–23

Grohmann, A. *Arabische Chronologie/Arabische Papyruskunde*, Handbuch der Orientalistik, Der nahe und mittlere Osten, Ergänzungsband ii, Leiden, 1966

Gruber, E. *Verdienst und Rang: die Faḍā'il als literarisches und gesellschaftliches Problem im Islam*, Freiburg, 1975

Grunebaum, G. von. 'The nature of Arab unity before Islam', *Arabica* x (1963) 5–23

—— 'Observations on the Muslim concept of evil', *Studia Islamica* xxxi (1970) 117–34

—— *Islam and medieval Hellenism: social and cultural perspectives*, London, 1976

—— 'Observations on city panegyrics in Arabic prose', *JAOS* lxiv (1944) 61–5

—— *Modern Islam: the search for cultural identity*, Berkeley, 1962

—— 'Islam and Hellenism', *Scientia* xliv (1950) 21–7

—— 'The convergence of cultural traditions in the Mediterranean area', *Diogenes* lxxi (1970) 1–17

—— 'The sources of Islamic civilization', *Der Islam* xlvi (1970) 1–54

Heffening, W. *Das islamische Fremdenrecht*, Hannover, 1925

Heintz, J. 'Oracles prophètiques et "Guerre Sainte" selon les archives royales de Mari et l'Ancien Testament', *Vetus Testamentum*, Suppl. xvii (1969) 112–38

Hengel, M. *Judaism and Hellenism: studies in their encounter in Palestine during the early Hellenistic period* i–ii, London, 1974

Horovitz, J. 'Salmān al-Fārisī', *Der Islam* xii (1922) 178–83

—— 'Die poetischen Einlagen der Sīra', *Islamica* ii (1926) 308–12

—— 'Alter und Ursprung des Isnād', *Der Islam* viii (1918) 39–47, 299

—— 'Noch einmal die Herkunft des Isnād', ibid. xi (1921) 264–5

—— *Koranische Untersuchungen*, Berlin–Leipzig, 1926

Hourani, G. 'The basis of authority of consensus in Sunnite Islam', *Studia Islamica* xxi (1964) 13–60

Ibn Ḥazm. *Al-Radd 'alā Ibn Al-Naghrīla Al-Yahūdī wa-rasā'il ukhrā* (ed. Iḥsān 'Abbās), Cairo, 1960

Ibn Isḥāq. *Al-Sīra al-Nabawiyya* (*l'ibn Hishām*) (ed. M. al-Saqqā *et al.*) i–ii, Cairo, 1375/1955

Ibn Kammūna. *Tanqīḥ al-abḥāth lil-milal al-thalāth* (ed. M. Perlmann), Berkeley-Los Angeles, 1967

Isser, S. *The Dositheans: a Samaritan sect in late antiquity*, Leiden, 1976

Jāḥiẓ. *Kitāb al-tarbī' wal-tadwīr* (ed. G. Van Vloten), Leiden, 1903

Jeffery, A. 'Ghevond's text of the correspondence between 'Umar II and Leo III', *Harvard Theological Review* xxxvii (1944) 269–332

Jolles, A. *Einfache Formen*, Tübingen, 1972

Jonas, H. 'Delimitation of the gnostic phenomenon—typological and historical' in U. Bianchi, *Le origini dello gnosticismo*, 90–108

Jones, M. 'Ibn Isḥāq and al-Wāqidī: the dream of 'Ātika and the raid to Nakhla in relation to the charge of plagiarism', *BSOAS* xxii (1959) 41–51

—— 'The chronology of the Maghāzī—a textual survey', *BSOAS* xix (1957) 245–80

Khoury, A. *Les Théologiens byzantins et l'islam*, Paris, 1969

Kindī. *Al-Risāla* (ed. Tien, SPCK), London, 1870

Kister, M. 'The expedition of Bi'r Ma'ūna', *Arabic and Islamic Studies in Honor of H. A. R. Gibb*, Leiden, 1965, 337–57

—— 'On a new edition of the Diwān of Ḥassān b. Thābit', *BSOAS* xxxix (1976) 265–86

—— 'Some reports concerning Mecca from Jāhiliyya to Islam', *JESHO* xv (1972) 61–76

—— '"Rajab is the month of God . . ."', *IOS* i (1971) 191–223

Klijn, A. and Reinink, G. *Patristic evidence for Jewish-Christian sects*, Leiden, 1973

Koch, H. *The growth of the Biblical tradition*, London, 1969

Kosmala, H. *Hebräer—Essener—Christen*, Leiden, 1959

Kraus, P. 'Beiträge zur islamischen Ketzergeschichte: das *Kitāb az-Zumurrud* des Ibn ar-Rāwandi', *RSO* xiv (1934) 93–129, 335–79

Laoust, H. 'La Classification des sectes dans "Le Farq" d'al-Baghdādī', *REI* xxix (1961) 19–59

Laoust, H. 'La Classification des sectes dans l'hérésiographie ashʿarite', *Arabic and Islamic Studies in Honor of H. A. R. Gibb*, Leiden, 1965, 377–86

Lausberg, H. *Handbuch der literarischen Rhetorik*, München, 1960

Lazarus-Yafeh, H. 'Is there a concept of redemption in Islam?', *Types of Redemption* (eds. Werblowsky–Bleeker), Leiden, 1970, 168–80

Lewis, B. 'An apocalyptic vision of Islamic history', *BSOAS* xiii (1950) 308–38

—— 'On that day: a Jewish apocalyptic poem on the Arab conquests', *Mélanges d'Islamologie* (Festschrift A. Abel), Leiden, 1974, 197–200

Lieberman, S. *Hellenism in Jewish Palestine*, New York, 1950

Löwith, K. *Meaning in history*, University of Chicago Press, 1949

Lüling, G. *Über den Ur-Qur'ān*, Erlangen, 1974

Maʿarrī. *Risālat al-Ghufrān* (ed. Bint al-Shāṭi'), Cairo, 1950

MacDonald, J. *The theology of the Samaritans*, London, 1964

Mach, R. *Der Zaddik in Talmud und Midrasch*, Leiden, 1957

Maier, J. *Geschichte der jüdischen Religion*, Berlin, 1972

Mālik ibn Anas. *Al-Muwaṭṭa'* (ed. M. ʿAbd al-Bāqī), Cairo, 1370/1951

McCarthy, D. *Old Testament covenant*, Oxford, 1973

Meeks, W. *The Prophet-King: Moses-traditions and the Johannine Christology*, Leiden, 1967

Meyer, E. *Der historische Gehalt der Aiyām al-ʿarab*, Wiesbaden, 1970

Meyerhoff, H. *The philosophy of history in our time*, New York, 1959

Meyers, C. *The Tabernacle Menorah: a synthetic study of a symbol from the Biblical cult*, Missoula, 1976

Mingana, A. 'The transmission of the Ḳur'ān', *Journal of the Manchester Egyptian and Oriental Society* (1915–16) 25–47

—— *Timothy's apology for Christianity*, Woodbrooke Studies ii, Cambridge, 1928, 1–162

—— ʿAlī Ṭabarī: *Kitāb al-dīn wal-dawla*, Cairo, 1923

——Id. (trans.): *The book of religion and empire*, Manchester, 1922

Morony, M. 'Religious communities in late Sasanian and early Muslim Iraq', *JESHO* xvii (1974) 113–35

Moubarac, Y. *Abraham dans les Coran*, Paris, 1958

Mowinckel, S. 'Psalm criticism between 1900 and 1935 (Ugarit and Psalm exegesis)' *Vetus Testamentum* v (1955) 13–33

Muir, W. *The apology of Al-Kindy*, London, 1887

Murray, R. *Symbols of Church and Kingdom: a study in early Syriac tradition*, Cambridge, 1975

Nallino, C. 'Ebrei e cristiani nell'Arabia preislamica', *Raccolta di Scritti* iii, Roma, 1941

Nau, F. 'Lettre du bienheureux patriarche Athanase', *ROC* xiv (1909) 128–30

—— *Les Arabes chrétiens de Mesopotamie et de Syrie*, Paris, 1933

Neusner, J. *Early Rabbinic Judaism*, Leiden, 1975

—— *Talmudic Judaism in Sasanian Babylonia*, Leiden, 1976

—— 'The religious uses of history: Judaism in first century AD Palestine and second century Babylonia', *History and Theory* v (1966) 153–71

Nöldeke, T. and Schwally, F. *Geschichte des Qorans*, Hildesheim, 1961

Norden, E. *Agnostos Theos: Untersuchungen zur Formengeschichte religiöser Rede*, Stuttgart, 1971

—— *Die antike Kunstprosa*, Stuttgart, 1958

Noth, A. *Quellenkritische Studien zu Themen, Formen und Tendenzen frühislamischer Geschichtsüberlieferung* i, Bonn, 1973

—— *Heiliger Krieg und heiliger Kampf in Islam und Christentum: Beiträge zur Vorgeschichte und Geschichte der Kreuzzüge*, Bonn, 1966

Nötscher, F. 'Himmlische Bücher und Schicksalsglaube in Qumran', *Revue de Qumran* i (1958–9) 405–11

Oppenheimer, A. *The ʿAm Ha-Aretz: a study in the social history of the Jewish people in the Hellenistic–Roman period*, Leiden, 1977

O'Shaughnessy, T. *Muhammad's thoughts on death: a thematic study of the Qurʾānic data*, Leiden, 1969

Pannenberg, W. *Revelation as history*, London, 1969

Paret, R. *Die legendäre Maghāzī-Literatur: arabische Dichtungen über die muslimischen Kriegszüge zu Mohammeds Zeit*, Tübingen, 1930

—— 'Der Koran als Geschichtsquelle', *Der Islam* xxxvii (1961) 21–42

—— *Der Koran: Kommentar und Konkordanz*, Stuttgart, 1971

Paul, A. *Écrits de Qumran et sectes juives aux premiers siècles de l'Islam*, Paris, 1969

Pedersen, J. *Israel: its life and culture* iii–iv, London, 1959

Pellat, C. 'Christologie Ǧāḥiẓienne', *Studia Islamica* xxxi (1970) 219–32

Perlmann, M. 'A legendary story of Kaʿb al-Aḥbār's conversion to Islam', *Joshua Starr Memorial Volume*, New York, 1953, 85–99

—— 'Another Kaʿb al-Aḥbār story', *JQR* xiv (1954) 48–58

Peters, J. *God's created speech: a study in the speculative theology of the Muʿtazilī . . . ʿAbd al-Jabbār*, Leiden, 1976

Petersen, E. 'ʿAlī and Muʿāwiyah: the rise of the Umayyad caliphate 656–661', *Acta Orientalia* xxiii (1959) 157–96

Pfister, F. *Alexander der Große in den Offenbarungen der Griechen, Juden, Mohammedaner und Christen*, Berlin, 1956

Philonenko, M. 'Une expression Qoumranienne dans le Coran', *Der Koran* (ed. R. Paret), Wege der Forschung cccxxvi, Darmstadt, 1975, 197–200

Popper, K. *The poverty of historicism*, London, 1963

Rabin, C. *Qumran studies*, Oxford, 1957

Rad, G. von. *Old Testament theology* i–ii, Edinburgh, 1962–5

Rahman, F. *Islamic methodology in History*, Karachi, 1965

—— *Prophecy in Islam: philosophy and orthodoxy*, London, 1958

Richter, G. *Der Sprachstil des Koran*, Sammlung orientalistischer Arbeiten (ed. O. Spies), Leipzig, 1940, Heft 3, 1–78

Richter, W. *Exegese als Literaturwissenschaft: Entwurf einer alttestamentlichen Literaturtheorie und Methodologie*, Göttingen, 1971

Roncaglia, M. 'Éléments ébionites et elkésaïtes dans le Coran', *POC* xxi (1971) 101–26

Rosenthal, F. 'The influence of the Biblical tradition on Muslim historiography', *Historians of the Middle East* (eds. B. Lewis and P. Holt), Oxford, 1962, 35–45

—— *Die aramaistische Forschung seit Th. Nöldeke's Veröffentlichungen*, Leiden, 1964

—— *Das Fortleben der Antike im Islam*, Zürich, 1965

Rössler, D. *Gesetz und Geschichte*, Neukirchen, 1962

Rubinacci, R. 'Il califfo ʿAbd al-Malik b. Marwān e gli Ibāḍiti', *Annali Istituto Universitario Orientali di Napoli* v (1953) 99–121

Rudolph, K. *Die Mandäer* i–ii, Göttingen, 1960–1

—— 'Probleme einer Entwicklungsgeschichte der mandäischen Religion', in U. Bianchi, *Le origini dello gnosticismo*, 583–96

Russell, D. *The method and message of Jewish apocalyptic*, London, 1964

Saadya Al-Fayyūmī, *Sefer ha-emunot weha-deʿot* (ed. Y. Qafeh), Jerusalem, 1970

Sabbagh, T. *La Métaphore dans le Coran*, Paris, 1943

Sahas, D. *John of Damascus on Islam*, Leiden, 1972

Samau'al Al-Maghribī. *Ifḥām al-Yahūd* (ed. M. Perlmann), New York, 1964

Sanders, E. 'The covenant as a soteriological category', *Jews, Greeks and Christians* (Festschrift W. Davies), Leiden, 1976, 11–44

Schacht, J. *The origins of Muhammadan jurisprudence*, Oxford, 1953

—— 'Sur l'expression "Sunna du Prophète" ', *Mélanges d'orientalisme offerts à Henri Massé*, Teheran, 1963, 361–5

—— 'Droit byzantin et droit musulman', *Convegno Volta* xii: *Oriente ed Occidente nel Medio Evo*, Roma, 1957, 197–218

—— *An introduction to Islamic law*, Oxford, 1964

Schiffman, L. *The Halakhah at Qumran*, Leiden, 1975

Schmucker, W. 'Die christliche Minderheit von Nağrān und die Problematik ihrer Beziehungen zum frühen Islam', in *Studien zum Minderheitenproblem im Islam* (ed. T. Nagel), Bonn, 1973, 183–281

Schoeps, H. *Theologie und Geschichte des Judenchristentums*, Tübingen, 1949

—— *Urgemeinde—Judenchristentum—Gnosis*, Tübingen, 1956

—— 'Judenchristentum und Gnosis', in U. Bianchi, *Le origini dello gnosticismo*, 528–37

Scholem, G. *Major trends in Jewish mysticism*, New York, 1974

Schreiner, J. *Einführung in die Methoden der biblischen Exegese*, Würzburg, 1971

Schreiner. M. 'Zur Geschichte der Polemik zwischen Juden und Muhammedanern', *ZDMG* xlii (1888) 591–675

Schützinger, H. *Ursprung und Entwicklung der arabischen Abraham-Nimrod-Legende*, Bonn, 1961

Schwarz, M. ' "Acquisition" (Kasb) in early Islam', *Islamic Philosophy and the Classical Tradition* (Festschrift Richard Walzer), Oxford, 1972, 355–87

Seale, M. *Muslim theology*, London, 1964

Seeligmann, I. 'Voraussetzungen der Midraschexegese', *Vetus Testamentum*, Suppl. i (1953) 150–81

Segal, M. 'The Qumran War Scroll and the date of its composition', *Scripta Hierosolymitana* iv (Jerusalem, 1965) 138–43

Sellheim, R. 'Prophet, Caliph und Geschichte: Die Muḥammed-Biographie des Ibn Isḥāq', *Oriens* xviii-xix (1965–7) 33–91

Sezgin, F. *Geschichte des arabischen Schrifttums* i, Leiden, 1967

Shahid, I. 'The Book of the Himyarites: authorship and authenticity', *Le Muséon* lxxvi (1963) 349–62

Shaked, S. 'Qumran and Iran: further considerations', *IOS* ii (1972) 433–46

Sister, M. 'Metaphern und Vergleiche im Koran', *MSOS* xxxiv (1931) 104–54

Smith, M. 'The image of God: notes on the Hellenization of Judaism, with especial reference to Goodenough's work on Jewish symbols', *BJRL* xl (1957–8) 473–512

Sourdel, D. 'La Classification des sectes islamiques dans "*Le Kitāb al-Milal*" d'al-Šahrastānī', *Studia Islamica* xxxi (1970) 239–47

Sperber, J. 'Die Schreiben Muhammads an die Stämme Arabiens', *MSOS* xix (1916) 1–93

Speyer, H. *Die biblischen Erzählungen im Qoran*, Hildesheim, 1961

Spicq, C. 'L'Épître aux Hébreux, Apollos, Jean-Baptiste, les Hellénistes et Qumran', *Revue de Qumran* i (1958–9) 365–90

Sprenger, A. *Das Leben und die Lehre des Mohammed* i–iii, Berlin, 1869

Steinschneider, M. *Polemische und apologetische Literatur in arabischer Sprache*, Leipzig, 1877

—— 'Apocalypsen mit polemischer Tendenz', *ZDMG* xxviii (1874) 627–59; xxix (1875) 162–7

Stetter, E. *Topoi und Schemata im Ḥadīṯ*, Tübingen, 1965

Stoebe, H. 'Geprägte Form und geschichtlich individuelle Erfahrung im Alten Testament', *Vetus Testamentum*, Suppl. xvii (1969) 212–19

Suyūṭī. *Al-Itqān fī 'ulūm al-Qur'ān* i–iv, Cairo, 1967

Szörenyi, A. 'Das Buch Daniel, ein kanonisierter Pescher?', *Vetus Testamentum*, Suppl. xv (1966), 278–94

Ṭabarī, 'Alī b. Rabbān. *See* Mingana

Ṭabarī, Muḥammad b. Jarīr. *Annales*, Leiden, 1879–1901

Tahānawī. *Kitāb Kashshāf iṣṭilāḥāt al-funūn*, Calcutta, 1862

Talmon, S. 'The "desert motif" in the Bible and in Qumran literature', *Biblical Motifs: origins and transformations* (ed. A. Altmann), Cambridge, Mass., 1966, 31–64

—— 'The calendar reckoning of the sect from the Judaean desert', *Scripta Hierosolymitana* iv (Jerusalem, 1965) 162–99

Teicher, J. 'The Dead Sea Scrolls–documents of the Jewish–Christian sect of Ebionites', *JJS* ii (1951) 67–99

—— 'The Damascus fragments and the origin of the Jewish Christian sect', *JJS* ii (1951) 115–43

Towner, W. 'Form-criticism of Rabbinic literature', *JJS* xxiv (1973) 101–18

Turner, B. *Weber and Islam: a critical study*, London, 1974

Urbach, E. 'Halakhah and history', *Jews, Greeks and Christians* (Festschrift W. Davies), Leiden, 1976, 112–28

Vermes, G. *Post-Biblical Jewish studies*, Leiden, 1975

Vollers, K. 'Das Religionsgespräch von Jerusalem (um 800 D)', *Zeitschrift für Kirchengeschichte* xxix (1908) 29–71, 197–221

Walzer, R. *Greek into Arabic: essays on Islamic philosophy*, Oxford, 1962

Wansbrough, J. *Quranic studies: sources and methods of scriptural interpretation*, Oxford, 1977

Wāqidī, *Kitāb al-Maghāzī* (ed. M. Jones) i–iii, Oxford, 1966

Watt, W. *Muhammad at Medina*, Oxford, 1956

—— *The formative period of Islamic thought*, Edinburgh, 1973

Wellhausen, J. *Reste arabischen Heidentums*, Berlin, 1961

—— *Das arabische Reich und sein Sturz*, Berlin, 1960

Wensinck, A. *A handbook of early Muhammadan tradition*, Leiden, 1960

—— *The Muslim creed*, Cambridge, 1932

Werblowsky, Z. *Beyond tradition and modernity: changing religions in a changing world*, London, 1976

—— and Bleeker, C. *Types of redemption*, Leiden, 1970

Widengren, G. *Religionsphänomenologie*, Berlin, 1969

—— 'Oral tradition and written literature among the Hebrews in the light of Arabic evidence, with special regard to prose narratives', *Acta Orientalia* xxiii (1959) 201–62

—— *Muhammad, the Apostle of God, and his ascension*, Uppsala–Wiesbaden, 1955

Wieder, N. *The Judean Scrolls and Karaism*, London, 1962

—— 'The Dead Sea Scrolls type of Biblical exegesis among the Karaites', *Between East and West: essays dedicated to the memory of Bela Horovitz* (ed. A. Altmann), London, 1958, 75–106

Wielandt, R. *Offenbarung and Geschichte im Denken moderner Muslime*, Wiesbaden, 1971

Wilckens, U. 'The understanding of revelation within the history of primitive Christianity', in Pannenberg, *Revelation as history*, 57–121

Wolfson, H. *The philosophy of the Kalam*, Harvard University Press, 1976

—— 'The double faith theory in Clement, Saadia, Averroes and St. Thomas, and its origin in Aristotle and the Stoics', *JQR* xxxiii (1942–3) 213–64

Yadin, Y. 'The Dead Sea Scrolls and the Epistle to the Hebrews', *Scripta Hierosolymitana* iv (Jersualem, 1965) 36–55

Yamauchi, E. *Gnostic ethics and Mandaean origins*, Cambridge, Mass., 1970

Zamakhsharī. *Al-Kashshāf ʿan ḥaqāʾiq al-tanzīl* i–iv, Beirut, 1967

Zimmermann, F. 'Some observations on Al-Farabi and logical tradition', *Islamic Philosophy and the Classical Tradition* (Festschrift R. Walzer), Oxford, 1972, 517–46

I

HISTORIOGRAPHY

THE structure of historical discourse is as effective, if not always so obvious, as that of poetry. In the light of current work in linguistics and literary criticism it is no longer possible (or necessary) to accept the classical (Aristotelian) distinction between the specific data of history and the general truths of poetry, or in later positivist terms, that there is a contest between history as science and history as literature. Some such dichotomy may be discerned in more recent discussions of history and myth, where in alleged defence of the former, 'significant content' is distilled and separated from the circumstances, local and temporal, of its transmission. Justification for this procedure seems to be epistemological and rests upon the implicit assumption of a qualitative difference between event and record, between occurrence and interpretation, in which the historian's participation in the historical process itself is tacitly ignored. The problems arising out of this intellectual salvage operation are common to all historiography, but appear to have been most sharply perceived by scholars concerned with the special form of record called salvation history (*Heilsgeschichte*). Central among the solutions proposed are those involving the concept of kerygma, a term often employed to define the 'message' of history, as contrasted with or opposed to its 'framework'. The latter may be described as myth and is frequently, if not invariably, regarded as incidental, accidental, or somehow tangential to the aim of salvation history, which is kerygma. It is tempting, but partly misleading, to describe this as a theological, not a historical, formulation. The notions of causality, teleology, and even linear movement are not the exclusive property of salvation history, though it is more than likely that they were first articulated there. These are structural concepts, and to the question whether they are imposed upon or elicited from the data of history any convincing reply must involve a careful scrutiny of the methods by which those data are thought to be verified. Casual or, as the case may be, urgent reference to 'myth' merely begs the question, unless it be acknowledged that myth is the (infinitely variable) linguistic code in which all experience is perceived and transmitted, and not merely a time-bound framework to be, when found obsolete, dismantled and eventually discarded.[1]

[1] Cf. H. W. Bartsch (ed.), *Kerygma and Myth: a Theological Debate* i–ii, London, 1972, esp. ii, 1–82.

My concern in these studies is with that version of salvation history composed by members of the early Islamic community to depict its origins and to direct its movement in response to a particular theophany. Now, the ground has been covered, perhaps as often as could have been wished, and I have elsewhere commented on what seemed to me typical products of that scholarship. Characteristic of the many treatments of this material is a distinctly positivist method: serious concern to discover and to describe the state of affairs at and after the appearance of Islam among the Arabs, a severely fluctuating willingness to acknowledge the presence there of notions and practices familiar from the study of earlier and contemporary cultures outside the Arabian peninsula, and finally, a nearly complete absence of linguistic and literary analysis. There have been of course honourable exceptions to the last of my allegations, but even there literary analysis has consisted mostly in the isolation of such components as theme and motif (*Stoffgeschichte*), seldom in the detection of morphological constants.[1] It is precisely with the latter that I intend here to experiment, and for that purpose have selected two of the earliest prose narratives dealing with the pre-history and history of the Islamic community: the *Sīra* of Ibn Isḥāq (d. 151/768) in the recension of Ibn Hishām (d. 218/834) and the *Maghāzī* of Wāqidī (d. 207/ 822).[2]

In my study of the Muslim haggadah I drew attention to two characteristic narrative techniques employed in the *Sīra*: exegetical, in which extracts (serial and isolated) from scripture provided the framework for extended *narratio*; and parabolic, in which the *narratio* was itself the framework for frequent if not continuous allusion to scripture. The relation between the two types is, however, not one of simple inversion. In the exegetical style scriptural extracts, however discrete and truncated, exhibit the canonical text; in the parabolic style scriptural allusions are implicit only, exhibiting diction and imagery but not the verbatim text of the canon. The exact nature of that allusion is something of a problem, which I attempted to solve by recourse to the term 'prophetical *logia*' designating sub-canonical versions of scripture, usually introduced at a secondary stage in reports of prophetical deeds. In such passages the priority of the report over the *logia* seemed certain.[3]

Yet another narrative technique is illustrated in passages containing

[1] e.g. R. Paret, *Die legendäre Maghāzī-Literatur: arabische Dichtungen über die muslimischen Kriegszüge zu Mohammeds Zeit*, Tübingen, 1930; W. Caskel, 'Aijām al-'Arab: Studien zur altarabischen Epik', *Islamica* iii (Suppl.) 1931; but cf. E. Stetter, *Topoi und Schemata im Ḥadīṯ*, Tübingen, 1965; A. Noth, *Quellenkritische Studien zu Themen, Formen und Tendenzen frühislamischer Geschichtsüberlieferung I: Themen und Formen*, Bonn, 1973.

[2] *Al-Sīra al-Nabawiyya l'ibn Hishām*, ed. M. al-Saqqā *et al.*, i–ii, Cairo, 1375/1955; *The Kitāb al-Maghāzī of Al-Wāqidī*, ed. M. Jones, i–iii, O.U.P. London, 1966.

[3] J. Wansbrough, *Quranic Studies: Sources and Methods of Scriptural Interpretation*, London Oriental Series vol. 31, Oxford, 1977, 122–31 (exegetical), 38–43 (parabolic).

scriptural extracts intoduced by paraphrastic versions of scripture in the form of anecdote. The literary unit is characterized by the distribution of keywords (*Leitworte*)[1] linking both parts of the composition in a tidy stylistic balance with remarkable economy of imagery. That style, which is neither exegical nor parabolic, can generate considerable narrative movement in time and space, and might thus be described as 'dynamic'. A well-known example (*Sīra* i, 358) is the jibe of Naḍr b. al-Ḥārith after listening to Muhammad's recitation of *qur'ān* and admonition with reference to the fates of vanished nations (*umam khāliya*): that Muhammad's parables were nothing but 'old wives' tales (*asāṭīr al-awwalīn*) copied out as they had always been copied out (*iktatabahā kamā 'ktatabathā*)'. Thereupon was revealed Q. 25: 5–6 (they say: old wives' tales copied out . . .), together with 67: 15 and 83: 13 (both containing the locution 'old wives' tales') and 45: 7, not so obviously relevant to that particular occasion.

All three styles may be described as midrashic, but differ according to the part played in each by its scriptural component, which can be (*a*) the specific object of exegesis, (*b*) exhibited only in paraphrastic and allusive form, or (*c*) the verbal complement to a related action. A variation of (*c*) is found in scriptural sequences appended to neutral, or at least not flagrantly theocentric versions of events such as military campaigns. There the role of scripture is ornamental rather than structural, and might be characterized as *ex post facto*. An example from the *Sīra* (i, 666–77) is Ibn Isḥāq's insertion of Q. 8: 1–75 at the end of the account of Badr, which itself contains only two or three references to scripture. The presentation is virtually exegetical but with this difference: it is scripture which provides commentary to the preceding historical report. The rhetorical effect could be described as *elevatio/anagoge*, that is, transfer of action/plot from human to divine agency. This style is found also in Wāqidī but there scriptural references in the historical report itself are both explicit and more frequent, exhibiting, at least for Badr, some concern for an integrated account (*Maghāzī*, 131–8). These narrative techniques are most easily observed and assessed in longer passages where their effect is cumulative and susceptible of broad statistical analysis. Though the corpus of *sīra-maghāzī* literature does contain non-midrashic material, its extent and quality is not such as to affect the impression gained from the midrashic styles.

A morphology of salvation history demands attention not merely to the typical units (forms) of narrative exposition, such as myth, legend, saga, and *memorabilia*, but also to the motives (*Geistesbeschäftigungen*) dictating their employment. It may be worth stating at once that the object of the

[1] M. Gertner, 'The Masorah and the Levites: an essay in the history of a concept', *Vetus Testamentum* x (1960) 274 n. 4 (Buber-Rosenzweig), 279 n. 1; W. Richter, *Exegese als Literaturwissenschaft: Entwurf einer alttestamentlichen Literaturtheorie und Methodologie*, Göttingen, 1971, 89 n. 44; I. Seeligmann, 'Voraussetzungen der Midraschexegese', *Vetus Testamentum*, Suppl. i (1953) 150–81.

exercise is not to discover the intention of the author (for which evidence anyway of a quite explicit kind is seldom lacking), but rather, to determine the significance of recurrent expressions (*Sprachgebärden*) in a particular language/literature, in this case Arabic. If the value of Jolles's work for such an undertaking is not readily apparent, it may suffice to recall that the 'einfache Formen' were studied not as primitive or inferior versions of history, but rather, as the basic and ubiquitous ingredients of narrative, including historical prose.[1] In current terminology the argument would be that the linguistic datum is inescapable, that logically no referent can be postulated as external to the mode of discourse, finally that 'kerygma' cannot be separated from 'myth'. The code, in other (and even more familiar) words, is the message. Naturally, a 'basic' or 'simple' form is not itself a literary work or genre, nor does a literary work ever represent the permutations of merely one (basic or simple) form. The prose narratives with which I am here concerned exhibit most, if not all, of Jolles's forms, the more easily perceived owing to the fragmentary character of composition. The lines of cleavage are signalled mostly, if not always, by the regular citation of sources (*isnād*.)

The passage *Sīra* i, 204–32 contains a fourfold account of the response, amongst various groups in the Arabian peninsula, to the earliest reports about the prophet Muhammad. The most easily observed feature of this account is the representative character of the four groups: soothsayers, Jews, Christians, and men in search of God. The reactions of each to signs that a new prophetical age was imminent are determined to some extent by typical features (respectively: daemonism, messianic expectation, ascetic piety, dissatisfaction with traditional worship), but also by the order of presentation: from the demonstrable inadequacy of the pagan oracle, the accurate though perversely rejected prognosis of the Jews, and Christian stress upon the role of the saintly teacher, to the confident identification by the *ḥanīfs* of genuine and unadulterated faith with the figure of Abraham. Illustrated in the sequence itself is the Islamic claim to have superseded earlier dispensations.

In the first section of the passage (204–11) the status of *jinn* as intermediaries between heaven and earth is established by explicit reference to Q. 72: 1–10 and 46: 30. There a portion of their number is described as saved by conversion (to Islam), others as barred from the councils of heaven by fiery comets. The specific role of *jinnī* as daemonic agent of the soothsayer (*kāhin*) is not, and for that matter cannot be, documented by scripture, though implicit allusion to Q. 6: 112 and 15: 18 (*shayāṭīn; man istaraqa 'l-sam'*) may be thought to furnish a conceptual link. It is in the narrative that the connection is explicitly made, and the comets (*shihāb/shuhub*) of scripture paraphrased 'falling stars' (*ramy bil-nujūm*) and interpreted as portending collapse of the familiar, natural order of

[1] A. Jolles, *Einfache Formen*, Tübingen, 1972, 91–5, 171–2, 266–8.

existence (lexical reflexes of Q. 6: 97 and 15: 20). The moral of the story was articulated by Muhammad himself, when asked much later by a group of the Anṣār (207): the movement of the stars signalled the demise of the soothsayer (*inqiṭā' al-kahāna*). An additional feature of the prophetical anecdote is acknowledgement of a hierarchy of angelic mediators culminating in the cherubim (*ḥamalat al-'arsh*; cf. Q. 40: 7 and 69: 17), while the daemons (*shayāṭīn*) of the soothsayers are alleged to have come only by stealth (*istaraq bil-sam'*) to whatever information from God they might have (i.e. Q. 6: 112, 15: 18). The bankruptcy of the *kāhin* is confirmed by two further anecdotes related of 'Umar b. al-Khaṭṭāb (210–11), but not before holders of that office were credited with having forecast Badr and Uḥud (imagery: *'aqr wa-nahr*; *shi'b*) and predicted the divine election and purification of Muhammad (imagery: *wa-ṣṭafāhu wa-ṭahhara qalbahu wa-ḥashāhu*; cf. Q. 3: 42). It is worth noting that implicit allusions to scripture outnumber by far explicit references, and that the purification ritual just mentioned can be related, circuitously, to Q. 94: 1–3.[1] The style is thus parabolic, rather than exegetical, and may be compared with that of the story of Ja'far b. Abī Ṭālib at the Ethiopian court (*Sīra* i, 336–7, in which scriptural imagery could be detected in sub-canonical form. Of some value for a historical analysis is the fact that elements of the pagan (*Jāhilī*) 'setting' are also found there, e.g. 'Thus we were, a people in ignorance worshipping idols . . . until'.[2]

In the second section of this passage (211–14) it is that very element ('We were polytheists, sectaries of idols . . .') which introduces the account of Jewish messianic expectations, uttered as a threat to the Arabs of Yathrib but in the event frustrated by the appearance not of a Jewish, but of an Arabian prophet. The prognosis is retailed in two forms: one by an anonymous preacher in Yathrib describing resurrection, judgement, eternal reward, and punishment (212); the other by one Ibn al-Hayyabān, a Syrian/Palestinian thaumaturge, come to the Ḥijāz in anticipation of the prophet (213–14). Neither account can be convincingly related to the lexicon of Jewish messiology, but both reflect nicely Quranic imagery on the one hand, the surrender of B. Qurayẓa on the other, and might be thought fair examples of *vaticinatio post eventum*. Ibn al-Hayyabān stressed that he had left Syria/Palestine for Arabia because 'here was the country of his (the prophet's) mission (*muhājaruhu*)'. That epithet (*muhājar*), had been applied to Yathrib/Medina earlier by two rabbis of B. Qurayẓa in an effort to save the sanctuary (*sic*: *ḥaram*) from destruction by As'ad Abū Kārib (*Sīra* i, 22), and later by a Christian monk in 'Amūriyya in his testament to Salmān Fārisī (218). The Jews' rejection of their own prediction was uniform, and is symbolized by the only explicit scriptural reference in this account,

[1] *QS*, 66–7.
[2] *QS*, 38–43.

namely Q. 2: 89. The eschatological imagery employed there is, however, also Quranic: *qiyāma*, *ba'th*, *ḥisāb*, *mizān*, *janna*, *nār*, *tannūr*.[1]

The third section (214–22) relates the odyssey of one man, Salmān Fārisī,[2] from the oppressive home of his Zoroastrian father in Iṣfahān through a series of novitiates with Christian religious in Syria, Mosul, Niṣibīn, 'Amūriyya, to slavery, passage to the Ḥijāz, conversion at Medina, and emancipation at the hands of the prophet. The attraction of Christianity lay in its ritual observance (*ṣalāt al-khams*: a phrase used, curiously, also of Ibn al-Hayyabān, 213), and each mentor is described as more devout than the last, despite an initial experience with a corrupt bishop in Syria. The testament (*waṣiyya*) of his dying master in 'Amūriyya recommended a new prophet in the Ḥijāz (*arḍ bayna ḥarratayn*) sent to proclaim the faith of Abraham (*dīn Ibrāhīm*) and bearing between his shoulders the seal of prophethood (*sic*: *khatam al-nubuwwa*). After considerable hardship, servitude with a Jewish master in Yathrib, and two visits to the prophet recently arrived from Mecca, Salmān was able to tell his story and to satisfy himself that he had reached his goal. The view of Christianity conveyed in this account is even more indifferent than that of Judaism in the preceding section. Neither can have been intended, by author or tradent, to serve as more than the most elementary *praeparatio evangelica*. Here the concluding anecdote, related by Salmān of his encounter with a healer in Syria, identifies Jesus as attesting the renewal in Arabia of the Abrahamic faith (221–2).

Thus the fourth section (222–32) is developed out of the equation *dīn Ibrāhīm*:*ḥanīfiyya*, which is assumed but never demonstrated. The facility with which three of the four celebrated God-seekers (*ḥanīf*) could be accommodated by conversion to Christianity emerges neither from the nature of their quest nor from the structure of the tale, the real substance of which is the odyssey of the fourth: Zayd b. 'Amr. He became neither Jew nor Christian, but did abandon the religion of his people (*dīn qawmihi*/*dīn al-'arab*)[3] and abstain from carrion, blood, sacrifice to idols, and the practice of burying alive unwanted daughters (*qatl al-maw'uda*). His travels in search of God took him to Mosul and all of the Jazīra, eventually to Syria/Palestine where a monk advised him to return to his native land for the imminent renewal there of the Abrahamic faith (231–2). He was attacked and killed, presumably by brigands, before reaching his goal. Affinity to the description of Salmān's quest is clear enough. Absent from both accounts is explicit reference to scripture, though allusions in each might be contained in the locutions 'seal of prophethood' (*sic*; cf. Q. 33: 40) and in Muhammad's observation with respect to Zayd that he

[1] Cf. *QS*, 31–3. [2] J. Horovitz, 'Salman al-Farisi', *Der Islam* xii (1922) 178–83.
[3] G. E. von Grunebaum, 'The nature of Arab unity before Islam', *Arabica* x (1963) 5–23.

would be pardoned (for not actually becoming a Muslim) since he by himself constituted a community/exemplum (*yub'ath ummatan waḥdahu*; cf. Q. 16: 120). A conspicuous difference from the story of Salmān is the presence here of lengthy extracts of Zayd's poetry (forty-five lines) bearing witness to his monotheism: the imagery is not Christian, nor particularly Jewish, despite references to Moses, Pharaoh, Jonah, and Abraham.

The passage as a whole represents, in the sense defined by Jolles,[1] a myth (*Wahrsage, Deutung*) devised to interpret the spiritual, intellectual, and social transformation brought about by the mission (*mab'ath*) of an Arabian prophet. That event is the only 'fact' here attested: the circumstantial evidence consists entirely in the historicization of theological concepts, e.g. exhaustion of the oracle (*inqiṭā' al-kahāna*), incipit of the messianic drama (*muhājar*), ritual observance (*ṣalāt al-khams*), restoration of order (*dīn*). These assume a kind of historicity by becoming themselves the Muhammadan proclamation (kerygma), without which they would be not only meaningless but non-existent except as linguistic data.

A similar process may be seen in an extended passage of the *Sīra* (i, 354–64) describing opposition in Mecca to the prophet. Adduced there are a dozen instances of conduct inimical to the activity of Muhammad, each the occasion of, and thus documented by, a Quranic revelation. It is the relation of event to scripture which requires to be examined: in the Muslim haggadah the exegetical device known as *ta'yīn al-mubham* (identification of the vague and ambiguous) served to establish a connection between scriptural phraseology and external referent, in the interest of narrative continuity. In halakhic exegesis the device was extended to become a kind of chronological grid known as *asbāb al-nuzūl* (occasions of revelation), employed to promote some and to eliminate other verses as the alleged bases of juridical decisions.[2] In the *Sīra*, on the other hand, history is itself generated by scriptural imagery or enhanced by scriptural reference. I have proposed designating the first style 'dynamic' and the second '*ex post facto*' or ornamental. The former exhibits a process of historicization, the latter one of exemplification: the difference between them lies in the quality of the non-scriptural component, that is, its position and expression in the narrative structure. In the passage to be examined here each 'event' (with three exceptions) precedes its scriptural counterpart and is related to it by a keyword or phrase (*Leitwort*). The first example is the story of Umm Jamīl (355) who, together with her husband Abū Lahab, the prophet's uncle, was consigned to eternal damnation (Q. 111). Her epithet 'firewood carrier' (*hammālat al-ḥaṭab*) is here referred to her having collected and thrown thorns in the path of the prophet. Neither the more subtle explanation found in later literature, that *ḥaṭab* was not firewood but malicious gossip (*namīma*), nor the obvious interpretation of the image as 'stoking

[1] Jolles, op. cit. 91–125. [2] *QS*, 135–6, 141–2.

the fires of hell' is adduced. In the light of that homespun exegesis it is odd to find the second anecdote about Umm Jamīl, recounting her physical assault upon the prophet (356), not provided with its customary scriptural embellishment (Q. 17: 45).[1] Nor is the role of Abū Lahab himself mentioned in this passage. It is anyway more than likely that Q. 111 contains not a historical reference, but an eschatological promise.

The second example (356) is the story of Umayya b. Khalaf, who irritated and provoked the prophet (*hamazahu wa-lamazahu*). Thereupon was revealed Q. 104: 'Woe to all who irritate and provoke . . .'. Here the scriptural imagery is also eschatological (*al-ḥuṭama*) and the historical reference probably secondary. In the third example (357) the link between narrative and scripture is not in fact literal but conceptual: in order to evade a financial obligation to one of Muhammad's companions, Al-'Āṣ b. Wā'il proposed deferment until their arrival in the next world where, as alleged by Muhammad himself, no one would be in want. Thereupon Q. 19: 77–80 was revealed, promising those who presumed to forecast their own destinies a special legacy (*wa-narithuhu mā yaqūl*). In the fourth example (357) the link, is, as in the first two, explicit: Abū Jahl threatened to curse (*lanasubbanna*) Muhammad's god if he did not desist from cursing (*sabb*) the gods of Quraysh, whereupon God revealed Q. 6: 108: 'Do not curse (*lā tasubbū*) those whom they worship beside God, lest they curse (*fa-yasubbū*) God in their enmity and ignorance.' The fifth example (358–9) is the story of Naḍr b. al-Ḥārith and the jibe 'old wives' tales' mentioned above, in which not merely one but three (of a total of nine) scriptural occurrences of that locution (*asāṭīr al-awwalīn*) were claimed on that occasion to have been revealed. The addition of Q. 45: 7 appears to be arbitrary, unless the teım *affāk* (liar) was intended to convey the special connotation 'forger/fabricator', in that context an allusion to Naḍr's own stories.

The composition of the sixth example (359–60) is more complex: the setting is, as often, an encounter between Muhammad and Quraysh, but the opening sally itself a scriptural citation, namely Q. 21: 98–9 'You, together with what you worship beside God, will be fuel for the fires of Hell (*ḥaṣab jahannam*).' This evoked from the poet 'Abdallāh b. al-Ziba'rā the disingenuous protest: 'But we (Quraysh) worship angels, the Jews Ezra, and the Christians Jesus . . . (*scil.* surely you do not mean, etc.).' His colleagues wondered at that, and when it was reported to Muhammad, the latter explained 'Anyone desirous of worship in God's stead will be together (*scil.* in Hell) with his worshippers, for they only serve daemons and what these order them to serve.' The 'revelation' at this point of Q. 21: 101–2 does not interrupt, but rather continues the dialogue: promise of reward for those who are not idolatrous, including Jesus and Ezra, the unwitting victims of error. The angelic daughters of God (*banāt allāh*) worshipped

[1] *QS*, 73.

by Quraysh are relegated by a second revelation (Q. 21: 26–9) to an appropriately subordinate position, and the exchange concluded by Q. 43: 57–61 which begins: 'And when (Jesus) ibn Maryam was adduced as example . . .'. Movement in this episode consists entirely of scriptural utterance (three separate passages) juxtaposed as rejoinder to Ibn al-Ziba'rā. Scripture is explicit, but not different in tone or imagery from non-scripture: the formal demarcation is arbitrary. Nor can the example be described as exegetical; the style is dynamic and the process historicization.

Similarly, the seventh example (360–1), which combines the figure of Akhnas b. Sharīq with the concept *zanīm* (affiiliate) of Q. 68: 10–3, upon which is commented 'God does not judge a man by his pedigree (*nasab*)': the material is genealogical and the point doctrinal. In the eighth example (361) Walīd b. Mughīra complains that he and Abū Mas'ūd, dignitaries of the two villages (*scil.* Mecca and Ṭā'if: *'aẓīmā' l-qaryatayn*), were passed over while revelation was vouchsafed Muhammad. Thereupon Q. 43: 31 was revealed: 'Had this qur'ān only been revealed to a dignitary of the two villages . . .'. In the ninth example (361–2) the technique is modified slightly: in the first of the two episodes related there the friendship beween Ubayy b. Khalaf and 'Uqba b. Abī Mu'ayṭ is described as intimate (*mutaṣāfin*), while the scriptural referent (Q. 25: 27–9) on the dangers of seduction contains the unembellished locution 'to adopt one as a friend' (*ittakhadha fulānan khālīlan*). When, however, in the second episode Ubayy interrogated Muhammad on the possibility of physical resurrection, the imagery employed is a tactile periphrasis of the scriptural locution 'after it is dust' (*wa-hiya ramīm*: Q. 36: 78–80):[1] 'he took an ancient and decaying bone, crumbled it in his hand, blew it into the wind in the direction of the prophet, saying . . .'. Again, in the tenth example (362), the proposition put to Muhammad by Aswad b. Muṭallib and his companions: 'let us worship that which you worship, while you worship what we worship (*scil.* to determine which is more effective)' becomes the nearly verbatim text of Q. 109.

The last two examples in this passage also belong to the category I have described as historicization derived from a keyword. In the first (362–3) Abū Jahl is made to utter 'Zaqqūm tree' and 'frighten' in a characteristic taunt at Muhammad's teaching, and these become in turn the eschatological imagery of Q. 44: 43 ("The Zaqqūm tree will be food for the sinner. . . ') and 17: 60 ('Like the cursed tree in the qur'ān with which we frighten them'). In the last example (363–4) it was the insistence of the blind Ibn Umm Maktūm upon being given instruction in the new faith while Muhammad was occupied with the conversion of others, that caused him to 'frown and turn away' from the unfortunate man and produced the imagery of Q. 80: 1 ('He frowned and turned away . . .')

[1] *QS*, 31–2.

Now, it would be simple, but equally simplistic, to argue either that *Sīra* i, 354–64 contains a reminiscence of the historical circumstances of the several scriptural revelations set out there, or that the 'historical setting' exhibits nothing more than an extrapolation from the scriptural passages adduced. All but three of the twelve examples depend upon a keyword in both scriptural and non-scriptural components, between which it would in most cases be difficult to insist upon a lexical or grammatical difference. Argument for a stylistic distinction is invariably reducible to the presence or absence of such rhetorical formulae as 'Woe to . . .', 'Have you not considered . . . ?', 'O you who . . .', 'Say . . .', that is, such as are characteristic of an apodictic, as contrasted with a narrative or expository style. Such of course are those conventions of Quranic usage which lend to that document an impression of unmediated theophany, and were intended to do so.[1] In some examples, where dialogue rather than exposition is dominant, even that distinction disappears.

It must be stressed that the unity of this passage (*Sīra* i, 354–64), in contrast to the one previously analysed (*Sīra* i, 204–32), is stylistic as well as thematic. There, historicization was achieved by reifying theological concepts (imagery typically associated with each 'confessional' group); here, it is achieved by the reification of scripture itself. For this passage a more appropriate epithet than unity might be uniformity: application of a single narrative technique does not eliminate, may in fact even accentuate, its episodic character. Some trace of a framework can, however, be discerned. At *Sīra* i, 393–6, for example, the same theme, Meccan opposition to Muhammad, is resumed: the same cast of characters either acting out the content of or providing the point of departure for a verse or two of scripture, e.g. 'Āṣ b. Wā'il and Q. 108, Naḍr b. al-Ḥārith and Q. 6: 8–9, Walīd b. Mughīra and Q. 6: 10. The imagery of the last verse, ridicule of the prophet (*mā kānū bihi yastahzi'ūn*, which is a Quranic formula), is developed in some detail at *Sīra* i, 408–10 employing Q. 15: 94, itself earlier adduced as introduction to that very theme (*Sīra* i, 262).

The over-all structure is admittedly loose and contains a good deal of not strictly relevant anecdote, but also considerable incidence of the by now familiar historicization. For example, at *Sīra* i, 270–2 an assembly of notables from Quraysh is described, convoked by Walīd b. Mughīra in order to agree upon an 'official' tribal policy towards Muhammad. Discussion turned in fact upon what to call him: soothsayer (*kāhin*), possessed (*majnūn*), poet (*shā'ir*), or sorcerer (*sāḥir*), each in turn rejected as not quite appropriate to the unfamiliar phenomenon represented by Muhammad. In the end 'sorcerer' was selected as least inaccurate, and was actively promulgated by Quraysh among the seasonal visitors to Mecca. At *Sīra* i, 289 the theme is exhibited in abridged form: 'and they accused him of (composing)

[1] *QS*, 12–20.

poetry, of (practising) sorcery and soothsaying, of (being) possessed'; and again (294) in the address of 'Utba b. Rabī'a to Quraysh exonerating Muhammad from those charges. These are the standard scriptural epithets employed to denigrate a prophet (e.g. Q. 51 : 39, 52 : 29–30), but the scriptural references are not given in these contexts nor was the term 'prophet' used by Quraysh. The narrative is parabolic (allusive), by means of which the (later) scriptural terms were endowed with specific historicity. That historicity is the fact of Meccan opposition to the novel proclamation of Muhammad.

A principal characteristic of the midrashic style so far examined is the discrete quality (that is, in relation to the canon) of the scriptural references, whether explicit or implicit. It is quite impossible to discern any pattern at all in their selection. Now, for the parallel accounts of Medinese and of Jewish opposition to Muhammad a pattern very gradually emerges, beginning with recurrent scriptural contexts and ending with deployment of (canonical) sequences of up to a hundred verses. The altered ratio of historical narrative to scriptural content provokes one question at least about the author's craft and his creative priorities. For the earlier passages analysed (*Sīra* i, 204–32 and 354–64) it seems to me rash to assume exclusive priority either of the historical reminiscence or of the scriptural locution. The basic datum is the keyword (*Leitwort*), itself the expression of a fundamental preoccupation with the fabric of salvation history. It provides the imagery of both the scriptural and non-scriptural components of the narrative. In the examples so far considered it is in my opinion difficult, if not impossible, to insist that the piece was inspired by the canonical text of scripture. Nor is the converse any more readily demonstrable, that is, that the canonical text of scripture represents the precipitate of an actual historical event. Thus, the very notion of a selection of *loci probantes* from scripture as points of departure for the composition of salvation history may be fallacious. Selection, on the other hand, of primary concepts (*topoi*) traditionally associated with the literature of salvation history might appear a viable alternative. These may be preserved as scriptural canon, but equally often as the non-canonical or sub-canonical data employed as testimony to the theophany. Within the framework of Islam such material is usually subsumed under the rubric 'sunna' (*exemplum*). I have elsewhere, in the interest of precision, proposed the terms 'prophetical *logia*' and 'Muhammadan *evangelium*'..[1] Though neither provides in itself a clue to priority, each term includes (theoretically) both canonical and non-canonical material, and thus need not be relegated, as merely exegetical, to a position of secondary importance, The well-known assessment of the *sīra–maghāzī* literature as interpretation, as extension, as confirmation of scripture requires assent to a gratuitous chronology (*asbāb al-nuzūl*). It also involves accepting the

[1] *QS*, 47–52, 63–85.

structural priority of scripture in every context in which it appears, and that I think belied by even the most elementary stylistic analysis. Where, however, deployment of the scriptural component coincides with extensive segments of the familiar text of the canon, it is clearly tempting to regard the product as exegesis. That view may be tested with respect to those passages of the *Sīra* which deal with Medinese and with Jewish opposition to the Arabian prophet.

Sīra i, 519–27 relates eleven episodes pertinent to the first of those themes, of which the keyword is hypocrisy (*nifāq*), intended to convey both disloyalty to Muhammad and backsliding after conversion to the new faith. The first example (519–20) was that of Julās b. Suwayd, who swore by God to the prophet that he had not in fact uttered the unflattering remark about him (namely, 'if that man is telling the truth then we are less than asses') reported to Muhammad by the talebearer ʿUmayr b. Saʿd. Thus was revealed Q. 9: 74: 'They swear by God that they did not express the rejection/disbelief which they did after their submission/conversion . . .'. The second example (520–1) is merely a sequel to the first, involving Ḥārith b. Suwayd, brother of Julās, and the revelation of Q. 3: 86: 'How will God guide a people who reject/disbelieve after having believed . . .?' In the third (521–2) one Nabtal b. al-Ḥārith, about whose malice Muhammad had been warned by Gabriel, is made to engage the prophet in conversation, then to report to his friends that Muhammad was nothing but a great gullible ear, believing everything told him. Thus Q. 9: 61: 'And some there are who insult the prophet, declaring that he is an ear . . .'. In the fourth (522) Thaʿlaba b. Ḥāṭib and Muʿattib b. Qushayr are described as 'those who undertook before God to believe and to conduct themselves piously in return for His bounty', but the scriptural reference (*scil.* Q. 9: 75) is not given. Muʿattib was then reported to have declared, at the battle of Uḥud: 'Had we any say in the matter we should not be dying here', whereupon Q. 3: 154: 'And a group, concerned for themselves and suspecting, in their pagan fashion, God unjustly, assert: had we any say in the matter . . .' Muʿattib was also alleged to have exclaimed, at the battle of Khandaq (*Aḥzāb*): 'Muhammad promised that we should enjoy the treasures of Chosroes and Caesar . . .', whereupon Q. 33: 12: 'Thus declare the hypocrites (*munāfiqūn*) and those sick in their hearts: what God and His messenger have promised us is nothing but deception.'

Here, and in the next example (522–3), is implicit allusion to Q. 9: 107 (*masjidan ḍirāran*) from which was fashioned the story of the notorious 'mosque of contention' (*masjid al-ḍirār*). A feature of this anecdote, with respect to 'Qur'ān reader' Mujammiʿ b. Jāriya, was to stress the allegation that those responsible for the *masjid* had no scriptural text of their own. In the sixth example (523) one of that group, Wadīʿa b. Thābit, is made to say on behalf of the enterprise: 'But we were only bantering and joking', whereupon Q. 9: 65: 'And if you ask them, they will say: we were only bantering and joking . . .'. In the next (523–4) Mirbaʿ b. Qayẓiyy, for not allowing Muhammad passage through his property on his way to Uḥud, provoked the censure: 'He is blind, blind in his heart and blind in his eyes', which may be compared with, though it is not adduced, Q. 22: 46 ('Blind are not their eyes, but rather their hearts . . .'). On the other hand, his brother Aws b. Qayẓiyy became, when he asked to be excused from Khandaq on the grounds that 'our houses are unprotected', the object of an explicit scriptural reference, namely Q. 33: 13: 'They will say: our houses are unprotected . . .' The eighth example (524–5) exhibits some confusion in its composition: the ostensible object of Q. 4: 107 ('those who betray themselves') is one Bushayr b. Ubayraq, not otherwise attested in the *Sīra*, but the substance of the narrative is the account of two men wounded in battle in the prophet's cause: Yazīd b. Ḥāṭib and one Quzmān, a confederate of B. Ẓafar. In parallel deathbed scenes the former was denied the comforts of Muslim salvation by his pagan father, and the latter by the fact of having taken his own life *in extremis*. They it is, of course, 'who betrayed themselves' or were betrayed. The argument is clear and the point a theological *topos*.

In the ninth example (526) reference is made to traditional (pagan) arbitration in a public dispute, the litigants being Julās b. Suwayd and his companions. By way of Q. 4: 60 it is made clear that recourse to soothsayers or pagan arbiters (*al-kuhhān ḥukkām ahl al-jāhiliyya*) was incompatible with the new proclamation. The tenth example (526) is straightforward: Jadd b. Qays was reported to have said to the prophet 'O Muhammad, grant me indulgence and do not put me in the way of temptation' (the circumstances are not specified), whereupon Q. 9: 49: 'Some there are who say: grant me indulgence and do not put me in the way of temptation . . .' The final episode in this narrative sequence (526–7) is related of the arch-enemy of Muhammad in Medina, ʿAbdallāh b. Ubayy b. Salūl. The first scriptural reference is naturally Q. 63 (*Al-Munāfiqūn*) and the only circumstantial allusion Muhammad's expedition against B. Muṣṭaliq (Muraysīʿ), upon which occasion Ibn Ubayy was heard to utter his celebrated threat to the political order in Medina: 'When we return the powerful will expel the weak.' The second reference is to his promise and, in the event, failure, to come to the assistance of B. Naḍīr during Muhammad's siege: 'If you should be expelled we will accompany you', whereupon Q. 59: 11–16: 'Have you not considered the hypocrites who say to their errant brethren: if you should be expelled we will accompany you . . .'

Collocation of explicit scriptural reference in this passage reveals dominance of *Sūra* 9, followed by 4, 3, and 33, with 63 and 59 represented once each. In itself perhaps of little significance, it exhibits retrospectively at least a narrowing range of selection. Rather more important is occurrence throughout of the term *qiṣṣa* (521, 522, 523, 526 (twice), 527), in the unmistakable sense of 'scriptural segment', or pericope. Standard usage appears to be, following a scriptural extract, 'to the end of the pericope' (*ilā ākhiri 'l-qiṣṣa*), save at 527: 'then the pericope from the *sūra* up to . . .' (*thumma 'l-qiṣṣa min al-sūra ḥattā* . . .). Now, in one instance (522) the formula occurs not after an explicit reference but merely an implicit allusion to scripture, namely Q. 9: 75, mentioned above in the episode concerning Thaʿlaba b. Ḥāṭib. As is well known, the root *q-ṣ-ṣ* is Quranic, most frequently employed in the sense of 'narration' (e.g. 7: 101), but also of 'recitation' (e.g. 6: 130), and its application to homily and paraenasis widely attested.[1] In the present context its application is clearly midrashic: an approximate equivalent of Rabbinic *parashah.* Like the latter, Arabic *qiṣṣa* contains an important ambiguity: reference may be to the pericope itself, to the accompanying interpretation, or to the combination of both. Its nucleus may be the verse itself, its commentary, or the verbal (occasionally conceptual) link between them.[2] In the three passages of the *Sīra* which I have adduced so far, the majority of separate episodes has been characterized by the presence of a keyword or concept, itself the single irreducible core of the narrative unit. Identification of that core for each unit is not difficult, as I hope to have shown. Of more value, and perhaps of more interest, is the next step: to detect a pattern in these keywords (*topoi*) which could shed some light both on their origins and on the motives in their selection. To some extent, the results of such an investigation will be statistically conditioned, that is, by the quantity of material analysed. But limits of space and of time demand selectivity, a procedure as unavoidably arbitrary as the alternative would be tedious. In anticipation of my conclusions in this chapter I would suggest, with due reservation, that the origin of these *topoi* was interconfessional polemic and that their selection was imposed upon the early Muslim community from outside.

In my fourth illustration from the *Sīra* (i, 530–72) there is evidence of a careful thematic transition: from the Medinese (Arab) mockery of Muhammad to his rejection by the Jews. As in the previous passages, the narrative here is episodic and the structure derived from a juxtaposition of anecdote and scripture. But unlike the previous examples, the scriptural components are here neither widely diffused in relation to the canon nor limited to just a few contexts, but rather, exhibit long and often uninterrupted sequences of the canonical text. The technical term *qiṣṣa* occurs (541 (twice), 549, 555, 558, 565,) of which one formulation (541) deserves notice: 'this pericope was then revealed' (*nuzilat hādhihi 'l-qiṣṣa*). The scriptural segments adduced are these: first two-thirds of *Sūra* 2, first half and end of *Sūra* 3,

[1] *QS*, 145–8.
[2] W. Bacher, *Die exegetische Terminologie der jüdischen Traditionsliteratur* i–ii, Hildesheim, 1965, i, 160–2, ii, 169–70.

portions from the middle and end of *Sūra* 4, and from the first half of *Sūra* 5, a miscellany from *Sūras* 6, 7, 9, 17, 39, 112, and (inserted earlier) a verse from *Sūra* 48. Within the passage one section (530–44) constitutes a structural unit separate from and introductory to the remainder. The style is unmistakably exegetical (short segments of scripture followed by rudimentary paraphrase with connective *ay*) but without the anecdote and identification (*ta'yīn*) characteristic of the haggadic style. In other words, the Quranic passage treated (Q. 2: 1–102) is left more or less anonymous, save for general allusion to B. Israel (vv. 1–7, 40–4, 57–8, 61, 73–8, 80-90, 94–102) and to the 'hypocrites' of B. Aws and Khazraj (vv. 8–24). At two points only is direct relation to contemporary events specified: 540–1 (*ad* Q. 2: 85–6) where the social and juridical aspects of Jewish-Arab association in Medina at the time of Muhammad's arrival are set out; and 543–4 (*ad* Q. 2: 97–102) where a modified version of the celebrated 'rabbinical test of prophethood'[1] is retailed together with a codicil on the disputed allegation that Solomon was a genuine prophet. Two further points may be noted: where the insistence of B. Israel upon seeing God face to face (*jahratan*) is mentioned (534) it is not Q. 2: 55 which is cited and which one would in this sequence expect, but Q. 4: 153, a minor, but from the point of view of the scriptural canon possibly significant variant. Second, following upon the description of Jewish–Arab relations in Medina (541) and explicit reference to Q. 2: 89 is the standard imagery of the pagan (*Jāhilī*) 'setting': 'We were polytheists, they in possession of scripture . . .'. Save for these unevennessess, it can hardly be doubted that composition of the entire section (530–44) was determined by the priority of scripture.

The remainder of the passage (544–72) exhibits reversion to the narrative technique with which I have so far been concerned. The first episode is formulated as a letter, from Muhammad to the Jews of Khaybar (544–5). Provided with a *basmala* and a few pious introductory formulae, the document comprises two elements: the text of Q. 48: 29, in which is stressed the fervent piety of Muhammad's companions; and a challenge to the addressees to acknowledge that Muhammad's prognosis was contained in Jewish scripture. The concluding formulae contain a paraphrase of part and an extract from Q. 2: 256: 'You shall not be compelled (though) truth will be distinguished from error.' Transmitted from 'Abdallāh b. 'Abbās, the letter is undated and without other marks of official or chancery origin. Not that such ought in this context to be expected: the polemical value of the 'document' is adequate explanation both of its composition and of its inclusion here, as prelude to a long series (thirty-eight items) of incidents attesting the doctrinal differences between Judaism and Islam.

The order of this series conforms to the sequence of Muslim scripture which, with some small overlapping margin, begins where the straight-

[1] *QS*, 122–46.

forward exegesis (530–44) had stopped. The first item (545–7) is an exercise in apocalyptic arithmetic derived from the Quranic sigla, and with particular reference to the *alif-lām-mīm* of Q. 2: 1. The challenge was articulated by Ḥuyay b. Akhṭab, who compelled Muhammad to consent to numerical interpretation (*gematria/ḥisāb al-jummal*) of the sigla and to divulge further examples from his revelation, producing thus a range of chronological speculation (from 71 to 734 years) on the duration of the new dispensation, a theme upon which much ink was to be expended in the exegetical tradition. It was the Jewish view, of course, that no prophet was granted such information, to which the Muslim reply was revelation of Q. 3: 7, of which one interpretation identified *mutashābihāt* with the Quranic sigla.[1] The next item (547) is the by now familiar assertion of Jewish perfidy attached to Q. 2: 89, according to which their expected prophet was sent to the Arabs and their own messianic hopes thus frustrated. In the following episode (547–8) Mālik b. al-Sayf denied that the Jews had ever accepted a covenant (obligation) from God with respect to Muhammad, whereupon was revealed Q. 2: 100: 'Every time they enter into an obligation a group of them rejects it.' Abū Ṣalūbā (548) challenged Muhammad: 'You have brought us nothing we recognize, nor has God revealed to you any sign at all that we can accept', to which the reply was Q. 2: 99: 'We have revealed to you clear signs, which only sinners reject.' And Rāfiʿ b. Ḥuraymila (548) said: 'Bring us a book sent from heaven which we can read, and cause water to gush forth, then we will accept you', provoking the revelation of Q. 2: 108: 'Or do you wish to try your apostle as Moses in the past was tried . . .?' Again (548) Ḥuyay b. Akhṭab and his brother were described as envious (*sic*) of the Arabs and determined to prevent conversions to the new faith, whereupon Q. 2: 109: 'Many of the Jews (*ahl al-kitāb*) wish out of envy (*ḥasad*) to bring about your apostasy . . .'

The *topoi* so far adduced include: alleged prognosis of Muhammad in Jewish scripture, Jewish perversity in rejecting fulfilment of their own messianic expectations, Jewish insistence upon miracles as credentials of prophethood, and Jewish perfidy in the interpretation of Muhammad's revelation. These are basic points of dispute that were to become constants in the literature of interconfessional polemic. Set out here, in what may be their earliest formulation in writing, they are fragmentary and undeveloped. But the primitive and rudimentary quality of this record might be thought evidence of its historicity: there is, indeed, a distinctly persuasive character about the circumstantial detail in which these polemical *topoi* are embedded. While, for example, it seems unlikely that the dialogue between Ḥuyay b. Akhṭab and Muhammad on the significance of the Quranic sigla actually took place, the language itself is witty, spicy, and undoubtedly authentic.

[1] *QS*, 149–50.

Rather less confidence can be placed in those briefer conversations generated by a keyword or concept, e.g. covenant/obligation (*'ahd*), sign (*āya*), challenge (*istiftāḥ*), envy (*hasad*), etc. A good example is the next episode in this series (549): upon the occasion of a Christian delegation to Muhammad from Najrān the Medinese Jews confronted the visitors in his presence, in order, apparently, to exchange the single recrimination: 'The Jews/Christians have no argument at all.' The *topos* is exhibited in the simultaneous revelation of Q. 2: 113: 'And the Jews say the Christians have no argument; and the Christians say the Jews have no argument, though both read scripture . . .' The anecdote is completed by an exegetical passage in which that recrimination was traced to the refusal by both parties to consult without prejudice their own scriptures. The polemical theme is of course the charge of scriptural falsification (*taḥrīf*) and its corollary: supersession by Islam of both earlier dispensations. The polemical 'fact' is undoubtedly real, its historicization unconvincing.

Again (549), Rāfiʿ b. Ḥuraymila challenged Muhammad to corroborate his mission by asking God 'to speak to us that we may hear His words', whereupon Q. 2: 118: 'And those who do not understand say: if only God would speak to us or send us a sign.' When (549–50) 'Abdallāh b. Ṣūriyā and the Christians (*sic*; presumably the delegation from Najrān) said to Muhammad: 'The only right way is ours; if you follow us you cannot fail', the scriptural version becomes (Q. 2: 135–41): 'They say: be a Jew or Christian and you will not fail . . .', a syntactic construction which, incidentally, was something of a problem to later masoretic exegesis.[1] Historicization of the *qibla* (direction of prayer) controversy is of particular interest (550–1): identification of the Jews (Ka'b b. al-Ashraf *et al.*) as those who objected to Muhammad's fixing of prayer in the direction of Mecca is, from the point of view of the scriptural sequence here (Q. 2: 142–7), gratuitous. But the *topos* itself (direction of prayer as sectarian emblem) was of ancient lineage in polemical literature, and a not unexpected element in the Muslim version of that literature. Similarly, the next episode (551), in which a group of the Anṣār asked some rabbis for a detail of the Torah which the latter concealed from them (*fa-katamūhum iyyāhu*), whereupon Q. 2: 159: 'Those who conceal the proofs and guidance which We have revealed (*inna 'l-ladhīna yaktumūna mā anzalnā . . .*).' The 'concealment' (*kitmān*) *topos* became an important component of the Muslim charge that God's word had been distorted and abused in the hands of faithless custodians. Further (552) the reply of the Jews when invited by Muhammad to join him: 'But we follow the path of our fathers', whereupon Q. 2: 170: 'They say: but we follow the path of our fathers . . .', exhibits an abundantly attested scriptural formula (*mā . . . 'alayhi abā'unā*), and one with ancient antecedents.

[1] *QS*, 233–4.

A recurring motif in this passage is, as has been noticed, the public dispute. Its course is more often than not predictable, but occasionally atypical, e.g. after Badr when Muhammad had assembled the Jews in the market of B. Qaynuqāʿ (552), they asserted that Quraysh knew nothing of war and that they (the Jews) would fare better if challenged by Muhammad. The ensuing revelation (Q. 3: 12): 'Say to those who reject/disbeleive: you will be overcome and delivered unto damnation . . .' is probably an eschatological threat and unrelated to the challenge of the Jews, itself hardly compatible with the inferior role assigned them in other reports of the political situation in Medina. But the next episode (552–3) is characteristic: Muhammad entered the Bet ha-midrash to argue the merits of Abraham and to summon the Jews (to return) to the Torah (*sic*). They refused (*sic*) and were described in Q. 3: 24 as ingenuously overconfident in their hope of salvation. In the following anecdote (553) the rabbis, again joined by the Christian delegation from Najrān, disputed the precise status of Abraham: whether Jew or Christian. The matter was settled by Q. 3: 65–8: neither Jew nor Christian but a Muslim seeker of God (*ḥanīfan musliman*), and assimilated thereby to a Judaeo-Christian dispute of long standing. On the next occasion (553) Jewish perfidy was illustrated, rather clumsily, in this way: a group of Jews conspired to accept Muhammad's revelation/mission in the morning (*ghudwatan*) and to reject it in the evening (*ʿashiyatan*), in order to confuse and to confound him. The scriptural version (Q. 3: 71–3) reads: 'O Jews, why do you confound truth with error . . . and a party of them say: accept what is revealed to them at the beginning of the day then reject it at its end'. When the Christians from Najrān and the rabbis again join forces (554) it was to ask whether Muhammad really expected to be worshipped/served as the Christians worshipped Jesus, a belief apparently shared by both groups but curtly dismissed by Muhammad himself and by scripture (Q. 3: 78–80). The session was concluded by reference to the prophetical covenant (Q. 3: 81) and Muhammad's expectation that the Jews at least would acknowledge its renewal.

To the four polemical *topoi* earlier noticed may be added: the Muslim charge of scriptural falsification, the Muslim claim of supersession, dispute about the direction of prayer, and about the roles in salvation history of Abraham and Jesus. The several occasions in this passage where Jews and Christians (the latter always from outside the Ḥijāz) appear as one man against the Arabian prophet exhibit some internal contradiction as well as undifferentiated confessional emblems, noted above in the initial descriptions of reactions to the Muhammadan kerygma. Evidence of stereotype is, however, not lacking. The Jew as *agent provocateur*, moved by envy (*ḥasad*) of the new community's solidarity, is an example (555–7): Shās b. Qays of B. Qaynuqāʿ sought to dispel this euphoria by reminding the Medinese converts from Aws and Khazraj of their former enmity at the battle of Bu'āth. He succeeded, and the two groups came to blows, stopped only by the timely intervention of Muhammad supported by a party of Meccan (*sic*) converts, whose words of pacification were reflected in Q. 3: 99–100. In the next illustration of that theme (557–8) the rabbis are made to say of their own converts to Islam (*Sīra* i, 513–8, 527–9): 'They are the worst of our number, had they been of the best they would never have abandoned the faith of their fathers.' To which the scriptural response (Q. 3: 113) was: 'They are not all alike, amongst the Jews (*ahl al-kitāb*) is a faction (*umma*: *sic*) who recite the words of God during the night and prostrate themselves.' Muhammad's companions were, none the less, forbidden alliance/intimacy (*biṭāna*) with them (Q. 3: 118–19). Jewish blasphemy (*sic*) is characterized by a dialogue in the Bet ha-midrash between Abū Bakr and the Rabbi Finhās (558–9): to the former's demand that the Jews finally acknowledge Muhammad and admit to his prognosis in their Torah and Gospel (*sic*), the latter replied: 'We have no need of God, but He needs (*faqīr*) us; we do not beseech Him as He beseeches us, for we can dispense (*ghanīy*) with Him, but not He with us . . .' Abū Bakr's anger and assault on the arrogant rabbi, who later denied having uttered those words, were brought to the attention of Muhammad and the dispute settled by revelation (Q. 3: 181): 'And God has heard the words of those who say: God is poor (in need) and we are rich (independent) . . .' with further allusion to the affair by way of Q. 3: 186–8. When, in the next episode (560), the Jews insinuate themselves into the confidence of the Anṣār and recommend their withholding contributions (*nafaqa*) to the maintenance of the struggling community, since they could 'not know what lay ahead', Q. 4: 37 was revealed: 'Those who are mean and who counsel meanness (*bukhl*) . . .' Again (560–1), when Rifā' b. Zayd the Jew spoke to Muhammad he would begin 'Lend me your ear, Muhammad', and then slander (*lawā lisānahu*) and attack (*ṭa'ana*) his religion, his conduct was reflected in scripture (Q. 4: 44–7): 'And amongst the Jews are those who say . . . lend us your ear, and then slander and attack (our) religion . . .'

Reflexes of traditional *topoi* are exhibited in the following episodes. The conspiracy (*scil. aḥzāb*) between Quraysh, Ghaṭafān, and the Jews (B. Qurayẓa and Naḍīr) became an occasion (561–2) for weighing the merits of Arabian paganism and Muhammad's proclamation. When consulted, the Jews assured Quraysh that they were closer to the truth than their erstwhile compatriot. By revelation of Q. 4: 51 the Jews were accused of idolatry (*yu'minūn bil-jibt wal-ṭāghūt*), a charge which may reflect a (very distorted) image from polemic internal to the Jewish community. Further (562–3), the Jewish claim that there had been no divine revelation since that granted to Moses, countered here by revelation of Q. 4: 163–6, exhibits a *topos* of Jewish sectarian polemic. A doublet of this dispute appears later in the passage (563–4), where the scriptural retort adduced is Q. 5: 19, in which was justified the interval (*fatra*) between past prophets and the appearance of Muhammad.

The status of the Arabian prophet in Medinese politics was the point of departure for several episodes combining polemical *topoi* with explicit reference to scripture. It was during a visit (563) of Muhammad to B. Naḍīr about an affair of blood-money (*dīya*) that he was saved by divine intervention from an attempt on his life, reflected in the revelation of Q. 5: 11. Called upon to arbitrate (566) in a similar affair between B. Naḍīr and B. Qurayẓa, he was granted divine guidance in the matter by Q. 5: 42. Invoked by wily rabbis (564–5) to pronounce judgement on two Jews found guilty of adultery, he avoided their snare and was confirmed in his decision by revelation of Q. 5: 41. On another occasion (567), in which the point of litigation is not specified, Muhammad rejected the blandishments of the rabbis, a tactic corroborated by revelation of Q. 5: 49–50. Now, these verses from Sūrat al-Mā'ida were to become the major *loci probantes* in halakhic speculation on the jurisdiction of the *imām*, the authority of the Qur'ān, and the means by which conflict between them could be harmonized.[1] In the *Sīra*, however, the context is haggadic and the *topoi* appropriate to interconfessional polemic about the credentials of prophethood, the corruption of Jewish scripture, and the validity of the new dispensation announced by God throught the agency of Muhammad.

Doctrinal niceties are rare in this passage. A rather crude formulation of unitarian Islam appears in a context (563) contrived to produce Q. 5: 18. In reply to Muhammad's sermon on divine recompense (*niqma*) the Jews are made to say: 'But we have no fear, we are the sons and beloved of God.' The author comments: 'Just what the Christians say!' And scripture: 'The Jews and Christians say: we are the sons of God and His beloved.' Later (570) the *topos* is differently treated, when a group of Jews complained to Muhammad that they could hardly accept him after he had abandoned their *qibla* and declared that Ezra was the son of God (*sic*). Thereupon was revealed Q. 9: 30: 'And the Jews say that Ezra is the son of God, while the Christians say that the Messiah is the son of God . . .' On yet another occasion (567) Muhammad, called upon by Jews to list just which prophets he did accept (*sic*), cited Q. 2: 136 and when he came to the name of Jesus his interlocutors objected: 'We will never believe in Jesus the son of Mary or in anyone who does believe in him.' To which the final retort was Q. 5: 59: 'O Jews, can you only plague us for believing in God and in what He has revealed, both to us and before our time . . .?' Jewish perfidy, here violation of the covenant (*mīthāq*) and concealing (*kitmān*) the real contents of the Torah, is the subject of a further dispute (568), in which the last word was

[1] *QS*, 185–95, 70–1; cf. J. Burton, *The Collection of the Qur'ān*, Cambridge, 1977, 68–86; cf. *BSOAS* xli (1978) 370–1.

Q. 5: 68: 'O Jews (*ahl al-kitāb*), you have no argument unless you hold fast to the Torah and the Gospel [*sic*] and what has been revealed to you by your lord . . .' It may be thought that this particular verse was badly matched to the context. The charge of idolatry had originally been levelled at the Jews only in the context of their conspiracy with Quraysh; later in the passage (568) the bald assertion that there were 'other gods than/with God' was ascribed to a group of Jews and rebutted by Q. 6: 19: 'Do you really testify that there are other gods than/with God? Say: I do not so testify. He is only one God, and I am free of your polytheism (*mimā tushrikūn*).'

Towards the end of this long passage (569) the apocalyptic theme which had introduced it is touched upon again. This time the Jews, who had previously asserted that no prophet had ever been told of the duration of his dispensation, asked Muhammad: 'When is the Judgment (*al-sā'a*) to be, if you are really a prophet as you claim?' The rejoinder was Q. 7: 187, which left the matter to God's discretion. Earlier the Jew Rāfi' b. Ḥuraymila had asked Muhammad for a book from heaven as bona fides of his mission; now (570–1) a party of Jews, dissatisfied with the disorder of Muhammad's revelation (*lā narāhu muttasiqan kamā tattasiq al-tawrāt*), ask 'for a book from heaven which we can read and recognize'. Then, the reply had been Q. 2: 108 complaining of their harassing tactics; now, it was Q. 17: 88, one of the celebrated *taḥaddī* verses, asserting the inimitability of the Quranic revelation.[1] The narrative framework is at least reasonable: polemic about the quality (rhetorical and otherwise) of Muslim scripture can only be derived from a Jewish milieu. At this point (571) there is a reference to the 'rabbinical test of prophethood', not to the modified Medina version mentioned above, but to the original Meccan recension, in which Quraysh had sought to pick the brains of the rabbis in Yathrib. The final episode (571–2) in this passage of the *Sīra* is, as might be expected, a public confrontation between Muhammad and a gathering of Jews, who now posed an Aristotelian problem: 'If God is responsible for this Creation, who then created God?' Muhammad lost his temper, but Gabriel arrived with the revelation of Q. 112, the pertinence of which may be thought at least questionable. The Jews were not impressed. They asked: 'But how did He do it? What limbs did He use?' Again Gabriel appeared, this time with Q. 39: 67: 'And they have estimated God falsely, for at the resurrection He shall grasp the entire earth and the heavens folded in His hand.' Muhammad's interrogators may not have been satisfied, but for the author of the *Sīra* the matter was closed.

This long and disjointed passage (*Sīra* i, 544–72) contains a series of *tableaux* with a single common element: Judaeo-Muslim polemic. Each of the scenes owes its expression to a commonplace (*topos*) of that polemic,

[1] *QS*, 79.

from which were derived both its scriptural and non-scriptural ('historical') components. Some of the juxtapositions are more felicitous than others. For example, introduction of the Christians is always gratuitous, and their alleged place of origin (Najrān) suspect. The motif itself, a delegation (*wafd*) to the Arabian prophet (549, 553, 554) figures elsewhere and may even contain a semblance of historicity. At *Sīra* i, 391–3 there is a report of a Christian delegation from Ethiopia (variant: Najrān!) to Muhammad at Mecca who became Muslims despite the public scorn instigated by Abū Jahl. At *Sīra* i, 573–84 a Melkite (*sic*) delegation from Najrān to Muhammad at Medina provided the occasion of a not very sophisticated outline of Christological controversy following the structure of Q. 3: 1–64. They were not converted, but parted amicably from Muhammad, taking with them a Muslim to fill the post of local arbitrator.

Of greater significance for this passage, however, is a second motif, the public dispute (*jadl/mujādala*) by means of which a forensic display of Muhammad's credentials is (repeatedly) achieved. Here the sequence of episodes may also be significant; chronology is anyway arbitrary since the scriptural references follow loosely the canonical text of the Qur'ān. That might seem to indicate a structural priority for scripture, as proposed for the relatively colourless exegetical passage (530–44). But again, as in the earlier passages analysed, the most conspicuous literary element in each *tableau* is the keyword, which may appear to justify the combination of scripture and non-scripture, even when as total entities they are not quite commensurate (e.g. the references in an exclusively Jewish setting to Gospel and polytheism). There is seldom in these narratives movement which cannot be immediately derived from the accompanying scriptural imagery. Conversely, there is very little in the scriptural component which cannot be, or have been, generated from the composition of the (nearly always) preceding anecdote.

The technique which I have called historicization can hardly be described as exegetical. It is in the frequent later insertions by the editor Ibn Hishām (which I have intentionally omitted from this analysis) that exegesis of a sort can be found, e.g. lexical, genealogical, topographical. The technique is also consistently elliptic. Never is the actual process of revelation made explicit, for example in the (elsewhere frequently attested) formulaic description of the prophet's 'seizure' (e.g. *Sīra* ii, 302: fever, perspiration, etc.), and very seldom by the agency of Gabriel, in the also fairly common *deus ex machina* formulation.[1] The standard locution in the passages so far examined is 'Thus/whereupon God revealed' (*fa-anzala 'llāh*), a mechanical insertion and often the only means of distinguishing the scriptural component from its immediate environment, as in the story of Ibn al-Ziba'rā and the polytheists. Apart from that device, evidence of scripture

[1] *QS*, 34–8, 61–3, 193 n. 5.

can be inferred only from a few quite fixed and much overworked rhetorical formulae (e.g. 'say', 'O you who . . .'. etc.). Moreover, the occasional glimpse of a narrative framework, as indicated above for the passage dealing with Meccan opposition to Muhammad (regular appearance of *dramatis personae*), and for that describing Jewish resistance (resumption of apocalyptic theme), could be thought to neutralize the priority of scripture there. The common denominator throughout, even when the term itself is not specified, is the midrashic pericope (*qiṣṣa*): a morphological constant based on a keyword/concept reflecting a polemical *topos*. In the analytical terminology of Jolles the *qiṣṣa* would be a speech-act (*Sprachgebärde*) and the *topos* a motive (*Geistesbeschäftigung*). The process of historicization is primarily mythic: the translation of strange, often hostile phenomena into familiar categories. The four passages of the *Sīra* seem to me in that sense mythic, illustrating four stages in the emergence of the Islamic kerygma: (*a*) initial proclamation, (*b*) pagan reaction, (*c*) opportunist and hypocritical submission, (*d*) Jewish rejection.

Application of the technique can be exaggerated. An example is the eschatological imagery of Q. 111, the first verse of which is usually rendered 'May the hands of Abū Lahab perish'. It appears at *Sīra* i, 351–2 and 355–6 juxtaposed to the complaint of one of Muhammad's uncles ʿAbd al-ʿUzzā, called Abū Lahab, that he could see nothing 'in his hands' of what the prophet had promised for the resurrection (*baʿd al-mawt*). The combination of 'Abū Lahab' (father of flame) with the description in Q. 111: 3 of hellfire as 'flaming' (*dhāt lahab*) and of his mate in Q. 111: 4 as 'stoker' (*ḥammālat al-ḥaṭab*) hardly requires a fixed historical context. The metaphorical value of 'hand' is in Muslim scripture formulaic, e.g. as 'power' (*qudra*) or 'mercy' (*raḥma*) *passim*, as 'deed or 'agent' (Q. 18: 57 *mā qaddamat yadāhu*), as 'obvious' (spatial) or 'imminent' (temporal) in the locution *bayna yadayhi*, *passim*. The anecdote itself may belong to that kind of 'history' known in Arabic as 'identification of the vague/ambiguous' (*taʿyīn al-mubham*), or appears at least to have been so understood in later exegetical literature, e.g. Zamakhsharī ad loc., on the value and origin of the symbolic *kunya* Abū Lahab (*Kashshāf* iv, 814). The 'märchen' attached to the figure of Umm Jamīl but, as has been noticed, not yet embellished by the 'screen' imagery of Q. 17:45, exhibits a form not often encountered in the *sīra-maghāzī* literature. It, too, may be read as mythic, that is, interpretation of the bizarre and unexpected as evidence of divine intervention in the affairs of men. Further witness to 'märchen' as myth may be found in two anecdotes about Muhammad's chief adversary in Mecca, Abū Jahl (also a symbolic *kunya*: *per antiphrasin* Abū Ḥakam): on both occasions he was compelled to submit to the prophet's greater strength, guaranteed by the unexpected and ferocious presence of a camel stallion (*Sīra* i, 298–9, 389–90: *faḥl min al-ibl*). Now, it is quite unnecessary to question the historicity of these 'events': more important is the combination of scriptural imagery and symbolic action which together make up the narrative/homiletic pericope.

Another instance of the historicization of an eschatological image is the well-known story of the Najrān martyrs (*Sīra* i, 31-7) and the 'men of the trench' (*aṣḥāb al-ukhdūd*) of Q. 85: 4. A reminiscence at least of the historical event is attested in sources outside the Islamic tradition. The scriptural locution is something of a problem: it may reflect a Biblical image, or more specifically the Qumranic lexicon, but can hardly be made to bear the burden of a historical allusion.[1] It may be supposed that the production of salvation history required scriptural witness that could be read 'historically'. The final result was the Qur'ān; an earlier stage is represented in the midrashic pericope.

Of that stage the canonical text of scripture contains vestiges. I have elsewhere described Quranic style as 'referential'[2] The epithet was intended to convey both its allusive and its elliptical character: allusion to an oral/literary tradition already familiar, and ellipsis in the intermittent and occasionally distorted treatment of that tradition. By way of illustration I attempted an analysis of *Sūrat Yūsuf* and *Sūrat al-Kahf*, both from within the exegetical framework of the haggadah.[3] It was only within that framework that either *sūra* achieved anything approaching narrative coherence. Shorn of the haggadah the canonical text was often meaningless, an observation which provoked the question of priorities and eventual recourse to the provisional (and hypothetical) term 'prophetical *logia*'. Quranic narrative is not merely repetitive and fragmentary, it is also proleptic. An example is Q. 38: 41, where Job knows already that it is Satan who was responsible for his misery.[4] Another is Q. 37: 102: 'O son, I saw in a dream that I am going to sacrifice you. What do you think of that?' The protagonists are of course Abraham and Isaac: into this single utterance the dramatic tension of Genesis 22: 1-8 was compressed, and thus eliminated. The Quranic verse is not simply a report of the event: it is commentary derived from the keyword 'sacrifice'. The dream motif may well be Rabbinic, and in that context familiarity with the Biblical passage was presupposed.[5] A similar phenomenon can be seen in Q. 12: 59, where Joseph's peremptory and, in the context, quite unexpected demand: 'Bring me a brother of yours from your father' requires, that any sense at all emerge, a knowledge of Genesis

[1] I. Shahid, 'The Book of the Himyarites: authorship and authenticity', *Le Muséon* lxxvi (1963) 349–62; M. Philonenko, 'Une expression Qoumranienne dans le Coran', in R. Paret (ed.), *Der Koran*, Wege der Forschung CCCXXVI, Darmstadt, 1975, 197–200.

[2] *QS*, 1, 40–3, 47–8, 51–2, 57–8.

[3] *QS*, 122–31, 131–9.

[4] H. Speyer, *Die biblischen Erzählungen im Qoran*, Hildesheim, 1961, 411.

[5] Speyer, op. cit. 164–5; G. Vermes, *Scripture and Tradition in Judaism*, Leiden, 1973, 194–8.

42: 3–13.[1] In all three instances the Muslim haggadah becomes a substitute for the Biblical passage, but does not relieve the harsh ellipsis of the Quranic utterance.

Another kind of prolepsis is exhibited in the Quranic version of a familiar *topos*: hardening of the heart. Two verses in particular are of interest in that the affliction is confidently acknowledged by its victims: 'Our hearts are veiled' (Q. 41: 5), and 'Our hearts are uncircumcised' (Q. 2: 88). The conventional Biblical image (e.g. Psalm 95: 8) is inverted and cause of the condition omitted.[2] The circumstances of literary or oral transmission in which a metamorphosis of that kind can take place are not easy to imagine. In the exegetical literature these ruptures and inversions are usually mended and straightened. In the midrashic pericope (*qiṣṣa*) the referential style of scripture is provided with a plausible external referent, or so it would seem. It may be, on the other hand, that the pericope, containing both report and *logia*, was prior in time and in conception to the forms in which both are now preserved.

I have referred to yet another midrashic style in which the role of scripture is less structural than ornamental (*ex post facto*). There the function of scripture is exegetical, its object of interpretation the neutral or profane historical report. From the point of view of style it is no longer, or at least not quite, as in the pericope, a matter of simple juxtaposition but rather, of parallel versions of the same action. For the relation between the two versions I suggested the term 'exemplification'. A specimen may be seen in the account of the battle of Badr (*Sīra* i, 606–77). The first version (606–66) contains a very circumstantial exposition of the prelude to, action during, and outcome of the first military engagement between Muhammad and the Meccans. The material of the description consists in, or is derived from, a number of themes and motifs familiar from the profane tradition of the *ayyām al-ʿarab*: e.g. clientship and loyalty, plunder and pursuit, challenges and instances of single combat. Documentation of oneiromancy and clairvoyance, e.g. the dream of ʿĀtika (607–9) and the vision of Juhaym (618), is part of that tradition; and the jibe of Abū Jahl to the effect that Quraysh seemed to be endowed with more than its due share of prophesying (*tanabbu'*) exhibits a modified reference to the pagan oracle. The behaviour of Quraysh throughout the account conforms to the ethos of the *ayyām*: to achieve honour and to avoid shame in a heroic society.[3] The conduct of Muhammad and his followers, on the other hand, does not offer quite the contrast to that of Quraysh found in the exegetical literature and in the

[1] *QS*, 134

[2] *QS*, 72–3; cf. H. Kosmala, *Hebräer—Essener—Christen*, Leiden, 1959, 6 (Heb. 3: 8, 15; 4: 7); H. J. Schoeps, *Theologie und Geschichte des Judenchristentums*, Tübingen, 1949, 156 (*sklerokardia*).

[3] Caskel, *Aijām*, 9–34; E. Meyer, *Der historische Gehalt der Aiyām al-ʿarab*, Wiesbaden, 1970, 5–24.

later *maghāzī* legend.[1] Formulae ('tags') such as consistent reference to Muhammad as Apostle of God (*rasūl allāh*) and mention of his frequent halts during the expedition to perform the ritual prayer (*ṣalāt*) may be discounted as structurally irrelevant. The action itself of the *ghazwa* which became a battle, the distinctly bedouin environment, and the motives ascribed to the protagonists correspond nicely to the same elements comprising the description of Quraysh. Despite fragmentary transmission and episodic presentation there is, indeed, a structural unity informing the account of Badr.

Two themes extraneous to the *ayyām* tradition may nevertheless be discerned: the divine promise (*wa'd*) to Muhammad at the outset, and the intervention of angels (*malā'ika*) during the battle. Neither is especially prominent. On three occasions (615, 621, 627) there is reference to God's promise that 'one of the two parties' (*iḥdā al-ṭā'ifatayn*: *scil.* the caravan or the army) would fall to Muhammad. There are also three allusions (633, 641, 647) to the role of the angelic hosts in the defeat of Quraysh. Neither theme (*topos*) is adduced as a specific cause of Muhammad's victory. The same may be said of two references to the role of Satan (Iblīs) in the deliberations of Quraysh: as challenge to Muhammad and his followers (612) and as responsible for their seduction (633) appear as ornamental rather than causal, and may be thought an appropriate counterpart to God and the angels. The satanic *topos* is elsewhere attested in the *Sīra*, e.g. in the plot of Quraysh to assassinate Muhammad (i, 480–2) and at the second meeting of 'Aqaba (i, 447), and seems to represent a conscious though crude modification of the pagan (*jinnī-shayṭān*) oracle to conform with a monotheist conception of the agencies of good and evil.[2] Of explicit reference to scripture in this section of the Badr account there are only three examples. Two of these document the angelic-satanic *topos*: Q. 4: 97 connects the angels with the fate of those Meccan Muslims who had in the event failed to migrate to Medina (641); Q. 8: 48 asserts the deceit and treachery of Satan, who had promised but not delivered aid to Quraysh (663). Of some interest in the latter example is appearance of the term 'shayṭān' in the verse and of the name 'Iblīs' in the gloss. The third scriptural reference is Q. 5: 24, on an earlier refusal of B. Israel to support Moses in battle, cited by Muhammad's companions in their assurance that they would not follow that example (615).

At no point in this account does scripture contribute to movement or to imagery. The literary type is thus not a pericope (*qiṣṣa*) in the sense defined above. It is, on the other hand, midrashic, and for the following reasons. Appended to the historical report is a section (666–77) consisting entirely of

[1] Paret, *Maghāzī-Literatur*, 1–10 (Badr), 170–211.

[2] *QS*, 59–61; cf. G. E. von Grunebaum, 'Observations on the Muslim concept of evil', *Studia Islamica* xxxi (1970) 117–34.

scriptural extracts related in somewhat arbitrary sequence to the account of Badr: a second version formulated, as it were, *sub specie aeternitatis*. The basic extract is Q. 8: 1–75 with some omissions (vv. 2–4, 18, 25, 28, 31, 37, 49–56, 58–9, 74) and one insertion (671), namely Q. 73. Exegetical in style (running commentary with connective *ay*), the passage provides the necessary *loci probantes* for the 'divine promise' (v. 7), the angelic hosts (v. 9), and the treachery of Satan (v. 48). But it provides even more: each verse is related to an event or figure in the preceding historical account, and is thus endowed with a specificity absent from scripture itself. The process cannot, however, be described as historicization, a term which I have reserved for the generation of 'history' otherwise unattested from a keyword or concept exhibiting more often than not a polemical *topos*. Here the more accurate epithet is exemplification, by which I mean the elevation of profane ('secular') action into a paradigm of divine causality. In other words, the battle (*yawm*) of Badr is transformed into an element of the Islamic theodicy (*ayyām allāh*).[1] Ostensible reason for adducing Q. 8 in connection with Badr is of course dispute about the division of spoils (*anfāl*: vv. 1, 41, 67–9). But the larger part by far of this section is concerned not with the spoils of war (property and prisoners), but rather with justification of God's design. Employment of such terms as *āya* (sign) and *'ibra* (*exemplum*: 673), *niyya* (intention) and *ḥisba* (reckoning: 674–5), *ribāṭ* (resolution) and *salm/silm/islām* (submission: 674–5),[2] reveals the purpose of this passage: transposition of *ghawza* into *jihād*.[3] What had been originally and primarily a comparison of strategic positions became retrospectively a demonstration of belief and right guidance, in brief: salvation history.

The relation of scripture to non-scripture in the account of Badr is thus loose and, to some extent, arbitrary.[4] It is quite impossible to argue that either element could in any way be derived from or dependent upon the other. It is equally impossible to doubt that structural priority in the composition belongs to the profane component. Scripture here is *ex post facto* as well as *ornatus*, and I would add, in anticipation of further samples of this style, that such is characteristic of the *maghāzī* literature, as contrasted with that of the *mab'ath*.

There is, however, evidence of variation and of development. In the slightly later work of Wāqidī the historical narrative of Badr covers 110 pages (19–128). Separated from this by two non-midrashic sections is a chapter (131-8) on the revelation of Q. 8 (*Sūrat al-Anfāl*). But already in the narrative itself the *topoi* of salvation history are abundantly attested and

[1] *QS*, 4–5.

[2] *QS*, 11, 185; A. Noth, *Heiliger Krieg und heiliger Kampf in Islam und Christentum*, Beiträge zur Vorgeschichte und Geschichte der Kreuzzüge, Bonn, 1966, 66–87.

[3] Cf. Noth, *Quellenkritische Studien*, 181 (Q. 30: 2 and Dhāt al-Ṣawārī).

[4] *Pace* F. Buhl, 'Ein paar Beiträge zur Kritik der Geschichte Muhammed's', *Orientalische Studien Theodor Nöldeke . . . gewidmet*, Giessen, 1906, i, 11 n. 3

carefully integrated, largely by means of scriptural citation. At the very start of his account (21) the author stressed the distinction between *ghazwa* and *jihād*, in reporting the opinion that had those (followers of Muhammad) who in the event did not participate understood that it was to be a question of *jihād*, they would surely have accompanied their leader, for they were 'men of pious intention and discernment' (*ahl niyyāt wa-baṣā'ir*). The dream of 'Ātika (29, 41–2, 122) is characterized as an omen/*exemplum* (*fa-laqad kāna dhālika 'ibratan*), as indeed were the hasty sacrifices of Abū Jahl (34, 96: *fa-kāna hādhā bayyinan*), and the warning of 'Addās that Quraysh were certain to meet their doom (35, 42). The satanic theme, formulated as the advice of Iblīs that Quraysh challenge Muhammad, is not omitted (38–9), but then neither is the *ayyām topos* that Quraysh (*scil.* Abū Jahl) took the decision with regard to their reputation amongst the bedouin (44: allusion to *qawl al-'arab*; cf. *Sīra* i, 618–19), condemned by reference to Q. 8: 47: '. . . those who act insolently and ostentatiously.' As in *Sīra* (i, 615), Q. 5: 24 is cited by Muhammad's followers to assure him of their loyalty (48), and in his selection of a camp site the prophet was advised by Gabriel (53–4). The 'divine promise' (*iḥdā al-ṭā'ifatayn*) is signalled by an implicit allusion to Q. 8: 7 and repeatedly asserted (49, 59, 67, 81, 112). The 'angelic hosts' (*malā'ika*) are introduced by explicit reference to Q. 8: 9–12 and the theme developed in some detail throughout the narrative (56–7, 70–1, 73, 75–80, 90–1), with implicit allusion (73) to the 'alleviation' (*takhfīf*) in Q. 8: 65–6. The challenge uttered (70) by Abū Jahl is documented by Q. 8: 19, and the story of the Meccan converts (72–4) prevented from emigrating by explicit reference to Q. 8: 49–63 as well as to Q. 4: 97–100, 29: 10, 12, and 16: 103, 106, 110. The disputes about allocation of spoils (98–9, 102, 104) are of course related to Q. 8: 1, 41 but also to Q. 3: 161, and those about the treatment of captives, execution or ransom (109–10), to Q. 21: 67, 14: 36, 5: 118, 71: 26, and 10: 88.

Now, there can be little doubt that the use of scripture by Wāqidī is of an order altogether different from that of Ibn Isḥāq. Remarkable is the stylistic integration of the two basic *topoi* symbolic of the theme 'holy war' (*jihād*): the 'divine promise' and the 'angelic hosts'. The former, after its introduction in the shape of a prophetical oracle (49), reappears in a sermon (59), in a dream (67), and in two separate prayers—one of entreaty (81) and one of thanksgiving (112). The latter, introduced by Gabriel as explicit revelation (56), figures in a later reminiscence of 'Alī (57), in a revelation to Muhammad (70–1), in reference to the Meccan converts (73), in a lengthy battlefield description (75–80), and in mention of their victims (90–1). The deployment, in addition to *Sūrat al-Anfāl*, of some twenty Quranic verses reveals a genuine concern for the rational allocation of scripture. The separate treatment, then, of Q. 8 might appear superflous (131–8): the style is exegetical (running commentary with connectives *ya'nī* and *yaqūl*) omitting, as in *Sīra*, some verses (vv. 3, 18, 21–6, 37, 40, 44, 51–3, 56, 59, 63, 70–1, 74) and inserting two (Q. 37: 176–7). The interpretative principle is that common to the haggadah: arbitrary connection of general scriptural statements with specific historical occasions (*taʿyīn al-mubham*). But here, as in the preceding historical report, reference is not limited to Q. 8: an appendix (136–8) contains an additional thirteen verses exhibiting a wide selection from the canonical text alleged to refer to Badr. Curiously, the only explicit mention of Badr in the canon (Q. 3: 123) is not included. Here, too, it would seem to be preoccupation with the meaningful distribution of scripture, rather than with salvation history, that lay behind this chapter of the Badr account, a concern which may be detected in the assignment (133) of Q. 8: 20 not in fact to Badr, but to the battle of Uḥud. An attribution more arbitrary than that is hardly conceivable, and the value of the whole exercise for the historical assessment of Badr might be thought negligible.

The historical report itself was, as we have seen, quite adequately furnished with theological *topoi*, with and without scriptural support. The process of exemplification in Wāqidī's work is thus more or less exegetical: the discovery of occasions of revelation (*asbāb al-nuzūl*) for the text of the canon. That such was not, or not exclusively, so for the same process in the *Sīra* has been indicated. The time-span between composition of the two works was, after all, two generations: the part played by scripture as canon, rather than as a corpus of diffuse prophetical *logia*, in formulating a suitable history of the community had increased considerably. This chronological observation corresponds to the evolution of exegetical method and to the emergence of the canonical text of scripture which I have elsewhere examined.[1] Comparison of the styles of Ibn Isḥāq and Wāqidī must, of course, include some notice of their respective treatments of scripture. It seems to me that on the evidence so far adduced it is difficult to argue that Wāqidī is closer than Ibn Isḥāq to the style of the popular preacher (*qāṣṣ*).[2] As a structural feature the *qiṣṣa* was employed by both writers, occasionally more developed in Wāqidī than in his predecessor, e.g. elaboration of the 'angelic hosts' *topos* (57, 70–1) by allocating command of its several military formations not merely to Gabriel, but as well to Michael and Isrāfīl. Similarly, on the origins of the Islamic 'fifth' in disputes about the spoils of battle, Wāqidī's account (17–18) of the events after the expedition to Nakhla is rather more sophisticated than that of Ibn Isḥāq (*Sīra* i, 603): the latter merely reports the fact, while the former is concerned to demonstrate explicit departure from the pagan (Jāhilī) practice of a 'fourth', and to relate it to the (at that point not yet revealed) provisions of Q. 8: 41. That was a halakhic problem

1 *QS*, 33–52, 119–21.

2 *Pace* J. M. B. Jones, 'Ibn Isḥāq and al-Wāqidī: the dream of ʿĀtika and the raid to Nakhla in relation to the charge of plagiarism', *BSOAS* xxii (1959) 46, 51.

and its historicization thus a matter of some importance: Wāqidī's version illustrates the transition from 'booty' to 'tribute' and the emergence of what became a theological concept (God's portion). To fix the occasion/date of a scriptural verse was a primary motive in this style, and might serve to explain the presence of the otherwise (i.e. for salvation history) quite superfluous tabulation of *Sūrat al-Anfāl* at the end of Wāqidī's account of Badr.

The example is not isolated: similar tabulations are found for Q. 3: 121–200 at the end of his report of the battle of Uḥud (319–29); for Q. 59 following his description of B. Naḍīr's expulsion from Medina (380–3); for Q. 33 appended to the description of Khandaq (494–5), etc. It must, however, be admitted that in the historical reports of these events references and allusions to scripture are not at all so plentiful as in the description of Badr. These 'scriptural supplements' owe their existence, at least in part, to the aim of exemplification, that is, to make of the neutral report a charged kerygma. For instance in the report (363–80) of B. Naḍīr's expulsion only two explicit references to scripture appear: Q. 59: 5 in the dispute on whether their crops could legitimately be destroyed (372–3), and 59: 7 on the division of their confiscated property (377–8). In the scriptural supplement the entire *sūra* (Q. 59) is adduced in relation to the event, and a comparison of this passage with the historical report reveals the manner in which circumstantial detail could be generated by scriptural imagery. In the account, as in Q. 59: 2, 'expulsion' is expressed *passim* by *akhraja/ikhrāj*, save at one point (374: also 178–9 concerning B. Qaynuqā') where the synonym *ajlā* is consciously introduced, which can only be an allusion to Q. 59: 3, where the term *jalā'* (exile) exhibits a reflex of the Hebrew cognate. That verse is explained in the supplement (381): 'their exile is (recorded) in the umm al-kitāb', which may be a reference to 'celestial register' or to the historical diaspora (*galut*). The probability of the latter gains some corroboration from the observation of one member of B. Naḍīr (371–2) faced with imminent expulsion: 'This is a trial decreed for us (*hiya malḥama* [*sic*] *kutibat 'alaynā*).' The historicity of the event need not be questioned, but the style of its report deserves attention. As evidence of salvation historiography this example could hardly be surpassed.

The techniques of historicization and exemplification so far analysed might appear to be typical respectively of separate periods in the history of the Muslim community: the prophetical mission (*mab'ath*) and the establishment of authority (*maghāzī*). Some such concern for authority is found, indeed, in Wāqidī's supplement to the B. Naḍīr episode (382): *ad* Q. 59: 8 'And what the prophet brings you accept, and from what he prohibits you desist' appears the paraphrase: 'Whatever commands and prohibitions the Apostle of God articulates are of the same authority as revelation (*bi-manzilat mā nuzila min al-waḥy*).' The argument is a halakhic promotion of the prophetical Sunna (*sunnat al-nabī*) but, and this is significant, promotion by means of a scriptural reference: it is the role of the Qur'ān within the community that is being stressed.[1] And it was in the history of the community that evidence would be sought, and found, for scripture as a source of authority. For the period (Meccan) depicted in the *mab'ath*, the *qiṣṣa* exhibits the simultaneous production of history and scripture. For the period (Medinan) of the *maghāzī*, that process was not (or no longer) adequate: historical data were present in such quantity that they had not (or no longer) to be contrived. The problem, rather, was to relate those numerous data to the prophetical *logia* being accumulated and fashioned as scripture. To that end the typical narrative process was the one I have described as exemplification. There is of course some overlap, but the two styles can, I think, be distinguished. The distinction is structural, and that may be less important than their shared motive, which is interpretation.[2]

The motive of all salvation history is interpretation, and to that extent salvation history is always mythic. I have chosen Jolles's terminology in order to avoid the common synonymity of 'myth and 'fiction'. The material of which myth represents an interpretation is seldom fictive; it is equally seldom that one can convincingly separate that material from its interpretation. This statement, at least since the demise of positivism, is a historiographical axiom and, however well known and generally accepted, may be from time to time usefully recalled. Salvation history is thus in no way exceptional, is in fact considered by many to exhibit an archetype of all historical writing.[3] That is not to deny the existence of other kinds of historiography, nor the possibility that much historical material may never be pressed into the service of salvation history. It is sometimes possible to trace separate developments of the same material inside and outside the framework of salvation history, as for instance in the biographical traditions attached to the figure of Alexander the Great[4]. And that very example provides a convenient illustration of the historian's problem: to recognize and to isolate the 'neutral' data of history from the interpretative (mythic) traditions in which they are usually transmitted.

For the study of salvation history the several efforts made to this end can be described from a survey of Biblical criticism during the past century.[5] From the positivist stance of the so-called 'literary' (documentary) criticism, to the refusal of form-critics even to consider (*pro* or *contra*) the facticity of their material, to tradition-critics' recognition of the formative influence

[1] *QS*, 77–84.

[2] Jolles, op. cit. 96–112.

[3] H. Meyerhoff, *The Philosophy of History in our Time*, New York, 1959, 5–9, 299–300; K. R. Popper, *The Poverty of Historicism*, London, 1963, 105–30; E. H. Gombrich, *In Search of Cultural History*, Oxford, 1974, 1–25.

[4] F. Pfister, *Alexander der Große in den Offenbarungen der Griechen, Juden, Mohammedaner und Christen*, Berlin, 1956, 24–35.

[5] H. Koch, *The Growth of the Biblical Tradition*, London, 1969, 68–78.

(patterning) of transmission techniques, to the latest 'literary' (structural) criticism and its concern with stylistic device and morphology, we have been able to observe a rise and fall in the value of facticity as an instrument of historical assessment. At the beginning of this chapter I alluded to the (in my opinion) false dichotomy between kerygma and myth, between the message and the code. That dichotomy has also been formulated as a distinction between 'proclamation' and 'documentation', in which the first term might be thought to reveal the concern of theologians to salvage something of 'fact' from the ruins left by Biblical critics. In so far as that can be a strictly theological problem (i.e. resting upon the opposition *Geschichte:Historie*), it is not actually relevant to my immediate concern, which is with the record as it has been preserved. It is from that record that the 'facts' must be elicited, but only, I think, to the extent that these remain necessary and rational truths (*notwendige Vernunftswahrheiten*) and do not degenerate into fortuitous data (*zufällige Geschichtstatsachen*).[1] The facts are of value if they are significant, and their significance lies in the way or ways in which they have been interpreted and preserved.

. . . . .

My observations have so far been directed to what I call midrashic styles in the earliest Islamic historiography. These account for a great deal but not quite all, of the substance of that literature. The non-midrashic material is preserved in a number of quite disparate forms: lists and documents, genealogies and chronologies, and last but certainly not least, poetry and formal prose. It may be of some value to examine the uses to which such material can be put in the composition of salvation history. The propensity to regard these forms as 'documentation', or the direct reflection of events, is less great today than in the past. Recognition of literary form and of the creative impulse even in such apparently neutral data as toponymy and chronology, in chancery documents and 'eye-witness' reports, has contributed to the greater caution and prudence of historians. Familiarity with the 'universal' motif, with the 'floating' *topos*, with the formulae and schemata of historical narrative, has tended to induce care, even hesitation, in selecting any single report, or combination of reports, as that/those most likely to reveal 'what really happened'.[2] Here again, the extent of such familiarity will be statistically determined: the further the net is cast the greater the likelihood of discovering the range, perhaps even the limits, of expression appropriate to recording and transmitting 'historical' data. Participation of the historian in the historical process, a circumstance to

[1] Cf. J. Schreiner, *Einführung in die Methoden der biblischen Exegese*, Würzburg, 1971, 14; K. Löwith, *Meaning in History*, University of Chicago, 1949, esp. 137–203; S. Brandon, *History, Time and Deity*, Manchester University Press, 1965, 106–205.

[2] *QS*, 139–40; Noth, *Quellenkritische Studien*, 9–28, 169–73.

which scholarly assent is now general if not absolute, could be thought to diminish the gap between event and record, or in the structure of salvation history, between 'proclamation' and 'documentation'.

Now, if the midrashic styles can be described as mythic, the non-midrashic material might be read as normative. By that I mean that the motive (*Geistesbeschäftigung*) in deployment of those forms lies in the articulation of an ethical ideal, of values by which conduct (individual and social) could be assessed and achievement measured. That an account of the past should be felt retroflectively to function as a norm for present and future is both widely attested and easily comprehended. That an account of the past should have been composed to function in that way requires to be demonstrated. I have alluded briefly to the notion of Sunna as *exemplum*, almost always in the Islamic lexicon a reference to the example of the prophet Muhammad. The tortuous path by which Sunna came to be identified with the specifically prophetical Sunna has been more than once documented.[1] And Sunna in that particular sense is abundantly attested in the *sīra–maghāzī* literature, the term '*sīra*' representing, indeed, a haggadic equivalent of the predominantly halakhic concept Sunna. But Sunna may also be defined rather more broadly as the practice of the Muslim community, and it is that definition which I am here concerned to explore. In the midrashic style the destiny of the community is depicted as the realization of a special theophany articulated as scripture, that is, the literary precipitate of divine revelation. That depiction is achieved by a variety of more or less direct links between God and His prophet. In the non-midrashic material it is the structure of the community which is depicted, in terms of actions and utterances from which an *exemplum* could be deduced. In the terminology of Jolles the 'basic forms' would be *memorabilia*, proposition, and maxim.[2] Elements of myth and of (mythic) 'märchen' are considerably less in evidence there than in the midrash. Legend and saga, on the other hand, in Jolles's sense (respectively) of emulation and kinship,[3] inform so much of the narrative as to be at once pervasive and elusive. In the former is symbolized the preoccupation of the entire corpus, in the latter the tribal ethos out of which the community emerged and of which it exhibited (at least in theory) the suspension.

The fact of kinship (*qawm*) furnishes not only a form, the genealogical filiation (*nasab*), but also a foil, the pagan (*Jāhilī*) 'setting' against which articulation of the community (*umma*) can be measured. An instance of its function as foil has been noticed: the story of Akhnas b. Sharīq and revelation of Q. 68: 10–13, by means of which the new dispensation was seen to cancel esteem (*ḥasab*) in terms of descent (*nasab*). However that may be,

[1] e.g. J. Schacht, *The Origins of Muhammadan Jurisprudence*, Oxford, 1953, 58–81.

[2] Jolles, op. cit. 200–17, 171–99, 150–70.

[3] Ibid. 23–61, 62–90.

a significant feature of the *Sīra* is the ubiquitous introduction of genealogies, in some contexts gratuitously, since identical information had been retailed in a previous episode dealing with the same person or persons. This practice has of course been remarked, as also the fact that a gradation of such information is discernible: from a complete pedigree to mere mention of tribal affiliation.[1] The device is generously employed in the *mubtada'* (genesis) chapters of Ibn Isḥāq's work (*Sīra* i, 1–157) derived from distorted Biblical and fictive South Arabian genealogies, e.g. those of the soothsayers Saṭīḥ and Shiqq (i, 15-19), whose prognosis of an Arabian prophet is contained in their interpretation of his dream for the Yemeni king Rabīʿa b. Naṣr. In the section dealing with Central and North Arabia (i, 73—157) genealogical information is dominant: Nizār, Khuzāʿa, Kināna, Naḍr, Fihr, Murra, Kilāb, Quṣayy, Hāshim, etc. Those pedigrees become the standard appellatives in the *mabʿath* (Meccan) chapters (i, 157–591): descent is agnatic and the string of patronymics can include up to twelve generations, e.g. ʿUrwa al-Raḥḥāl (184), Khadīja bt. Khuwaylid (187 and 189), Zayd b. Ḥāritha (247), and all the earliest Companions (250–64), for whom identical data are repeatedly adduced (the sequence: '... ʿAbd Manāf b. Quṣayy b. Kilāb b. Murra b. Kaʿb b. Lu'ayy b. Ghālib b. Fihr, etc.'). This same information appears more frequently, and more significantly, in another form: descriptive lists subdivided by tribal membership. That device is attested at the end of the *mubtada'*, viz. the allocation of wells in Mecca (i, 147–50), and becomes standard practice in the *mabʿath*: emigrants to and from Ethiopia (322–30, 364–9), participants at the ʿAqaba meetings (428–33, 443–4, 454–67), Meccan opposition to Muhammad (408–9), Jewish opposition (513–16), Medinese opposition (519–27), Jewish converts to Islam (527–9), those who offered sacrifices before Badr (664–6), etc. The last example belongs to the *maghāzī* (Medinan) chapters (i, 591–ii, 642), in which all description of participants, prisoners, casualties, etc. is set out in precisely the same manner. Whatever the motive in this presentation[2]—political, social, administrative, or historical—the descriptive list provided with genealogical rubrics accounts for a considerable portion of Ibn Isḥaq's work. In that of Wāqidī, limited to the *maghāzī* proper, genealogical information is restricted to such lists, and very seldom adduced extensively at the mention of individual persons. It might be argued for the latter that the *dramatis personae* were familiar, or that such social and political factors as cohesion and loyalty could/should be indicated by other means, e.g. membership of Quraysh, Muhājirūn, or Anṣār. Naturally, the bedouin and the Jews, who were not included in these groups, continued to be described in tribal contingents.

[1] Noth, *Quellenkritische Studien*, 38–9.

[2] I. Goldziher, *Muhammedanische Studien* i–ii, Halle, 1889–90, i, 177–207; Noth, op. cit. 90–6.

One use of genealogical identification common to both Ibn Isḥāq and Wāqidī appears in their reports of the composition of the early raids and expeditions, e.g. Nakhla (*Sīra* i, 601–2; Wāqidī, 13), in which is stressed exclusive participation of Muhājirūn ('Quraysh'). For reasons clear from the course of later Islamic history that particular *topos* became generally useful. On the battlefield at Badr Muhammad is made to utter misgivings about the deployment of Anṣār away from Medina (*Sīra* i, 615; Wāqidī, 68), and conflicting reports on the respective roles of Muhājirūn and Anṣār have been preserved, e.g. for the early expeditions led by Ḥamza (Wāqidī, 9) and Sa'd b. Abī Waqqāṣ (Wāqidī, 11) as well as for the later campaign at Bi'r Ma'una (Wāqidī, 352).[1] Here of course tribal affiliation had become secondary to status as a Muslim, and would at least in theory remain so until with the later recruitment/conversion of bedouin tribes for garrison settlement during the period of expansion (*futūḥ*), the two modes of identity came into conflict on a much larger scale.[2]

Both as historical fact and as literary form chronology is scarcely attested in the *mubtada'* chapters of the *Sīra*, though of 'traditional' dating by reference to major events (e.g. battles and reigns) there is some evidence.[3] With the *mab'ath* concern for chronology increases, generating the narrative structure which I have elsewhere described as the 'Muhammadan *evangelium*'. Enclosed within the span marked by the Year of the Elephant (A.D. 570) and the Hijra (A.D. 622), the time-sequence is signalled, if not actually fixed, by regular use of the standard formulae: 'and when' (*fa-lammā*), 'then' (*thumma*), 'so/thus' (*fa-*), 'when' (*idh*), 'and it was' (*wa-kāna*), 'thus it was' (*fa-kāna*), etc. Explicit reference to the age of Muhammad is rare, but frequent enough to evoke a general impression of movement in time and to date significant events, e.g. six years at the death of Āmina (*Sīra* i, 168), eight at the death of 'Abd al-Muṭallib (169), fourteen or fifteen at the outbreak of Ḥarb al-Fijār (184). Crucial moments, like the purification (164–5) and the ominous journey to Syria (182–4), are thus tacitly dated by virtue of their position in the narrative. This 'distributional chronology' is notional but effective, and the only basis for dating a considerable part of early Muslim history.[4]

That basis was not substantially, and certainly not immediately, modified by introduction of the Hijra calendar. But the formal evidence is significant: in the *maghāzī* literature proper an explicit and meticulous chronology is not merely attested but becomes its organizing principle. It is thus that each episode is introduced: 'and that was so many months after the Hijra (*'alā ra's . . . ashhur min muhājarat rasūl allāh*).' The very detail of

[1] M. J. Kister, 'The expedition of Bi'r Ma'ūna', *Arabic and Islamic Studies in Honor of H. A. R. Gibb*, Leiden, 1965, 337–57.
[2] Noth, op. cit. 51–3, 115–17.
[3] Cf. A. Grohmann, *Arabische Chronologie*, Leiden, 1966, 1–15.
[4] Noth, op. cit. 40–5, 155–8.

this mode is deceptive. Though employed by both Ibn Isḥāq and Wāqidī it seldom produced the same result, and in the work of the latter it appears to be a matter of tidiness/completeness rather than of accuracy. For so many discrepancies in an account of eighty-five campaigns over a period of ten years it is imperative to suppose either conflicting reports or considerable distance in time from the events related.[1] Despite its questionable probative value the form exhibits an important preoccupation: the rational distribution of community activity from its newly acquired base of operations (Medina) and under its recently established charter (the 'Constitution' or Umma document).

A further, and equally significant, impulse is evident: a concern to fix the dates of first occurrences (*awā'il*), e.g. the first battle standard (*liwā*) bestowed by Muhammad (Wāqidī, 9: to Ḥamza), the first shot fired in the cause of Islam (Wāqidī, 10: by Sa'd). Solicitude for 'origins' produced eventually a genre of Arabic literature whose *raison d'être* was not so much historical as juridical. Whether, in the context of *maghāzī* reports, the *awā'il*, unlike notices of genealogical affiliation, reveal genuine curiosity about the past can be at least seriously debated. For a community whose positive law was to be derived exclusively from precedent (*sunna/imām*) it might be thought that here is further evidence of normative composition. Indeed, the role of chronology in such basic Muslim sciences as those pertaining to scripture and halakhah is too central to permit a casual reading of the *maghāzī* literature. The annalistic structure of later historiography might, on the other hand, indicate nothing more than concern for tidy presentation.[2]

The insertion of documents into historical narrative poses a number of problems, of which the most important for the historian is the question of authenticity.[3] For structural analysis that is irrelevant, and my concern here is with the stylistic value of such insertions. It may be worth remarking that documents (treaties, letters, decrees), like orations and poetry, lists and genealogies, are not aesthetically or logically intrusive in this literature. The style of the *sīra–maghāzī*, whether or not midrashic, is always episodic and fragmentary, the lines of cleavage usually but not invariably marked by mention of one or more tradents (viz. the *isnād*). The narrative unit might as easily contain/be a document or poem as a report or anecdote. Thus to speak of 'insertion' may be misleading, there being in that term some connotation of superfluity or dispensability. The function here of documents, and of poetry, is testimonial, that is, witness to action as cause and effect. As in the midrashic-style scripture, so in the non-midrashic material

[1] J. M. B. Jones, 'The chronology of the Maghāzī—a textual survey', *BSOAS* xix (1957) 246–58, 262–4, 272.

[2] *QS*, 175–86; Noth, op. cit. 97–100.

[3] Noth, op. cit. 60–80, 131–49.

document and poem are employed to that end, though both are found in the midrash: for instance, the poetry of the *ḥanīf* Zayd b. ʿAmr and Muhammad's letter to the Jews of Khaybar. Another example is Ibn Isḥāq's account (*Sīra* i, 467–8) of divine authorization to wage Holy War, introduced by the *basmala* and derived from the imagery of Q. 22: 39 and 2: 193. There the form is 'documentation', the substance 'proclamation'.

As components of narrative, documents seldom conform with chancery prescription, though an approximation may be achieved where they are transmitted as *separata* (appendices), for example by Ibn Saʿd.[1] In the *Sīra* and in Wāqidī, where documents are of comparatively rare occurrence and where they promote rather than interrupt the narrative, such niceties of chancery procedure as date, scribe, witness, and authentication are almost always absent. Essential, and always present, is only the introductory formula: 'he wrote' (*kataba*), lending to the report a dimension (*scil.* attested, reliable, 'official') not contained in such introductions as 'he said' (*qāla*) and 'he related' (*ḥaddatha*). Documents, in brief, provided emphasis of a sort not otherwise available. An illustration may be seen in the circumstances of revelation for Q. 39: 53–5, where a reference to the spiritual conduct of the Anṣār is 'documented' by a written (!) record of the verse, made for Hishām b. al-ʿĀṣī by ʿUmar (*Sīra* i, 475–6). Similarly, expressions of solidarity and/or affiliation (i.e. of normative value for the history of the community), like the interdict on B. Hāshim (350–1, 374–81), the 'constitution' of Medina (501–4), and the pacts of brotherhood between Muhājirūn and Anṣār (504–7), are either adduced as documents (*ṣaḥīfa*, etc.) or alluded to as somehow figuring in documentation (*dīwān*, etc.). For the interdict on B. Hāshim there is even reference to archival safekeeping (*scil.* in the Kaʿba), a point which combines nicely chancery procedure with sanctuary tradition.

Occasionally, narrative and documentation conflict, as in the elaborate descriptions of the embassy from Najrān and the matter-of-fact terms of the treaty alleged to have been granted by Muhammad.[2] Here the narrative is composed entirely of midrashic *topoi* (derived from Q. 3: 1–64) and of lexical items from the tribute clauses of the treaty (stuffs manufactured in Najrān). The result might be seen as a blend of mythic and normative historiography. A similar combination is exhibited in the story of Ḥudaybiyya, especially as compiled by Wāqidī (571–633): the keyword is in fact 'documentation' (*kitāb*) culminating in the text of the treaty between Muhammad and Quraysh (611–12). As essential and final stage in the negotiations, the 'document' is earlier signalled: during the report of

1 J. Sperber, 'Die Schreiben Muhammads an die Stämme Arabiens', *MSOS* xix (1916) 1–93 (following Wellhausen).

2 Sperber, art. cit. 88–93; W. Schmucker, 'Die christliche Minderheit von Nağrān und die Problematik ihrer Beziehungen zum frühen Islam', in T. Nagel (ed.), *Studien zum Minderheitenproblem im Islam*i (Bonn, 1973) 183–281, esp. 234–81.

ʿUmar's histrionic protests (606), during Suhayl's insistence that his son be returned before conclusion of the treaty (608), and during the dispute about protocol (*basmala* or not) and Muhammad's designation (610: *rasūl allāh* or not). Afterwards, negotiations about the conduct of Abū Baṣīr, which imperilled the substance of the treaty, were similarly 'documented' (624, 627, 629).[1] Equally central to the account is stress upon the 'historical' significance of the affair at Ḥudaybiyya: despite Muhammad's submission to the demands of Quraysh and ʿUmar's repeated remonstrations, it was interpreted as a major victory (*fatḥ*) and sealed by revelation of Q. 48 (609–10, 617–23). Variants in the transmitted texts of the treaty itself may reflect some consciousness of ambiguity in Muhammad's action, the normative value of which increased with distance in time from the event.[2]

In narrative characterized by informal dialogue utterance in formal register, whether prose or poetry, is conspicuous.[3] Like 'documentation', oration and verse attract attention, and their stylistic value derives principally from their precise location within the narrative. An example from the *Sīra* (i, 500–1) is the insertion of Muhammad's earliest Medinan oration (*khuṭba*) between a report of the first mosque built there and a text of the 'constitution' (*umma* document). By means of three separate devices, each a manifestation of the prophet's recently acquired status, the founding of the new community was thus synchronically symbolized. Like most instances of reported speech in historical narrative, the *khuṭba* and other forms of oratory represent a dramatic impulse, the purpose of which is both to entertain and to underline. That much may be said also of poetry, which like oratory in early Islamic society belonged to the register of forensic or liturgical expression. The social occasions of utterance for both were thus approximately the same. For such occasions in the *sīra–maghāzī* literature poetry was the dominant mode.

A good deal of scholarship has been devoted to the question of that poetry's authenticity, rather less to its part in the narrative structure.[4] One function I have already suggested is testimonial, e.g. the lines ascribed to the *ḥanīf* Zayd b. ʿAmr (*Sīra* i, 226–30), or Abū Ṭālib's long apologia for Muhammad (272–80). Neither example can be described as embellishment: each contributes to the narrative as much as, if not more than, the corresponding prose. This 'integrated' style contrasts with the more

[1] Cf. Sperber, art. cit. 16–18.

[2] W. Heffening, *Das islamische Fremdenrecht*, Hannover, 1925, 167–9.

[3] Caskel, *Aijām*, 45–6; Noth, op. cit. 81–90.

[4] e.g. J. Horovitz, 'Die poetischen Einlagen der Sīra', *Islamica* ii (1926) 308–12; W. ʿArafat, 'Early critics of the authenticity of the poetry of the Sīra', *BSOAS* xxi (1958) 453–63; id., 'An aspect of the forger's art in early Islamic poetry', *BSOAS* xxviii (1965) 477–82; id., 'The historical significance of later Anṣārī poetry I–II', *BSOAS* xxix (1966) 1–11, 221–32; but cf. M. J. Kister, 'On a new edition of the Dīwān of Ḥassān b. Thābit', *BSOAS* xxxix (1976) 265–86; for Zayd b. ʿAmr cf. T. Nöldeke–F. Schwally, *Geschichte des Qorans*, Hildesheim, 1961, i, 18–19.

common practice of appending to a descriptive passage all the poetry alleged to have been recited at, composed for, or inspired by the depicted event, e.g. Badr (*Sīra* ii, 8–43), Uḥud (129–68), Ḥunayn (459–78), etc. Poetry so presented might be described as a counterpart to the similar application of scripture which I have called 'exemplification'. But the similarity may only be positional, not functional: poetry as appendix does not enhance the narrative but, rather, commemorates the event. Within the narrative, poetry need not be simply embellishment, but of some structural value, as for example, the elegy and lampoon composed by Ka'b. b. al-Ashraf for Quraysh after Badr (Wāqidī, 121–2). Like the 'document' at Ḥudaybiyya, the poem itself is an agent in the development of relations between Medina and Mecca. Assessment is, however, not always so simple. As in the *ayyām al-'arab*, so in the *sīra–maghāzī* literature it is impossible to discern a single (constant) relationship between prose and poetry, that is, in terms of compositional priority.[1] Wāqidī displays a more disciplined use of verse than does Ibn Isḥāq, but their aims may well have been different: the *Sīra* is not merely a biography of the prophet of Islam; it is also an anthology of Arabian lore.[2]

The extent to which that anthology can be even approximately equated with an objective historical account is, and will remain, a problem.[3] Authenticity can be as much a result of (successful) narrative technique as of veracity. The extensive use of dialogue in the *sīra–maghāzī* literature, and the frequent occurrence there of situations familiar from (modern) observation of bedouin life, may certainly provide 'authenticity' but not necessarily 'historicity'. A 'realistic' feature like Abū Sufyān's coproscopy (*qiyāfa*) at Badr, when twice employed in different contexts (*Sīra* i, 618, ii, 396), becomes suspect as a kind of rustic motif consciously introduced by the author to inject local colour.[4] As such, it is not qualitatively different from the (also twice employed) 'märchen' of Abū Jahl and the camel stallion, mentioned above. Its value for my analysis is not thereby reduced, merely altered. For the non-midrashic material I have listed here, one might claim a kind of perennial relevance, that is, more or less valid witness to the Arabian environment of Muhammad's community, but not to specific historical realia. It belongs thus as much to the Islamic kerygma as does the midrashic material: it is precisely the Arabian origin of Islam which is proclaimed in both.

. . . . .

The very fact of having produced a history of its origins distinguished

[1] Caskel, *Aijām*, 59–75.

[2] Grunebaum, 'Arab unity before Islam', 5–23.

[3] R. Sellheim, 'Prophet, Caliph und Geschichte: Die Muḥammad-Biographie des Ibn Isḥāq', *Oriens* xviii–xix (1965–6/67) 73–91; cf. *QS*, 58.

[4] Buhl, 'Ein paar Beiträge', 10 n. 2.

the Islamic community from most of the sectarian expressions based on Judaeo-Christian tradition. Formulation of a history, instead of or in addition to cultic prescriptions and theological concepts, implies a degree of social and political confidence as well as a sense of participation in an evolutionary process whose general terms were familiar. Now, the concept of salvation (redemption/resolution) as a historical process is of course Biblical, and the precise expression of the archetype has been much discussed.[1] Both substance and modality of its Judaeo-Christian development are found in Islamic historiography, and it seems likely that where conditions (social/intellectual) either permitted or provoked a specifically historical formulation, the only model possible was in fact Biblical.[2]

I have sought in the preceding pages to identify the primary components in the Islamic adaptation of that model, and am concerned in the following to show that these were largely derived from the discourse of interconfessional polemic. There is in this proposition nothing unusual: any description of confessional formation presupposes acquaintance with doctrine in the event rejected as heterodox. Of special interest in the *sīra–maghāzī* literature is the articulation of doctrine, orthodox and heterodox, as event in the life of the Arabian prophet. By means of the narrative techniques here designated historicization and exemplification, polemical *topoi* were introduced as incidents, and thus provided with an apparently authentic *Sitz im Leben.*

Most of the standard *topoi* appear in that remarkable passage of the *Sīra* (i, 544–72) summarizing Muhammad's encounter with the Jews of Medina. What might justifiably be called the basic themes of Muslim polemic are there adduced in anecdotal form:

(*a*) Prognosis of Muhammad in Jewish scripture
(*b*) Jewish rejection of that prognosis
(*c*) Jewish insistence upon miracles for prophets
(*d*) Jewish rejection of Muhammad's revelation
(*e*) Muslim charge of scriptural falsification
(*f*) Muslim claim to supersede earlier dispensations.

The context is thus emphatically Jewish: allusions to Christianity and to Christian opposition are inconsistent and confused and, save for the Christological dispute with the delegation from Najrān, appear only in the framework of Jewish polemic. Even the formulaic expression of asceticism,

[1] e.g. G. von Rad, *Old Testament Theology* i–ii, Edinburgh, 1962–5, i, 105–28, ii, 99–125; H. J. Stoebe, 'Geprägte Form und geschichtlich individuelle Erfahrung im Alten Testament', *Vetus Testamentum*, Suppl. viii (1969) 212–19; and the references *apud* Richter, *Exegese*, 95 n. 70, 170 n. 21.

[2] F. Rosenthal, 'The influence of the Biblical tradition on Muslim historiography', in B. Lewis and P. M. Holt (eds.), *Historians of the Middle East*, O.U.P. London, 1962, 35–45; J. Obermann, 'Early Islam', in R. Dentan (ed.), *The Idea of History in the Ancient Near East*, Yale University Press, 1955, 237–310.

ṣalāt al-khams, is not limited to the enigmatic figure of Salmān Fārisī, but, as has been noticed, was applied also to the Syrian Jew Ibn al-Hayyabān.

Of those themes the most prominent, and the one destined to bear the major burden of Muslim external polemic, was the charge of scriptural falsification, levelled originally at the Jews, later the Christians, and finally employed for polemic internal to the community. The charge was traditional: between Jews and Samaritans, Jews and Christians, Pharisees and Sadducees, Karaites and Rabbanites. One of the most interesting formulations (for my purpose here) was that of the Ebionites, who attributed fabricated passages (*pseudeis perikopai/falsa capitula*) in the Pentateuch to diabolical intervention in the process of transmission.[1] Whatever the origin of that motif (Marcionite?), it is unmistakably reflected in the role of the satanic agent in the Islamic theories of scriptural abrogration (e.g. Q. 22: 52: *alqā 'l-shayṭān* . . .). There the argument was adduced ostensibly in support of the divine annulment of 'false' revelation (e.g. the celebrated 'satanic' verses: Q. 53: 19–23), though its primary application within the Muslim community was to the necessity of superseding prescription, usually by reference to authority outside the canonical text of scripture.[2] It is not unlikely that what became the doctrine of abrogation (*naskh*) was originally a polemical *topos* employed to justify a new dispensation, and hence readily transferable within the sectarian milieu.[3] Not merely its expression but also the motive (*Geistesbeschäftigung*) underlying employment of the *topos* was to a considerable extent uniform. Much as the Ebionite theory of 'false pericopes' provided support for rejection by that sect of the Temple sacrifice and the Davidic monarchy, the charge of scriptural falsification within the Muslim community was adduced by the Shīʿa against the authority of the Sunnī *khilāfa* in favour of the ʿAlid *imāms*.[4] Whatever the context, the charge itself exhibits an (admittedly indirect) exegetical procedure, and corroborates rather than weakens, the notion of authority based upon exclusive appeal to scripture.

A related *topos* is that pertaining to the temporal, as contrasted with the spatial, extent of revelation. There the dispute turned upon admission/rejection of post-Mosaic revelation, in the Muslim context an allusion to Muhammad's claim, but in sectarian literature a traditional (at least as early as the Samaritan schism) quarrel about the sources of legislative authority. Formulation might be in terms of what could/should be included

[1] Schoeps, *Judenchristentum*, 148–55, 366–80; Epiphanius, *apud* A. F. Klijn and G. J. Reinink, *Patristic Evidence for Jewish–Christian Sects*, Leiden, 1973, 188–9.

[2] *QS*, 60–1, 174–88; J. Burton, 'Those are the high-flying cranes', *JSS* xv (1970) 246–65.

[3] *QS*, 10, 70–1.

[4] Schoeps, *Judenchristentum*, 155–9, 219–47; I. Goldziher, *Die Richtungen der islamischen Koranauslegung*, Leiden, 1920, 263–4; cf. J. Eliash, 'The Shīʿite Qur'ān: a reconsideration of Goldziher's interpretation', *Arabica* xvi (1969) 15–24.

in the canon (e.g. for Samaritans, Hellenistic Jewry, Christians), or as the date beyond which prophecy/revelation was no longer operative in Israel (e.g. in Rabbanite–Karaite polemic).[1] For the latter it was of course a question of prescription derived either exegetically from the canon, or directly from a source parallel and of an authority equal to the canon. That particular formulation was eventually to be as central to Islam as it was to Rabbinic Judaism, and it is thus not surprising to find it recorded among the earliest polemical *topoi*. Accessory to the problem of effective prophecy was that of valid prophetical credentials, specifically: miracles. Demand for such as evidentiary signs was traditional and so general in the Judaeo-Christian environment as hardly to require documentation, though the specific demand for 'scripture' can only have originated in a Torah-centric (Jewish or Ebionite) milieu.[2]

What I have called the basic themes of polemic were supplemented by others:

(*g*) The direction of prayer (*qibla*)
(*h*) Abraham and Jesus in sectarian soteriology
(*i*) Solomon's claim to prophethood
(*j*) Sectarian Christology
(*k*) The 'sons of God'
(*l*) The 'faith of the fathers'.

These, too, occur primarily in Jewish contexts, but could be extended to Judaeo-Christian combinations, and the last two even to the pagan (Jāhilī) milieu. Like the search for scriptural testimonia and the charge of scriptural falsification, the *qibla* controversy reflects a *topos* much older than the history of the Muslim community. Its appearance here is not unexpected: the direction (compass point) in which prayer was performed was not merely a ritual nicety but a sectarian emblem, a token of separatism and, for example, a matter of acute contention in the Ebionite community.[3]

Similarly, disputes about the role of Biblical figures, particularly Abraham and Jesus, but also Solomon, represent adaptations from earlier tradition. The eligibility of Solomon for the office/rank of prophet was a *topos* of both Rabbinic and Ebionite literature, and the role of Abraham as the object of divine election prior to the Mosaic revelation a theme exploited particularly in Christian polemic.[4] Absence of the Biblical prophets from the Islamic and Ebionite series of 'prophets' has been the subject of

[1] S. Lieberman, *Hellenism in Jewish Palestine*, New York, 1950, 194–9; N. Wieder, *The Judean Scrolls and Karaism*, London, 1962, 259–63.

[2] *QS*, 73–9: references there to Andrae, Jeffery, and Khoury.

[3] Schoeps, *Judenchristentum*, 141, 340.

[4] *QS*, 54–6; Schoeps, op. cit. 244–6; cf. J. Finkel, 'Jewish, Christian, and Samaritan influences on Arabia', *MacDonald Presentation Volume*, Princeton, 1933, 163–6.

considerable speculation: in neither case is a Samaritan source necessary, nor can the possibility be altogether excluded.[1]

Reference to Christological doctrine in the *Sīra* is, as has been noted, the only instance of specifically Christian polemic and is intrusive in that exposition of Islamic origins, as indeed seem to me most of the references to delegations from Najrān. A link with Jewish polemic is none the less discernible: by means of the *topos* 'sons of God', bracketing thus the figures of Jesus and Ezra.[2] Further transfer to the lexicon of pagan (Jāhilī) polemic was achieved by identifying Christian soteriology as polytheistic and combining that allegation with rejection of the 'daughters of God' (*banāt allāh*) of Quraysh. I have alluded to the function of the pagan environment in Islamic salvation history: as foil to the era inaugurated by the new dispensation, the whole derived from a fairly tidy correspondence between superseded and superseding phenomena. One means of achieving that correspondence was transposition of, say, Jewish into pagan Arab custom, in turn abrogated or modified by Islam, e.g. the fast of 'Ashūrā'.[3] It may be that the Islamic description of pagan idolatry owes something to that process. The designation 'daughters of God' reflects of course the epithet 'sons of God' (*abnā' allāh/benī elōhīm*) adduced in the context of Jewish polemic (*Sīra* i, 563 *ad* Q. 5: 18; 570 *ad* Q. 9: 30), and traditionally in exegetical literature on the referent in Q. 18: 4 (*ittakhadha 'llāh waladan*).[4] As depicted in the Muslim tradition, the 'Jāhilī syndrome' is markedly derivative, a genuine *praeparatio evangelica*.

In more or less the same way the *topos* 'faith of the fathers' could be deployed in polemic with both Jews and pagans, though its Jewish origin can hardly be doubted. A Biblical expression (*elōhē abōtēnū*), the image was perpetuated in sectarian writing, e.g. the Qumranic 'covenant of the fathers' (*berit ha-abōt*), and the Mishnaic 'sayings of the fathers' (*pirqē abōt*), in each of which the emphasis is upon tradition and continuity.[5] Naturally, the formula may also contain or conceal innovation of a radical kind, though sectarian usage tends to be reactionary. It is to some extent a question of pronouns: in Muslim scripture 'what *our* fathers worship' (Q. 11: 62) as contrasted with 'God is your lord and the lord of *your* fathers' (37: 126). The appeal to authority is the same: the context is public dispute and the location symbolic, on the one hand, of resistance to change, on the other, of the need to restore ancient values.[6]

[1] Schoeps, op. cit. 159–69, 335–6; J. MacDonald, *The Theology of the Samaritans*, London, 1964, 204–11.

[2] *QS*, 123–4. [3] *QS*, 183. [4] *QS*, 123.

[5] C. Rabin, *Qumran Studies*, Oxford, 1957, 84 n. 2 (Mish. Nid. 4. 2 v. Sadducees).

[6] A. Alt, *Kleine Schriften zur Geschichte des Volkes Israel* i–ii, München, 1953, i, 1–78: 'Der Gott der Väter'; cf. G. Fohrer, *Geschichte der israelitischen Religion*, Berlin, 1969, 20–7; D. Flusser, 'The Dead Sea Sect and pre-Pauline Christianity', in C. Rabin and Y. Yadin (eds), *Aspects of the Dead Sea Scrolls*, Scripta Hierosolymitana IV Jerusalem, 1965, 239; J. Maier, *Geschichte der jüdischen Religion*, Berlin, 1972, 47–9.

Now, there is little in Muslim polemical literature which cannot be directly related to one of these twelve themes. A series of minor *topoi* ought, however, to be mentioned here, since they are first attested in the *sīra-maghāzī* literature:

(*m*) 'Seventy-one years'
(*n*) Idolatry
(*o*) Cessation of revelation
(*p*) 'Dieu a besoin des hommes'
(*q*) Creation
(*r*) Resurrection
(*s*) Jurisdiction
(*t*) Hypocrisy
(*u*) Exile
(*v*) Satan
(*w*) 'Face to face'.

Muslim appropriation of these perpetuated with minor modification the Judaeo-Christian legacy. When pressed into the service of dispute the context was likely to be pagan, e.g. the attitude of Quraysh to Muhammad's preaching of resurrection,[1] or the introduction of a satanic *topos* as the monotheist adaptation of pagan daemonism.[2] The topics 'creation' and 'exile' were introduced in Jewish contexts, but as data conceded rather than as points disputed.[3] Polemical treatment of the former suggests a philosophical dispute about the mode of divine creation rather than about the fact itself, and may derive from a later theological (anti-Aristotelian) argument.

The *topos* 'seventy-one years' is apocalyptic: the datum was theological, not historical, but figured fairly extensively in the literature of polemic.[4] In the *Sīra* it is adduced in the context of 'prophetical credentials' and thus may be classed with the prognosis–miracle themes. The charge of 'idolatry' is notably not limited to polemic with Arabian paganism but, as has been noticed, was linked by way of the locution 'sons of God' to dispute with Jews and Christians. Another literary connection is conceivable: in Jewish sectarian usage 'idolatry' was figuratively employed for practices/prescriptions thought not to derive from God (e.g. by Qumran sectaries and Karaites), based upon exegesis of Ezekiel 14: 3–4 and 20: 39 (*gillūlīm*).[5] Arguments about the cessation of divine revelation belong to 'scriptural' polemic and are of exclusively Jewish origin, as is the *topos* 'face to face',

[1] *QS*, 31–2.
[2] *QS*, 59–61.
[3] *QS*, 7–8.
[4] F. Rosenthal, *Die aramaistische Forschung seit Th. Nöldeke's Veröffentlichungen*, Leiden, 1964, 252 n. 5; cf. Wieder, *Judean Scrolls*, 87; K. Rudolph, *Die Mandäer* i, Prolegomena: Das Mandäerproblem, Göttingen, 1960, 23 n. 5.
[5] Wieder, op. cit. 151–3.

representing conjecture about the modality of revelation.[1] Jurisdiction became a polemical theme owing to its juxtaposition with arguments about the bona fides of prophethood and about the distinction between divine and secular authority, both invariably historicized in a Jewish context.[2] Hypocrisy, on the other hand, is the basic *topos* in accounts of Medinese Arab opposition to Muhammad. The concept itself belongs of course to the lexicon of internal Jewish polemic, later adopted by Christianity from the Old Testament prophets, and of common currency in sectarian dispute.[3] Comparatively isolated is the *topos* 'Dieu a besoin des hommes' developed from the imagery *faqīr* (needy/poor): *ghanīy* (self-sufficient/rich), exhibiting in all likelihood a (later) philosophical dispute about the attributes of God.

Comparison of all this material with the basic themes of the Quranic theodicy provokes and/or confirms the impression that Muslim scripture is a torso. There, the imagery is limited (retribution, sign, exile, covenant),[4] and the concept of a 'saving history' absent. Here, in the *sīra–maghāzī* literature, the former is expanded, the latter supplied. The relation between the two is, however, not exegetical. I should rather describe it as complementary: two versions of Judaeo-Christian polemic adapted to the Arabic language and the Ḥijāzī environment. The actual instrument of adaptation was the midrashic pericope and, to some extent, the scriptural parallel appended to a theologically neutral report. Each of the twenty-three *topoi* listed above has a literary history chronologically antecedent to the origins of Islam. Most exhibit specific sectarian disputes. For many it may be possible to determine, and to date, a *Sitz im Leben*. Others represent basic and, so to speak, 'perennial' themes in the articulation of monotheist doctrine. Notice of these is essential, if only for the pragmatic, and rather pedestrian, purpose of taking a position with regard to the originality ascribed to the Arabian prophet. It can hardly be disputed that the discovery, and appropriation, of ancient ideas is always something of a personal achievement, perhaps even an intellectual necessity (can experience ever be transmitted etc.?), but not quite relevant, I submit, to the task of historical description.[5] By its own express testimony, the Islamic kerygma was an articulation (whether traditional, progressive, or radical is immaterial) of the Biblical dispensation, and can only thus be assessed.

A number of shared data facilitate this task. Essential, for instance, to the theme of supersession is the notion of covenant. As much, I think, as can be said about the covenant in Muslim scripture I have recorded

[1] *QS*, 34–6.

[2] *QS*, 185–93.

[3] Wieder, op. cit. 135–40; M. Gertner, 'The terms pharisaioi, gazarenoi, hupokritai: their semantic complexity and conceptual correlation', *BSOAS* xxvi (1963) 266–7.

[4] *QS*, 2–12.

[5] But cf. J. Fück, 'Die Originalität des arabischen Propheten', *ZDMG* xc (1936) 509–25; R. Paret, 'Der Koran als Geschichtsquelle', *Der Islam* xxxvii (1961) 24–42.

elsewhere.[1] Its limited role there is in Muslim salvation history similarly restricted: symbolic of man's obligation to God the covenant was betrayed by the Jews, restored by Muhammad, and manifests neither differentiation nor development.[2] 'Covenant' is thus a calque, but necessary to the Islamic theophany, for which it provides a summary of all previous theophanies. That symbolic quality is characteristic of most of the Biblical components of Islamic salvation history. I have mentioned application of the *topos* 'exile' in the *Sīra* to a particular event: expulsion of the Jews from Medina. Explicit there was the semantic equivalence *jalā'*: *ikhrāj*. As a saving act in Muslim history 'exile' is expressed by *khurūj/hijra* (*Sīra* i, 321–41) and illustrated by the emigration of Muhammad's followers to Ethiopia.[3] Further historicization of the theme is achieved in the account of a second emigration, to Medina (Yathrib) and establishment of the new community (*Sīra* i, 468–501). In the story of Abū Salama, the first of the Companions to go to Medina, the two emigrations are explicitly linked. A formal difference between the two is the enumeration of emigrants to Ethiopia in tribal contingents, to Medina in small groups and as individuals. That difference may be itself insignificant, but probably not fortuitous: the first emigration was placed squarely within the pagan tribal environment, the second described in a manner appropriate to the cohesion of the new community.

Now, the Biblical employment of genealogies has been fairly exhaustively explored.[4] The fashion in which both the original occupation of Canaan and the return to Palestine from Babylonian exile were described in terms of kinship may be thought a literary, if not historical, model for similar events in the Islamic *sīra–maghāzī* literature. The common theme—emergence of a nation out of tribal groups sharing a theophany— is in my opinion further evidence of the symbolic nature of salvation history.

Treatment of the theme 'holy war' is pertinent. I have adduced the accounts of Badr from Ibn Isḥāq and Wāqidī to illustrate the midrashic transposition of *ghazwa* into *jihād*. Of the two versions Wāqidī's is the more polished and persuasive, even to inclusion of an epilogue relating the prayers of thanksgiving offered by the Ethiopian Najāshī upon hearing of the Muslim victory (120–1). The notion of war as divine instrument is conveyed by employment of such imagery as 'trial/ordeal' (*malḥama*: 372 B. Naḍīr; 503, 506, 514 B. Qurayẓa), 'yoke/snare' (*qarana fil-ḥibāl*: 120, 185 Badr; *rabaṭa/kattafa*: 177 B. Qaynuqā'; 509 B. Qurayẓa), and allusion to the 'divine promise' (*wa'd*). A possibility of stylization in similar Biblical accounts has often been proposed, and the pre-Biblical history of some of

[1] *QS*, 8–12.
[2] D. J. McCarthy, *Old Testament Covenant*, Oxford, 1973, 10–34, 53–6.
[3] *QS*, 38–43.
[4] Fohrer, op. cit. 75–83; Maier, op. cit. 9.

the imagery investigated.[1] Of its further development as *topoi* in the literature of apocalyptic[2] there is in Muslim writing ample evidence, but later than the *sīra–maghāzī*, where warfare is not yet eschatological. But the Biblical concept of holy war as a means of purification/sanctification is here not quite absent, exhibited in anecdotes defining eligibility for martyrdom,[3] e.g. the stories of Yazīd b. Ḥāṭib and Quzmān.

These themes (covenant, exile, genealogy, holy war) and the *topos* 'faith of the fathers' belong to, indeed comprise, the Biblical 'wilderness tradition' (*Wüstentradition*), which was of particular significance in sectarian history as (retrospective) programme for reform and the restoration of earlier (and better) times.[4] In the several patterns of sectarian formation during and after the period of Hellenist hegemony in Palestine the 'wilderness' syndrome was a constant. Its presence therefore in the *sīra–maghāzī* literature is not without interest. It cannot, however, be made to account for the whole of Islamic salvation history, which exhibits such additional Biblical material as reference to sanctuary and calendar, to messiology and authority, as well as to the function of élites in the confessional community. These themes might be described as components of an 'institutional tradition', and as symbolic of a direction diametrically opposed to the tendency of the 'wilderness tradition'. Now, that postulate may appear too schematic, and ought probably not to be pressed too far. But the aim of the *sīra–maghāzī* literature was to depict the origins of the community, and it seems justified to seek at that stage of its emergence evidence of a dominant type.

Islamic sanctuary traditions, related of course to Mecca and Medina, turn upon a basic lexicon made up of the terms *ḥurma*, *muhājar*, and *ḥajj*. The epithet *muhājar* (scene of migration/mission) was, as has been remarked, regularly applied to Yathrib/Medina in stories designed to convey its role in the *praeparatio evangelica* (*Sīra* i, 20–3). For Mecca, on the other hand, it is its pre-Islamic status as sanctuary (*ḥurma*/*ḥaram*) for all Arabs which was stressed (23–6), not least in competition with the monophysite Christianity established in the Yemen (43–62).[5] In that context pilgrimage (*ḥajj*) and intercalation (*nasī'*) were adduced as perquisites of the sanctuary

[1] Fohrer, op. cit. 109; J. G. Heintz, 'Oracles prophetiques et "Guerre Sainte" selon les archives royales de Mari et l'Ancien Testament', *Vetus Testamentum*, Suppl. xvii (1969) 112–38.

[2] e.g. M. H. Segal, 'The Qumran War Scroll and the date of its composition', *Scripta Hiero.* iv, 138–43; Wieder, op. cit. 120–3.

[3] *QS*, 170–3; J. Pedersen, *Israel: its Life and Culture* iii–iv (London, 1959) 1–32; Noth, *Heiliger Krieg*, 66–92.

[4] Cf. C. Barth, 'Zur Bedeutung der Wüstentradition', *Vetus Testamentum*, Suppl. xv (1966) 14–23; von Rad, *Theology* i, 280–9; but also S. Talmon, 'The "desert motif" in the Bible and in Qumran literature', A. Altmann (ed.), *Biblical Motifs: Origins and Transformations*, Cambridge, Mass. 1966, 31–64.

[5] M. J. Kister, 'Some reports concerning Mecca from Jahiliyya to Islam', *JESHO* xv (1972) 61–76; C. Nallino, 'Ebrei e cristiani nell'Arabia preislamica', *Raccolta di Scritti* iii (Roma, 1941) 121–9.

authorities, together with miscellaneous data on the number, identity, and ordinances of the sacred months. The polemical moment is at least implicit in emphasis upon Ramaḍān at the expense of Rajab[1] (*Sīra* i, 235–6, 239–40), and explicit in the revelation of Q. 9: 7 prohibiting intercalation (43–5). Calendar traditions might also figure in halakhic dispute, for instance, whether to date the Nakhla expedition in Rajab or Shaʿbān (*Sīra* i, 601–6; *Maghāzī*, 13–9).[2] But more significant than such niceties was the introduction of a new calendar based on lunar reckoning and dating from the Hijra.

Like fixing the direction of prayer, adoption of a special calendar was by tradition a sectarian emblem, well attested in the literature of inter-confessional polemic.[3] Equally traditional are the fairly abundant references to the Meccan sanctuary, e.g. expulsion of earlier custodians (*scil.* B. Jurhum) for desecration (*Sīra* i, 113–14), dedication before birth (Ghawth b. Murr) to sanctuary service (119), investiture (Quṣayy b. Kilāb) with sanctuary privileges (124–6), miraculous character of Zamzam (110–14, 142–7, 150–1), restoration of the Kaʿba by Quraysh (192–9), supersession of the pagan cult (199–204), and of the sacrificial ordinances (76–7, 89–91, 151–7).[4]

The remaining three components of what I have called the 'institutional tradition' are directly related to expression of authority in the community. Now, whatever may have been the source of Muhammad's authority amongst his followers, his status in Islamic salvation history is that of agent/spokesman for God (*rasūl allāh/nabī*). Title and office are charismatic, and it must be presumed that their Arabic versions corresponded somehow to notions long since crystallized in the Judaeo-Christian tradition. It may of course be that the designation 'prophet/apostle' was distinctly messianic, and only retrospectively applied to the founder of the Muslim community. I have elsewhere described the messianic symbolism of the 'Muhammadan *evangelium*' (*dalāʾil al-nubuwwa*):[5] in the *Sīra* the imagery is fairly stereotyped, e.g. prognosis of an 'apostle' in the Ḥijāz (i, 15–18, 69–70), divine selection of the name 'Muḥammad' (157–8), interpretation of the name 'Muḥammad' as 'protected/favoured' (356), identification of 'Muḥammad/Aḥmad' with the Paraclete (232–3), etc.[6] It is none the less difficult to infer from the messianic imagery a messianic proclamation. It was as founder/leader of the community that Muhammad was designated 'apostle' and 'prophet', not as herald of the eschaton, of which there

[1] M. J. Kister, ' "Rajab is the month of God . . ." ', *IOS* i (1971) 191–223; cf. Maier op. cit. 94.

[2] Jones, 'Ibn Isḥāq and al-Wāqidī', 47, 51.

[3] e.g. S. Talmon, 'The calendar reckoning of the sect from the Judaean Desert', *Scripta Hiero.* iv, 162–99; Wieder, op. cit. 172, 210 n. 1, 255.

[4] J. Wellhausen, *Reste arabischen Heidentums*, Berlin, 1961 (1897), 112–29.

[5] *QS*, 65–74.

[6] Nöldeke-Schwally, *GdQ* i, 9–10.

is in fact little trace in the *sīra–maghāzī* literature. That could of course be merely the result of its composition 150–200 years after the death of Muhammad, by which time the expectation of a messianic age had receded if not altogether vanished. In fact, authority in the *sīra–maghāzī* can best be defined as a matter of secular arrangements with divine sanctions. There is in practice no hint of conflict between the two, though the theoretical possibility is not quite ignored: a reflex of the Biblical theme 'monarchy *v.* theocracy' is exhibited in the story of Quraysh and the rabbis of Medina (*Sīra* i, 282–314), as also in disputes between Muhammad and the Jews about cessation of prophecy.[1] It would be impossible to insist that both contexts are exclusively literary, but also difficult to overlook there the symbolic function of Biblical material. Successful composition of salvation history required some familiarity with established techniques: the paradigm was not far to seek.

It could thus be argued that salvation history is to some extent nomothetic rather than idiographic: the laws may be literary (that is, historiographical, not historical) but are for that not less binding. Salvation history is also cumulative: adoption of the Biblical paradigm imposed a linear continuum affecting not merely temporal but also causal sequence. Both its structure and its logic were dictated by the language of that paradigm; local modification is less important than the shared concept of movement in history as purpose and design.

Almost entirely absent from the Islamic version of salvation history is the element of apocalyptic[2] associated with the intertestamental period. In view of the regular occurrence in Muslim scripture of eschatological imagery, the mundane preoccupation of the *sīra–maghāzī* literature is striking. But like the document of revelation, the historical version is a torso. For the comprehensive portrait of the early Muslim community eventually transmitted to the medieval and modern periods, both scripture and *sīra* had to be supplemented, by recourse to the literary forms conventionally designated haggadah and halakhah. I use the term 'form' advisedly: the substance of the entire literature is more or less constant. It is in its expression and mode of preservation/transmission that emphasis varies.[3] And of course the process took time: it is worth recalling that specifically Islamic literature first appeared in Mesopotamia at the end of the second/eighth century.

1 *QS*, 122–9; Fohrer, *Geschichte*, 114–22, 131–43.

2 D. S. Russell, *The Method and Message of Jewish Apocalyptic*, London, 1964, 205–34, 263–84.

3 *QS*, 49–51, 182–3.

II

AUTHORITY

WITHIN the monotheist tradition the organizing principle of a confessional community may be located in its definition of authority. By 'authority' I mean the immediate and tangible instruments of legitimation: those means by which the sanctions of a transcendent deity are realized in practice, those terms within which a theodicy becomes credible and workable. Certain data had by all such communities to be accommodated:

(*a*) a historical theophany;
(*b*) an existential task;
(*c*) an agent as recipient for (*a*) and executor for (*b*).

The terms of that proposition are schematic and phenomenological; in community records they become diffuse and historical. Preserved as documentation, theophany is in fact a disputed corpus of scripture, the task a welter of detailed and conflicting prescription, and the figure of recipient/executor a peg for unstable and contentious assessment of paradigmatic types. It is in the historical expression of these terms that the variety of sectarianism becomes manifest and the criteria for differentiation available. A corresponding and equally schematic set of theologoumena may be discerned in the structure of the monotheist confession:

(*a*) the nature of creation;
(*b*) the means of salvation;
(*c*) the renewal of dispensation.

These represent ultimately the substance of dogmatic theology, but long before their deposit in the form of doctrine characteristic of a clearly defined confessional community, they are exhibited as recurring points of dispute in sectarian polemic. Argument about creation may, in primitive polemic, contain little more than assertions of the deity's existence or attributes; salvation will be discussed in terms of ethical conduct and social justice; and dispensation in terms of covenant renewal and extension of the theophany. The use of such material in historical descriptions of sectarianism is obviously difficult, and nowhere more so than in a study of the origins of the Muslim community. Enumeration of the standard polemical themes employed in Islamic salvation history ought to have made quite clear the role of tradition in composing that literature. Naturally, the whole Judaeo-Christian tradition is not represented there, and it may be that from omissions (e.g. circumcision, baptism, eucharist, priesthood, etc.) as much information may be gleaned as from inclusions (e.g. scripture, prophet, miracles, angels, etc.). The traditional *topoi* are perhaps not quite random phenomena: it may also be that with sufficient patience in their analyses some hint of configuration or system in their Islamic deployment could emerge.

By way of methodological caveat: the simple collation of phenomena common to two or more confessions in the monotheist tradition is seldom adequate to more than demonstration of the equally simple assertion that a confessional community belonging to the Judaeo-Christian tradition must exhibit some, and probably will exhibit other, traditional features. An example is Rabin's list of terminological parallels between Islam and Qumran.[1] The circular argument cannot be avoided, even if each of its items were unexceptionable, by postulating historical continuity: namely, that Islam represented a late expression/remnant of the Qumranic confession. For that it would be necessary to show that such central features of the latter as stress upon ritual, indeed levitical, purity, upon asceticism, and upon the governing function of a genealogically designated priesthood, could also have been factors (at any stage) in the development of Islam. Such is hardly possible. Whatever the common origin of features shared by the two confessions, historical descent from one to the other requires more imaginative reconstruction than seems justified. Moreover, the Islamic data are there drawn from a varied (temporally and qualitatively) range of source materials, and require for their interpretation (in Rabin's thesis) a heretical Jewish community at Mecca/Ṭā'if with whom Muhammad had contact prior to his encounter with presumably 'orthodox' (Rabbinic) Judaism in Yathrib, that is, 'the prominently Aaronid city of Medina' (*sic*). To propose that the appearance in Palestinian Judaism of 'certain ideas of the Qumran sect' might be attributed to the Muslim conquerors in the company of their heretical Jewish allies is extraordinary, and that the apocalyptic 'Secrets of Simeon b. Yoḥayy' could be adduced as documentation of that process, seems to me to be, from the point of view of historical method, quite unsound. The occurrence in Arabic of such calques as *malḥama*, *rāhib*, *dajjāl*, *aḥbār*, *ummī*, and *iblīs*, need not after all be traced to a single source.

Another, rather more substantial, effort along these same lines was undertaken by Schoeps in his exhaustive study of the Ebionites.[2] There at least some of the shared phenomena were fundamental both to Islam and to that particular manifestation of Judaeo-Christianity, e.g. identity

[1] Rabin, *Qumran*, 112–30; cf. *QS*, 50–1; E. Bishop, 'The Qumran scrolls and the Qur'ān', *MW* xlviii (1958) 223–36.

[2] Schoeps, *Judenchristentum*, 334–42, 305–15; M. Roncaglia, 'Éléments Ébionites et Elkésaïtes dans le Coran', *POC* xxi (1971) 101–26; A. Sprenger, *Das Leben und die Lehre des Mohammed* i–iii, Berlin, 1869, i, 18–42.

of 'scriptural' revelation and celestial register, the charge of scriptural falsification, absence/rejection of Biblical prophets, adoptionist Christology. Several subsidiary items, like baptism, prohibition of wine, and dispute about the direction of prayer, belong to the standard emblems of dissent and are of less value to a description of Islamic origins. Schoeps's exposition was a development of hypotheses originally expressed by Sprenger, Harnack, and Schlatter, stressed the anti-gnostic character of Ebionism, and identified in somewhat dogmatic fashion the presence of gnostic elements in Judaeo-Christianity with the contemporary (or slightly later) syncretist expression associated with the name Elkesai. That characterization has been, and continues to be, a matter of dispute; but as a heuristic postulate in the analysis of Islamic origins it could be of some value.[1] An extreme, and in my opinion bizarre, formulation of Schoeps's argument, with which the theses of Andrae have been compounded, is the recent attempt by Lüling to establish an Ebionite Vorlage for Islam on the basis of a new redaction history of Muslim scripture. There the operative components are thought to be a sacrificial fertility cult and an angelic Christology, rejected by Arabian Christianity (*sic*) and endorsed by primitive Islam. The author's thesis is provocative, his evidence unsound, and his method undisciplined.[2]

Common to all these attempts are certain tacit assumptions about the Islamic theophany, its eclectic character, and the value of exegetical literature distant from seventh-century Arabia some several hundred miles and at least two centuries. The comparative method itself has distinguished antecedents, though it may be doubted whether its diachronic application has ever been justified. The now fairly ancient quarrel about Qumran and the Karaites illustrates the best, and the worst, aspects of this method. But the example can be instructive: for Qumran a primary enigma is, indeed, identification of the community. On that subject the literature is well known, and could anyway not be summarized or evaluated here. One point may, however, be recalled: existence of the community is not unambiguously attested outside its own literary (and archaeological) remains. This fact has served as stimulus to conjecture of quite extraordinary range, of which some at least is methodologically useful. Like Qumran, the Muslim community, as explicit articulation within the Judaeo-Christian tradition, was for most of the first two centuries of its existence attested

[1] H. J. Schoeps, *Urgemeinde—Judenchristentum—Gnosis*, Tübingen, 1956, 30–67; id., *Judenchristentum*, 325–34; id., 'Judenchristentum und Gnosis', in U. Bianchi (ed.), *Le Origini dello Gnosticismo*, Leiden, 1970, 528–37 (v. K. Rudolph, 'Probleme einer Entwicklungs-geschichte der mandäischen Religion', ibid. 583–96; cf. Klijn–Reinink, *Patristic Evidence*, 54–67; E. Yamauchi, *Gnostic Ethics and Mandaean Origins*, Cambridge, Mass., 1970, esp. 53–67.

[2] G. Lüling, *Über den Ur-Qur'ān*, Erlangen, 1974, esp. 174–85, 347–400; T. Andrae, *Les origines de l'islam et le christianisme*, Paris, 1955, 15–38, 145–61.

only by Islamic literary witness. To the Arab conquests, as territorial expansion, as political, economic, and social innovation, there is of course external testimony, but largely irrelevant to description of the religious phenomena these were later claimed to be. For both Islam and Qumran the internal evidence is substantial, but not sufficient to satisfy curiosity about the comparative silence of contemporary sources. For Qumran that silence was broken by identifying the Dead Sea sect with the Essenes, a proposal for which there is today widespread if not quite general acceptance. But external witness could be multiplied in other ways.

One example is Flusser's application of the Bultmann thesis with respect to the kerygma of the Hellenistic Church.[1] His method was to isolate a series of thematic constants, that is, of elements central, indeed indispensable, to any confessional expression in the Judaeo-Christian tradition, and from these to construct a minimal theology. The themes included: dualism of good and evil, predestination, election of grace, the community of God, the new covenant, baptism, spirit as the gift of wisdom, and the opposition between flesh and spirit. The flavour is unmistakably Christian, but it can hardly be doubted that each of these subjects was one about which some decision had to be taken in the course of polemical strife.

A different but related approach may be illustrated by reference to the several efforts to identify Qumran with the addressees in the Epistle to the Hebrews.[2] The method, most meticulously applied in the work of Kosmala, consists in matching the imagery and lexicon of the Epistle with those of the sectarian scrolls, a process made complex by the coexistence of several strands of correspondence in Hebrew–Greek translation. From the basic doctrine of Hebrews (6: 1–3): rejection of 'dead' actions, acceptance of faith, baptism, the laying on of hands, resurrection, and judgement, it could be argued that the substance of the Epistle reflects an essentially eschatological preoccupation, its central argument that Jesus was in fact the expected messiah (Christ). Similarly, the scrolls exhibit an eschatological emphasis: preparation in the wilderness, a calendar and priesthood peculiar to the sect, rejection of the Temple sacrifice, stress upon fraternity and perseverance, and the employment of prognostic exegesis. The basis of the correspondence lies in the messianic imagery common to both: the arguments put forward by the Epistle in favour of Jesus fit more or less the qualifications set out in the scrolls.

The limits of such an exposition are obvious: discovery of yet another corpus of literature even closer in concept and vocabulary to Hebrews

[1] Flusser, 'Dead Sea Sect', 215–66; cf. R. Bultmann, *Theology of the New Testament* i–ii, London, 1965, i, 1–183.

[2] Kosmala, *Hebräer*, esp. 1–43; Y. Yadin, 'The Dead Sea Scrolls and the Epistle to the Hebrews', *Scripta Hiero.* iv, 36–55; C. Spicq, 'L'Épître aux Hébreux, Apollos, Jean-Baptiste, les Hellénistes et Qumran', *Revue de Qumran* i (1958–9) 365–90.

would demolish that carefully constructed edifice. Prior to discovery of the scrolls, the classical solution to the puzzle had of course been a Judaeo-Christian sect. The circle was completed by Teicher, who regarded the scrolls, as well as the Damascus Document, as products of a Judaeo-Christian community, in fact the Ebionites, a possibility recognized but not accepted as conclusive by Schoeps.[1] The substance of Teicher's argument was, on the one hand, identification of Jesus with *moreh ha-ṣedeq* of Qumran, and on the other, comparison of the stringent legalism of the Damascus Document with that attested in Ebionite literature.

Now, it must be clear that once adopted the method of selected parallels is of virtually unlimited application but also likely to be productive of little more than tautologies. Required is some means of determining the origin or native habitat of 'universal' theologoumena. In his study of the dualism common to Qumran and the Iranian religions, Shaked's criterion was the comparison of theological 'systems', based upon the reasonable supposition that the greater degree of internal consistency among the components of any system was likely to indicate the origin of a particular concept.[2] It might be added that, in eclectic and syncretist theologies where all components are recognizably alien, there remains the problem of identifying the processes of adaptation, modification, and incorporation, which can alter the appearance of the most familiar theologoumena. But recognition of a system is itself something of a problem, to which solutions tend to present themselves only at a late stage in the development of a confessional community, that is, after the crystallization of dogma. For the earlier stages one must make do with something less than a system, perhaps with something like a general sectarian orientation, if even that much can be elicited from the inevitable scrappy and biased witness of confessional polemic. By 'sectarian orientation' I would understand both the avowed aim of the community and its visible organization. That of course is also the understanding of sociologists working in the field of Islamic studies, for whose increasingly prolific analyses Weber provided the foundation.[3] Results have so far been rather disappointing: owing partly to shortcomings in Weber's own synthesis (uncritical selection of data, retrojective interpretation, inflexibility of the basic model), and partly to the methods of his successors, (perhaps) ideally suited to the empirical study of contemporary Islam, but less to the structural analysis of medieval literature. But all is not lost: some compensation may be found in Weber's isolation of ideal types, though the method is seldom productive of strictly historical

[1] J. Teicher, 'The Dead Sea Scrolls—documents of the Jewish–Christian sect of Ebionites', *JJS* ii (1951) 67–99; id., 'The Damascus Fragments and the origin of the Jewish Christian sect', ibid. 115–43; Schoeps, *Urgemeinde*, 68–86.

[2] S. Shaked, 'Qumran and Iran: further considerations', *IOS* ii, 433–46; cf. also Yamauchi, *Mandaean Origins*, 68–89.

[3] Cf. B. Turner, *Weber and Islam: a Critical Study*, London, 1974, esp. 22–38, 137–50.

conclusions. A typology of monotheist confessions is bound to be abstract. It is possible, indeed likely, that no historical community would correspond to a single type. But like Jolles's 'einfache Formen', such a typology would permit tentative conclusions about the 'motive' (*Geistesbeschäftigung*) or organizing principle of the confession. It would have to account for the basic data of monotheism (theophany/task/agent) as well as for the corresponding theologoumena (creation/salvation/dispensation), and finally, to provide some evidence towards determining the notion of authority implicit in the organization of these data. As an aid to further analysis I propose reference to the following priorities:

1. primitivist;
2. scripturalist;
3. ritualist;
4. eschatological;
5. gnostic.

While these rubrics are meant to convey 'sectarian orientations', it can be objected that neither are they mutually exclusive nor does any one of them adequately describe the historical trajectory of a single confessional community. For both reasons I stress the term 'confessional' with its theological implications, rather than 'community' for which social, economic, and political factors must be reckoned. My object here is analysis of salvation history, in which causality is by tradition, and necessity, monochrome: all action is interpreted *sub specie aeternitatis*. An appropriate example is the view of early Christianity's evolution from eschatological to ritualist confession as consequence, not of contact through mass conversion with the ideologies of imperial Rome, but of the interminably delayed parousia.

To begin with a few conventions: rubric (5) 'gnostic' is a reference to gnosis as knowledge of the divine mysteries reserved for an élite, rather than to Gnosticism as concrete expression of an ontological-theological-anthropological system.[1] My use of 'gnostic' is thus essentially epistemological, and includes the social and organizational implications of that use since these are important for a definition of authority. Rubric (4) 'eschatological' is intended to convey not only concern with the eschaton (death/judgement/reward/punishment), but also with the beliefs and imagery belonging to apocalyptic, e.g. primordial, messianic, and cosmic.[2] By (3) 'ritualist' I understand preoccupation with the Law: not simply observance, but also interpretation, extension, and often creation. The impetus would be halakhic: to make the Law relevant and applicable to every

[1] Bianchi, *Gnosticismo*, xxvi–xxix; H. Jonas, 'Delimitation of the gnostic phenomenon—typological and historical', ibid. 90–108.

[2] Russell, *Apocalyptic*, esp. 104–39, 345–50.

aspect of individual and community existence.[1] For (2) 'scripturalist' preoccupation would be with the theophany: the explicit intervention of God in the history of the community/individual, as the matrix of belief (existential) and of action (liturgical).[2] Finally, under (1) 'primitivist' I subsume those confessional formulations exhibiting reaction to change and defining excellence by allusion to a remote and ideal past. In that syndrome moral purity is equated with austerity and/or simplicity, and it is thus attested most commonly in community development at points of sophistication and complexity.[3]

The *topoi* of Islamic salvation history exhibit a dominant concern with the notion of authority: acceptance or rejection on the basis of a scriptural dispensation in the possession of a prophet. In dispute are the authenticity of the former and the qualifications of the latter. Towards a solution to the question which of the several expressions of Judaeo-Christian sectarianism could have been the source of those *topoi*, the primitive polemic of the *sīra–maghāzī* literature yields very little. For location of the confessional type, as contrasted with identification of a specific sect, the same material may be less refractory. Of gnostic and eschatological values there is little or no evidence. Knowledge of the deity is throughout equated with scripture, distorted and concealed owing to the perfidy of faithless custodians, but not identified with arcane wisdom reserved for an élite. Allusion to the eschaton is limited to assertion of the facts of resurrection and eventual judgement, and altogether free of primordial or cosmic significance. Something of the 'wilderness tradition', and hence of data belonging to the primitivist type, is found there and may represent a reaction to the urban milieu in which that literature was composed.[4] To preoccupation with ritual, apart from regular emphasis upon the duty of public prayer (*ṣalāt*), there is little witness. Pilgrimage (*ḥajj*) might be thought an exception, though treatment of that subject lay outside the sphere of polemic, unlike, for example, discussion of the direction of prayer (*qibla*). Provision for the abrogation of pagan (Jāhilī) ritual, within the framework of sanctuary traditions, is almost perfunctory, and never the occasion of doctrinal or ideological dispute.

Thus, both positively and negatively, the confessional type delineated in the *sīra–maghāzī* literature is scripturalist, due not merely to the centrality of Muslim scripture, but also to constant mention of what was alleged to be 'Jewish' and/or 'Christian' scripture. (*tawrāt/injīl*). But that conclusion, which is hardly surprising, could also be misleading: 'scripture' is here an exclusively polemical concept, alluding either to mode of theophany or to prophetical credential, never to the source of prescriptive

[1] C. Albeck, *Einführung in die Mischna*, Berlin, 1971, esp. 4–93.
[2] McCarthy, *Covenant*, esp. 1–9, 53–6.
[3] Von Rad, *Theology* i, 36–84, 280–9.
[4] Sellheim, 'Muḥammad-Biographie', 33–46.

regulation. Even apparent exceptions, such as the anecdotes relating Muhammad's encounters with the rabbis of Medina, are not in fact: the argument there is about integral transmission/preservation of scripture and the forensic demonstration of 'true prophethood'. The function of scripture seems to be testimonial, of which mere possession constituted a valid claim to participate in the process of Biblical salvation history. Evidence of the halakhic and liturgical functions of scripture, attested in the literature of tradition (*ḥadīth*) and exegesis (*tafsīr*), is absent.

Selection of the confessional type 'scripturalist' is thus of restricted utility, based after all only upon witness of the *sīra–maghāzī* literature. The standard description of Islam as 'religion of the book' is not without value, merely undifferentiated. To achieve at least a degree of clarity in the continued employment of that description, two problems require to be examined and may be articulated more or less as follows: (*a*) what are the actual functions of scripture in the Muslim community, and (*b*) what are the actual sources of prescriptive authority there? It would, I believe, not be too simplistic to state that the traditional response, in Muslim and in orientalist scholarship, is an equation of scripture with authority, that is, to solve either of the problems by casual reference to the other. They are, of course, related but also distinct, and each, in my opinion, would benefit from separate treatment.

The literary uses, and hence communal functions, of scripture might be (roughly) isolated as four: polemic, liturgical, didactic, and juridical, in descending order of importance and (approximate) chronological order of appearance. I believe that this set of priorities can be demonstrated from the Muslim exegetical literature, which I have elsewhere examined in some detail to that end.[1] Those functions are prior to and part of the process of canonization, not a consequence of the accomplished fact. The pre-canonical history of Muslim scripture is, for a number of fairly cogent reasons, mostly a matter of conjecture. The structure of the Qur'ān itself, the transparent polemic of the canonization traditions, and the character and chronology of the exegetical literature pose far more problems than can be solved by study of the hitherto available sources. My own, emphatically provisional, conclusion was that the canonical text of scripture exhibited separate *logia* collections which had for some time prior to their final redaction been in liturgical and homiletic use in one or several related communities.[2]

For the canonical status of scripture a number of distinct criteria may be adduced.[3] Such as 'word of God' and 'of divine inspiration' are general coinage and are equally attested outside and within the monotheist tradition. Similarly, the yardstick of 'antiquity' and reference to the canon as

[1] *QS*, x, 119–21.

[2] *QS*, 43–52.

[3] G. Widengren, *Religionsphänomenologie*, Berlin, 1969, 574–93; B. Gerhardsson, *Memory and Manuscript: Oral Tradition and Written Transmission in Rabbinic Judaism and Early Christianity*, Copenhagen, 1964, 67–70; F. Nötscher, 'Himmlische Bücher und Schicksalsglaube in Qumran', *Revue de Qumran* i (1958–9) 405–11.

replica of a 'celestial register', are nearly universal phenomena but perhaps especially characteristic of Middle Eastern religions. Notions like 'messianic' and 'apostolic' authority may be thought typical of Christianity, or at least of the Christian canon, but certainly are not absent from Jewish and Muslim concepts of communal regulation. Finally, sanctification through liturgical (ritual) usage is as valid a criterion of canonicity as any of the foregoing, and moreover reflects, in contrast to those, acknowledgement of practical exigency.

Now, as unmediated theophany the Muslim scriptural canon reflects a concept of authority as the word of God. The articulation of dogmas relating to its uncreatedness and its formal as well as substantive inimitability, however logical as corollaries they might be, seem to me to be secondary to acceptance of scripture as prophetical bona fides.[1] The notion of 'apostolic' transmission can thus not be entirely excluded from the Islamic formulation of canonicity, nor of course the idea of 'celestial register' underlying the two dogmas. Muslim theology is in fact characterized by a number of scriptural ('textualist') dogmas, of which the uncreatedness and inimitability of the Qur'ān are only the most important. Enjoined upon the believer are quite explicit doctrinal positions with regard to such matters as the mechanics of revelation (*tanzīl*), its redaction (*jam'*), and its apparatus of self-correction or abrogation (*naskh*). Concern for the form and pedigree of the canon is easily documented. Interpretation of its content was the subject of an extensive exegetical literature. My interest here is in the practical application of scripture during the process of community formation.

The polemical use of 'scripture' as testimonial, dominant in the *sīra–maghāzī* literature, was never entirely abandoned. It is, however, worth recalling that those sources which may with some assurance be dated before the end of the second/eighth century (and thus before Ibn Isḥāq) contain no reference to Muslim scripture.[2] A possible exception might be the much cited and recently disputed chapter of John Damascene's *De Haeresibus*. I am myself disposed to accept Abel's arguments for later compilation and pseudepigraphy, but were the document authentic it could anyway not be adduced as evidence for a canonical text of Muslim scripture.[3] Upon the vexed question of a Vorlage for Ghevond's text of the

[1] *QS*, 77–84.

[2] A. Mingana, 'The transmission of the Ḳur'ān', *Journal of the Manchester Egyptian and Oriental Society*, 1915–16, 25–47; E. Fritsch, *Islam und Christentum im Mittelalter: Beiträge zur Geschichte der muslimischen Polemik gegen das Christentum in arabischer Sprache*, Breslau, 1930, 96–102.

[3] A. Abel, 'Le Chapitre CI du Livre des Hérésies de Jean Damascène: son inauthenticité', *Studia Islamica* xix (1963) 5–25; but cf. A. T. Khoury, *Les Théologiens byzantins et l'islam*, Paris, 1969, 47–67; D. J. Sahas, *John of Damascus on Islam*, Leiden, 1972, 58–95; W. Eichner, 'Die Nachrichten über den Islam bei den Byzantinern', *Der Islam* xxiii (1936) esp. 144–57.

alleged correspondence between Leo III and ʿUmar b. ʿAbd al-ʿAzīz I am unable to offer an opinion, though it is of some interest to note that connection of a composition/redaction of the Qur'ān with the figure of Ḥajjāj b. Yūsuf, included in both the *Risāla* of ʿAbd al-Masīḥ Kindī and the 'Jerusalem dispute' ascribed to one Ibrāhīm Ṭaberānī, is also found there.[1] That motif, as well as several others in the same correspondence, was characteristic of polemical literature not in the first/seventh but in the third/ninth century. Its point would seem to be a quarrel about the authenticity of a Muslim scripture, in the sense of valid supersession of the Biblical dispensations. On the other hand, the witness of both the Patriarch Timotheos[2] and of the Christian tract contained in Heidelberg Papyrus 438,[3] possibly contemporary with the author of the *Sīra* (d. 151/768), might reflect the circumstances obtaining within the Muslim community.

An impression of those circumstances is of course also to be had from the sequence of exegetical types set out in my study of that literature: the social function of the haggadah corresponds perfectly not merely to its literary form but also to the fluid state of the scripture of which it represents a popular and rather primitive commentary. In that type the homiletic impulse is everywhere evident: the purpose was of course didactic, an exercise in communal edification.[4] Something of the same purpose may be seen in the composition of salvation history, though possibly for a restricted (literate) public. Later exegetical types, specifically the masoretic and rhetorical, were the product of private and, to some extent, pedantic scholarship.

. . . . .

As is well known, a considerable portion of Muslim scripture consists of disjointed paraenesis, developed from traditional Judaeo-Christian imagery appropriate to the articulation of prayer. Assessment of the Arabic style is difficult, but perhaps no more so than were the earliest efforts at form-critical analysis of the Hebrew Bible. The major obstacle there, as here, is the absence of a concurrent profane literature by which rhetorical modification could be measured.[5] But the challenge was not abandoned: medieval

[1] A. Jeffery, 'Ghevond's text of the correspondence between ʿUmar II and Leo III', *Harvard Theological Review* xxxvii (1944) 297–9; K. Vollers, 'Das Religionsgespräch von Jerusalem (um 800 D)', *Zeitschrift für Kirchengeschichte* (Gotha) xxix (1908) 48; W. Muir, *The Apology of al-Kindy*, London, 1887, 77–9 (Arabic text of *Risāla*, London, 1870, 80–5); cf. Nöldeke–Schwally, *GdQ* iii, 6 n. 1, 104 n. 1.

[2] A. Mingana, *Timothy's Apology for Christianity*, Woodbrooke Studies ii, Cambridge 1928, 1–162; L. Cheikho, 'Al-Muḥāwara al-dīniyya . . . bayna 'l-khalīfa 'l-Mahdī wa-Tīmāthāus al-jāthalīq', *Al-Machriq* xix (1921) 359–74, 408–18; cf. L. E. Browne, 'The Patriarch Timothy and the Caliph Al-Mahdi', *MW* xxi (1931) 38–45.

[3] G. Graf, 'Disputation zwischen Muslimen und Christen' (Dialoge PSR Nr. 438, PER, Arab. Pap. 10000), in F. Bilabel and A. Grohmann (eds.), *Veröffentlichungen aus den badischen Papyrus-Sammlungen*, Heft 5, Heidelberg, 1934, 1–31.

[4] *QS*, 145–8.

[5] *QS*, 94–8.

Muslim exegesis dealt with scripture from the points of view of lexicon, syntax, and metaphor, always from the premiss that Quranic phenomena exhibited perfection of the type. The canon had perforce to be normative.[1] The restricted value of that approach for historical analysis of the scriptural style must be obvious.

Studies of the liturgical use of Muslim scripture, from which I exclude the homily or haggadic *narratio*, are few and uneven. Those which deserve mention (e.g. of Goitein, Andrae, Baumstark, and Richter)[2] are valuable but limited, by common assent to a view of Muslim scripture as the rhetorical achievement of one man. Underlying them all is the monumental work of Norden, variously interpreted and applied, but uniformly acknowledged.[3] As is also well known, Norden's merit was to establish the schematic and typological character of both the evangelical homily and the communal hymn, and further: to document an approximate *Sitz im Leben* for their components. For a study of early Christian literature (Greek or Latin) there was no lack of earlier and contemporary *exempla* from the profane tradition. Comparative analysis is thus possible in a way that does not quite obtain, at least for scripture, in either Hebrew or Arabic. An understandable if not quite defensible wish to reduce or even to ignore that obvious disadvantage has led a number of scholars, in Biblical and Islamic studies, to stress substantive parallels at the expense of formal calques. What ought to be, and originally was, an exercise in philology and literary criticism has tended more and more to become a search for phenomenological similarities with a predictable retreat into the vagaries of 'oral tradition' as somehow explaining an alleged uniformity of expression in the religious literature of the Middle East.[4] To be fair, that uniformity is not merely an arbitrary invention of modern scholarship. There are many similarities which cannot be ascribed to accident or even polygenesis; it is their documentation which, in the absence of explicit literary links and of criteria for assessing the chronological (!) progress of *topoi* and motifs employed in literary and oral tradition, proves so difficult. Norden's method required an abundance of comparative material that

[1] *QS*, 202–46.

[2] S. D. Goitein, 'Das Gebet im Qor'ān', Diss. Frankfurt, 1923 (unpub.), see id., *Studies in Islamic History and Institutions*, Leiden, 1966, 17 n. 1, 73–89; T. Andrae, *Origines*, 67–199; A. Baumstark, 'Jüdischer und christlicher Gebetstypus im Koran', *Der Islam* xvi (1927) 229–48; G. Richter, 'Der Sprachstil des Koran', in *Sammlung orientalistischer Arbeiten* (ed. O. Spies), Leipzig, 1940, 3. Heft, 1–78.

[3] E. Norden, *Agnostos Theos: Untersuchungen zur Formengeschichte religiöser Rede*, Stuttgart, 1971 (1913).

[4] Cf. Norden's caveat, op. cit. 117; S. Mowinckel, 'Psalm criticism between 1900 and 1935 (Ugarit and Psalm exegesis)', *Vetus Testamentum* v (1955) 13–33; diametrically opposed approaches are found in G. Widengren, 'Oral tradition and written literature among the Hebrews in the light of Arabic evidence, with special regard to prose narratives', *Acta Orientalia* xxiii (1959) 201–62, and I. Engnell, 'Methodological aspects of Old Testament study', *Vetus Testamentum*, Suppl. vii (1960) 13–30.

has been hardly available for Old Testament studies, and not at all for the Qur'ān.

Now, the formulaic character of Quranic phraseology is more or less generally acknowledged. Its actual extent has not, I believe, been computed, but would (however tedious the procedure) undoubtedly provide statistical evidence of the document's curiously repetitive structure.[1] It is a task for data processing equipment, not for the unaided eye, so subtle are the syntactic and morphological variations which can make of a simple formula a complex formulaic system. The most easily established taxonomy is of course one based on thematic categories, but these tend to be both fairly obvious and structurally inconclusive. An example of the limits of such classification may be seen in Andrae's study of eschatological imagery in the Qur'ān, as well as in treatments of scriptural metaphor (e.g. Sister and Sabbagh) and in Allard's cumbersome 'analyse conceptuelle'.[2] Surprisingly perhaps, a more valuable base for structural analysis was created by the medieval masoretes, whose studies of polysemy and synonymy (*wujūh/naẓā'ir/mushtabihāt*) included phraseological as well as lexical collocation.[3]

The point of departure for all such analysis is naturally the recurrent phrase (formula). For Muslim scripture it is in my opinion that feature, rather than thematic continuity, which makes of the document an unmistakably homogeneous composition. Without the computer, discussion of this homogeneity will be to some extent impressionistic, but a few specimens may help to support my argument that in both form and function the origins of Muslim scripture were liturgical. Now, easiest of access are those formulae inserted as refrain into litanies, e.g.

fa-bi'ay ālā'i rabbikumā tukadhdhibān (Q. 55)
(So which of your Lord's bounties will you deny)

wayl yawma'idhin lil-mukadhdhibīn (Q. 77)
(Woe on that day to those who deny)

inna fī dhālika la-āya/la-āyāt (Q. 16, 26, 30)
(In that there is a sign/signs)

wa-inna rabbaka la-huwa 'l-'azīz al-raḥīm (Q. 26)
(And your Lord is indeed mighty and merciful)

innī lakum rasūlun amīn (Q. 26)
(I am a trusted messenger unto you)

[1] *QS*, 12–20, 47–8, 112–18.

[2] e.g. Andrae, *Origines*; M. Sister, 'Metaphern und Vergleiche im Koran', *MSOS* xxxiv (1931) 104–54; T. Sabbagh, *La Métaphore dans le Coran*, Paris, 1943; M. Allard, *Analyse conceptuelle du Coran sur cartes perforées*, Paris, 1963; cf. *QS*, 215–16, 238–9.

[3] *QS*, 208–16.

wa-taraknā ʿalayhi fil-ākhirīn (Q. 37)
(And we left him among those who followed)
illā ʿibāda ʾllāhi ʾl-mukhlaṣīn (Q. 37)
(Save for the chosen creatures of God)
inna ka-dhālika najzī ʾl-muḥsinīn (Q. 37)
(Thus do we reward the pious)
fa-ttaqū ʾllāha wa-aṭīʿūn (Q. 26)
(So fear God and obey)

These vary a great deal in frequency of occurrence, but each in its context contains or indeed constitutes the pausal (rhyme) phrase. In respect of public recitation that is a feature of some significance, and as much may be said for at least half the Quranic formulae. Their liturgical function is thus assured not by semantic content but by syntactic position. Infinitely employable in this role are those phrases with *allāh* as subject plus predicate (after *inna*) in the nominative, or (after *kāna*) in the accusative, and usually of a *faʿūl/faʿīl* measure, e.g.

inna allāha ghafūr raḥīm
(God is forgiving, merciful)
wa-kāna ʾllāhu ʿalīman ḥakīman
(God is knowing, wise)

Such are structural formulae, in which the slots (of which one includes the rhyme syllable) can be filled by any adjective of seemly content and requisite morphology. Their regular distribution throughout the text of scripture is a fact of primary importance for its periodization, that is, division into rhythmic units of recitation.

The mechanism is simple and productive: the rhymes *-an/-ūn/-īn* are generated by the insertion of *kāna*, *laʿalla*, a genitive construct, or an adverbial/prepositional phrase, e.g.

bal kāna ʾllāhu bimā taʿmalūna khabīran
(But God is aware of what you do)
wa-mā kāna aktharuhum muʾminīn
(But most of them do not believe)
dhālika khayrun lakum laʿallakum tadhkurūn
(That is a benefit for you that you may recall)
wa-huwa khayru ʾl-rāziqīn
(And he is the best of providers)
wa-huwa arḥamu ʾl-raḥīmīn
(And he is the most loving)
wa-kafā billāhi shahīdan
(May God suffice as witness)

Of these the actual permutations are nearly unlimited. And yet, for a span of 78,000 words, the recurrence of particular forms is quite remarkable.

One may, indeed, speak of fixed or stereotyped pausal phrases in which not merely the rhyme word but also the preceding five or six appear repeatedly without the slightest variation, or with at most substitution of a synonym or morphological variant. Such formulae may be employed from five to twenty-five or more times, always in the position of segment-marker and entirely irrespective of context, e.g.

mā kānū bihi yastahzi'ūn
(What they used to ridicule)

inna 'llāha yuḥibbu 'l-muttaqīn
(For God loves the pious)

inna 'llāha lā yuḥibbu 'l-ẓālimīn
(For God does not love the impious)

wa-lā taziru wāzira wizra ukhrā
(And no one shall bear the burden of another)

inna 'llāha ʿalīmun bi-dhāti 'l-ṣudūr
(For God knows what is in men's hearts)

wa/thumma ilayhi/ilaynā turjaʿūn/yarjiʿūn/rājiʿūn
(Then to him/us you will be returned/they will return)

wa/fa-anbatat/anbatnā fīhā min kulli zawjin karīm/bahīj
(And there has grown/we have caused to grow there every noble/splendid sort)

wa-lā/lan tajida li-sunnati 'llāhi/li-sunnatinā tabdīlan/taḥwīlan
(And you will find in God's way/in our way no change)

fa-lā khawfa ʿalayhim wa-lā hum yaḥzanūn
(And they need have no fear nor will they regret)

fa-mā lakum kayfa taḥkumūn
(Why then do you judge so)

wa-ilā 'llāhi tarjiʿ/tasīru 'l-umūr
(And with God all things find their end)

wallāhu lā yahdī 'l-qawma 'l-ẓālimīn
(And God does not guide an impious people)

wa-lākin kānū anfusahum yaẓlumūn
(But they did wrong themselves)

wa-mimā razaqnāhum yunfiqūn
(And they give of that which we have provided)

matā hādhā 'l-waʿd in kuntum ṣādiqīn
(When is this promise to be, if you are truthful)

dhālika (huwa) 'l-fawzu 'l-ʿaẓīm
(That is the great victory)

wa/fa-ulā'ika hum al-mufliḥūn
(And those are the successful ones)

wa-mā 'llāhu bi-ghāfilin ʿammā tafʿalūn
(And God is not heedless of what you do)

Those represent stereotypes at the level of clause-structure. Single words, e.g. *jamīʿan/ajmaʿīn* (all together), and phrases, e.g. *hum fīhā khālidūn/khālidīn fīhā* (abiding therein), or *ʿalā kulli shay'in qadīr/shahīd* (capable/observant of all things), are as frequently attested in the role of segment-marker. The style is formulaic and might seem to indicate oral composition, in any case oral delivery.

Arabic morphology permits a wide lexical range in the formation of pausal (rhyme) phrases: neither the crucial syllable nor the metric structure need be altered by one-to-one substitution, e.g. *wallāhu khayru 'l-rāziqīn/nāṣirīn/ghāfirīn/mākirīn* (and God is the best of providers/helpers/guardians/plotters). But the formulaic style is not limited to refrains and other segment-markers; it is also attested in 'incipit-formulae' and what may be called conventional or stereotyped collocation. Examples of the former are usually employed as narrative introductions (protokollon):

hal atāka ḥadīth . . .
(Have you heard the story of . . .)

wa-laqad ātaynā . . .
(And we have granted . . .)

wa-min āyātihi . . .
(And among his signs are . . .)

a(wa)-lam tara/yaraw . . .
(And have you/they not seen . . .)

wa-law tara . . .
(And if you could see . . .)

a(fa)-ra'ayta . . .
(And did you not see . . .)

wa-mā adrāka mā . . .
(How do you know what . . .)

wa-mā yudrīka laʿalla . . .
(How do you know whether . . .)

wa-idhā qīla lahum . . .
(And when they were told . . .)

wa-ka'ayyan min . . .
(And how many of . . .

kadhdhabat/fa-kadhdhabūhu . . .
(They rejected/so they rejected him . . .)

wa-lammā jā'a amrunā . . .
(And when our decree fell . . .)

(wa)-yas'alūnaka ʿan . . .
(And they will ask you about . . .)

(wa)-mā as'alukum ʿalayhi min ajrin/ajran . . .
(And I expect nothing of you . . .)

wa-sakhkhara lakum . . .
(And he has subjected to you . . .)
wa-dhkurū ni'mata 'llāhi 'alaykum . . .
(And recall God's favour to you . . .)
(*wa*)-*kadhālika nufaṣṣilu 'l-āyāt . . .*
(And thus we set out the signs . . .)

The count is by no means exhaustive, but the formulae listed here are characteristic of the scriptural incipit, invariably introductory to a homily or paraenasis. Their frequency and distribution suggests a conscious if simple notion of public oratory. But within the rhetorical units, whether homily or hymn, the same tendency towards stereotyped collocation is manifest, e.g.

ṣirāṭun mustaqīm
(a straight path)
shadīdu 'l-'aqāb
(violent of punishment)
sarī'u 'l-ḥisāb
(swift of reckoning)
khuṭuwātu 'l-shayṭān
(the steps of Satan)
al-insu wal-jinn
(men and daemons)
'adhābun alīm
(severe punishment)
sulṭānun mubīn
(clear proof)
asāṭīru 'l-awwalīn
(ancient dicta: 'old wives' tales')
ajalun musammā
(fixed term)
lā rayba fihi/fihā
(there is no doubt)
(*fī*) *ḍalālin mubīn*
(in manifest error)
fa-lā junāḥa 'alaykum/fa-laysa 'alaykum junāḥ
(and there is no blame upon you)
illā bi-idhni 'llāh
(save with God's permission)
thumma 'stawā 'alā 'l-'arsh
(then he seated himself upon the throne)
yaqūlu lahu kun fa-yakūn
(he says be! and lo! it is)

sū'u 'l-ʿadhāb
(grim punishment)

inna 'llāha (rabbī/rabbaka) yabsūṭu 'l-rizqa li-man yashā'u wa-yaqdir
(For God distributes bounty to whom he will in measure)

hal/in/mā hādhā/anta illā bashar
(is he/are you anything but a mortal)

al-ladhīna ūtū . . .
(those who have been granted . . .)

jannātin tajrī min taḥtiha 'l-anhār
(gardens under which rivers flow)

a-wa-lam/a-fa-lam yasīrū fil-arḍi fa-yanẓurū kayfa kāna ʿāqiba
(and have they not gone out into the world to see what was the destiny)

sīrū fil-arḍi fanẓurū . . .
(go out into the world and see . . .)

yā qawmī uʿbudū 'llāha mā lakum min ilāhin ghayruhu
(my people, worship God for you have no other god than him)

al-ladhīna āmanū wa-ʿamilū 'l-ṣāliḥāt
(those who believe and do good works)

These collocations belong to the scriptural style, so much so that they could almost be described as bound. From the point of view of phraseology, not merely initial and final but also medial positions are characterized by formulae, both lexically and syntactically circumscribed to a reasonable degree of predictability. Quranic imagery is naturally not limited to such formulations, but these are in presence sufficient to merit some statistical attention.

To proper formulaic systems witness is less readily accessible: it is here, more than in detection of formulae, that computer processing could be helpful. By 'formulaic system' I mean here permutations based on fixed lexical and grammatical items, e.g.

al-ḥayāt al-dunyā+matāʿ:

wa-mā 'l-ḥayāt al-dunyā illā matāʿu 'l-ghurūr
(And this life is nothing but the chattels of deception)

fa-mā matāʿu 'l-ḥayāt al-dunyā fil-ākhira illā qalīl
(And of the chattels of this life there is in the hereafter but little)

innamā baghiyukum ʿalā anfusikum matāʿu 'l-ḥayāt al-dunyā
(You have only oppressed yourselves (with) the chattels of this life)

al-ḥayāt al-dunyā+laʿb wa-lahw:

wa-mā hādhihi 'l-ḥayāt al-dunyā illā lahwun wa-laʿb
(And this life is nothing but pleasure and play)

al-ladhīna 'ttakhadhū dīnahum lahwan wa-la'ban ghurratuhum al-ḥayāt al-dunyā
(Those who take their religion as pleasure and play: their deception (lies in) this life)

al-samāwāt wal-arḍ+khalq/mulk:
wa-min āyātihi khalqu 'l-samāwāti wal-arḍ
(And among his signs is the creation of the heavens and earth)
mā ashhadtuhum khalqa 'l-samāwāti wal-arḍ
(I have not called them to witness the creation of the heavens and earth)
wa-lillāhi mulku 'l-samāwāti wal-arḍ
(And God's is dominion in the heavens and earth)
am lahum mulku 'l-samāwāti wal-arḍi wa-mā baynahumā
(Or have they dominion of the heavens and earth and what lies between)

mā 'alayhi+abā'unā:
bal nattabi'u mā alfaynā 'alayhi abā'anā
(But we follow the precedent of our fathers)
a-ji'tanā li-talfitanā 'ammā wajadnā 'alayhi abā'anā
(Do you come to turn us from the precedent of our fathers)
a-tanhanā an na'buda mā ya'budu abā'unā
(Do you forbid that we worship what our fathers worship)

shurakā'+za'ama/da'ā:
ayna shurakā'ī 'l-ladhīna kuntum taza'mūn
(Where then are my partners whom you alleged)
hā'ulā'i shurakā'unā 'l-ladhīna kunnā nad'ū min dunika
(These are our partners to whom we pray instead of you)

iftarā+kadhib/ifk:
wa-man aẓlamu miman iftarā 'alā 'llāhi kadhiban
(And who is more impious than one who fabricates a lie against God)
wa-lākinna 'l-ladhīna kafarū yaftaruna 'alā 'llāhi 'l-kadhib
(But those who reject fabricate a lie against God)
wa-dhālika ifkuhum wa-mā kānū yaftarūn
(And that is their lie and what they fabricate)

maṣīr/mihād/ma'āb/ma'wā/mathwā:
wa-bi's al-maṣīr
(And grim is the destiny)
wa-ilā 'llāhi 'l-maṣīr
(And God's is the destiny)
wa-ilayhi 'l-maṣīr
(And His is the destiny)
wa-bi's al-mihād
(And grim is the destiny)
wa-husnā ma'āb
(And a fine destiny)

ilā rabbihi ma'āb
(Destiny is his lord's)
wa-ilayhi ma'āb
(Destiny is His)
la-sharra ma'āb
(An evil destiny)
fa-inna 'l-janna hiya 'l-ma'wā
(For (their) destiny is heaven)
fa-inna 'l-jaḥīma hiya 'l-ma'wā
(For (their) destiny is hellfire)
ma'wākum al-nār
(Your destiny is hell)
wa-bi'sa mathwā 'l-ẓālimīn
(And grim is the destiny of the impious)
al-nāru mathwākum
(Hell is your destiny)
a-laysa fī jahannama mathwan lil-kāfirīn
(Is there not in hell a destiny for those who reject)

More or less synonymous, the five terms I have rendered 'destiny' in the last example generate nearly identical phraseology, and thus attest the limits as well as the utility of a formulaic system.

Whether, on the other hand, designation of these several Quranic phenomena as 'formulaic' is strictly accurate may be something of a problem. If such usage presupposes exclusively isometric substitution, it can, clearly, not always be applied. Extensive passages of Muslim scripture do not scan, either quantitatively or accentually, though it is equally clear that the refrains and other pausal phrases do exhibit regular stress (cadence) and/or a constant quantity of syllables. In a passage such as Sūra 26 (Shu'arā') this feature is striking: there pausal phrase corresponds with verse division and the rhyme scheme itself is remarkably uniform (*īn/ūn/īm/ūm*, with only four exceptions: [*banī isrā'*]*īl*, in 227 verses), with an average syllable count per verse of fifteen to twenty (seriously breached only by the first and last verses). And there are very few verses in that *sūra* which cannot be related to a formulaic interpretation of Quranic imagery. Though none of the preceding categories of formula can be exhaustively treated without a computer, it may seem that the material is at least appropriate to such analysis.

Now, after Norden's meticulous analysis of basic prayer structure from the spheres of Hellenism, Judaism, and Christianity, it can be observed as a matter of course that the equivalent Muslim expressions conform to type. For the eulogy, doxology, and basileia, Baumstark has noted the phraseological correspondence (*tabāraka/subḥān/al-ḥamd/mulk/mā fil-samāwāt wal-arḍ*).[1] Such rhetorical devices as parallelism, alliteration, anaphora, and

[1] Baumstark, art. cit.

isokola are common to all four literatures, and certainly suggest a shared legacy.[1] Save for the categories of incipit and stereotyped collocation, which may or may not be liturgically employed, what I have described as Quranic formulae exhibit the same rhetorical devices and appear to have filled the same liturgical functions. A line like *wa-lā taziru wāziratun wizra ukhrā* (And no one shall bear the burden of another) is a perfect example of rhythmic prose, characterized by assonance (alliteration) and anaphoric stress: in each of its five occurrences (Q. 6: 164, 17: 15, 35: 18, 39: 7, 53: 38) it constitutes an internal or the final rhyme phrase. The development of formal rhyme from conceptual rhyme (parallelism) is, I believe, more or less generally conceded, and underlying the latter is of course the principle of formulaic language. That the context of that development was not poetry but prose, Norden has demonstrated.[2]

Despite the strong theoretical possibilities alluded to above, the practical quest for prototypes of Quranic diction is hindered both by the transmission history of the document and the absence of trustworthy comparative material. The recent conjectures of Lüling with regard to the essentially hymnic character of Muslim scripture are not unreasonable, though I am unable to accept what seems to me his very subjective reconstruction of the text. The liturgical form and function of the Qur'ān is abundantly clear even in the traditional recension, as well as from the traditional literature describing its communal uses. The detection of strophic formations is certainly not difficult, and the theological (as opposed to rhetorical) nature of orthodox insistence upon the absence from scripture of poetry and even (though less unanimous) of rhymed prose must be acknowledged.[3] But for all that we are no closer than we have ever been to the actual forms of pre-Islamic Arabic and, in the present state of documentation, a change in these conditions seems unlikely.[4] One additional piece of evidence for a liturgical/cultic use of the Qur'ān may lie in the collective designation *qurrā'*, variously attested in accounts of Bi'r Ma'ūna, Ṣiffīn, and Kufan society, and traditionally glossed as *ḥamalat al-qur'ān* (bearers of *qur'ān*). From what is known of the services in battle of such groups as the Biblical *shōṭerīm* and Qumranic *mesōrōt* (*anshē ha-ṣerekh*), e.g. exhortation, proclamation of statutes, fixing of inscriptions on standards, an analogous function for the *qurrā'* may be thought possible, in which case they could of course have been literally 'bearers of *qur'ān*', and not simply those who had preserved in their memories the text of scripture.[5]

[1] Norden, *Agnostos Theos*, 156; id., *Die antike Kunstprosa*, Stuttgart, 1958 (1909), 156–61.

[2] Ibid. 810–960.

[3] Lüling, *Ur-Qur'ān*, 119–73; cf. Ibrāhīm Anīs, *Musiqā 'l-shi'r*, Cairo, 1952, 300–10.

[4] J. Blau, 'Sind uns Reste arabischer Bibelübersetzungen aus vorislamischer Zeit erhalten geblieben?', *Le Muséon* lxxxvi (1973) 67–72 (v. Baumstark).

[5] Nöldeke–Schwally, *GdQ* ii, 12 n. 2 and references; cf. Kister, 'Bi'r Ma'ūna', 337–57; Gertner, 'Masorah and Levites', 257–9.

Witness to the polemical, liturgical, and didactic (homiletic) value of Muslim scripture is thus not hard to come by. Its exploitation as a source of halakhic authority is also attested, but in a manner complicated by factional dispute and an elaborately ambiguous technical vocabulary. It was, however, precisely that alleged function of scripture which brought about its canonization, or so I have argued elsewhere.[1] It seemed to me that both the chronology and the character of the literary evidence demanded that, or a very similar, conclusion. But the actual historical circumstances may have been quite different. There are at least two considerations involved in further discussion of the problem: (*a*) that, given its unmistakably formulaic structure, cultic use alone may have produced the text in its present canonical shape; and (*b*) that, despite the quantity of halakhic argument to the contrary, it is doubtful whether the Qur'ān ever became a primary source of community regulation. That it had to be seen to be such was, of course, the point of the argument: halakhic exegesis can in no case be discounted as a factor in the process of canonization. The value of that literature lies in its witness to the enduring *uṣūl* (sources) controversies, from which it is often just possible to deduce what, if not the text of scripture, was the source of juridical prescription. Whatever consensus might be elicited from that literature, it can only point to a generic concept of 'revelation', which included both the text of scripture (*waḥy matluw*) and material of equal authority outside scripture (*waḥy ghayr matluw*), *scil.* the prophetical Sunna. From my observations above on the liturgical function of the Qur'ān, it may be supposed that the terms *matluw/tilāwa* (recited/recitation) were of considerable significance in establishing a typology of authority. The canon was 'recited', that is, used in prayer; it was not, for all that, the exclusive source of prescription. As I have earlier stated:[2] 'Whatever the linguistic and logical assertions made about the *ipsissima verba* of scripture, halakhic exegesis turned upon the assumption of a chronological, and hence causal, relation between Qur'ān and (prophetical) Sunna. The question of priority, though hedged with qualification, was generally answered in favour of the latter.'

. . . . .

The Islamic concept of authority can be fairly described as 'apostolic'. In the midrashic styles of salvation history the functions of scripture were to generate (historicization) and to embellish (exemplification) a portrait of the early community, and simultaneously to provide bona fides of its covenantal dispensation. Dominant there is the charismatic figure of the Apostle of God in an essentially public posture. Informing the narrative is a polemical concern to depict the emergence of a religious polity (*umma*)

[1] *QS*, 148–202; but see Burton, *Collection*, 172–87; and *BSOAS* xli (1978) 370–1.
[2] *QS*, 188.

out of a more or less traditionally articulated theophany (*waḥy*). The difference between *Sīra* and Sunna as literary forms might be expressed as the transition from polemic to paradigmatic description, of the Apostle as well as of life in the early community. The formative principle of Sunna is *exemplum*, an intentionally ambiguous notion whose various applications may be discerned in the Arabic term *imām*. The range of reference, from leader of the community (*ma'mūm/umma*) to canonical text of scripture (*muṣḥaf*) to celestial register of divine decrees (*lawḥ maḥfūẓ*), reflects a number of distinct doctrinal positions, the most important of which was identification of authority with scripture.[1] Save in this somewhat constrained context of technical terminology, the equation was neither realistic nor in practice taken seriously: the alternative designations of 'revelation', *kitāb allāh* (book of God) and *kalām allāh* (word of God), included both the canon (*imām:muṣḥaf*) and the Sunna.[2]

In Muslim sectarian (Shī'ī) usage the term *imām* is unambiguous: reference is always to the leader of the community, in the enhanced and particular sense of legitimist and ordained (*waṣiyya/naṣṣ*) recipient of the prophetical legacy (*mīrāth al-nubuwwa*). The *imām* is sinless (*ma'ṣūm*), the source of prescription (*aṣl-al-fiqh*), and the sole possessor of gnosis (*jafr*).[3] That here, amongst similar and even more extremely formulated qualities, are to be found the origins of such 'scripturalist' dogmas as those of inimitability and uncreatedness, seems more than likely. Indeed, the designation *imām* for the scriptural canon may reflect the same environment. There, in any case, the priority of Apostle over Book was repeatedly and consistently expressed.[4]

Acknowledgement in the early Muslim community, as in Rabbinic Judaism, of an authority outside scripture was invariably qualified by assertion that the relation between the two sources was exegetical. That, of course, is the major problem in assessment of the sources of authority, namely, the distinction between derivation and independent origins. Halakhic terminology is designed expressly to convey the impression that scripture is the sole source of authority, and must be judged accordingly. Elaboration of such terminology exhibits a secondary stage of argument, and may usefully be compared with earlier formulations of halakhot in which *exemplum* (*imām*) is invariably a reference to an action or utterance of the Apostle. There is a further consideration: the hermeneutical discipline (with its terminology) was the invention, and monopoly, of a

[1] Q. 11: 17, 36: 12, 46: 12; Suyūṭī, *Al-Itqān fī 'ulūm al-Qur'ān*, Cairo, 1967, i, 170; cf. Nöldeke–Schwally, *GdQ* iii, 6–18.

[2] *QS*, 51–2, 56–7, 74–8.

[3] I. Goldziher, *Vorlesungen über den Islam*, Heidelberg, 1910, 215–30; id., *Richtungen*, 263–309; T. Andrae, *Die Person Muhammeds in Lehre und Glauben seiner Gemeinde*, Stockholm, 1918, 290–390.

[4] e.g. *QS*, 162 n. 4 (Q. 45: 29).

scholarly élite, whose social role in the process of community formation requires at every stage to be assessed. It seems not unreasonable to suppose that efforts to establish an exegetical (and, hence, to some extent subordinate) relation of Sunna to Qur'ān might be attributed to that quarter.

Now, all these problems: the ambiguity of *exemplum*, the bias of halakhic terminology, and the vested interests of a clerical élite, are pertinent to what I have proposed was the Islamic concept of 'apostolic' authority. The resolution of each may be observed in the classical compilations of Muslim halakhot, of which an example is the *Ṣaḥīḥ* of Bukhārī (d. 256/870). By that date the principle of 'apostolic' authority was fully achieved, articulated, and unanimously acknowledged as the 'prophetical Sunna'. But its history is much older, and already the *Muwaṭṭa'* of Mālik b. Anas (d. 179/795),[1] not well known for his insistence upon *exempla* from the prophetical Sunna, illustrates the paradigmatic, as opposed to midrashic, style. Any sondage would do: I have selected four chapters that deal with ordinances pertinent to sacrifice.

Kitāb al-ḍaḥāyā (ch. 23, pp. 482–7)

1. A prophetical tradition (*ḥadīth*) on the kinds of blemish that disqualify sacrificial victims.

2. Same subject; Mālik: And this is the best that I have heard (*wa-hādhā aḥabbu mā sami'tu ilayya*).

3. A tradition from 'Abdallāh b. 'Umar recommending, but not prescribing, shaving of the head.

4. A tradition from Bushayr b. Yasār on not sacrificing before the Prophet had done so.

5. A prophetical tradition on not sacrificing too early on the Day of Sacrifice (*yawm al-aḍḥā*).

6. A prophetical tradition prohibiting consumption of a sacrificial offering after the passage of three days.

7. A prophetical gloss on the preceding: the object being charity to the poor (*dāffa*).

8. Same subject: prophetical specification, modification, rescission.

9. A prophetical tradition on the number of sacrificial victims per group.

10. Same subject: one sacrifice per individual or household, and inadvisability of sacrifice shared outside household; Mālik: And the best I have heard . . . (*wa-aḥsanu mā sami'tu . . .*).

11. A prophetical tradition: one victim per household.

12. A tradition from 'Abdallāh b. 'Umar on the duration of the Feast of Sacrifice (*yawm al-aḍḥā*). The same from 'Alī b. Abī Ṭālib.

[1] Mālik b. Anas, *Al-Muwaṭṭa'*, ed. M. 'Abd al-Bāqī, Cairo, 1370/1951; see Schacht *Origins*, 22–7, 61–9, 83–5, but also 113–19, 311–14 (systematic reasoning).

13. A tradition from ʿAbdallāh b. ʿUmar stating that sacrifice may not be offered on behalf of an unborn child. Mālik: The sacrifice is customary, not obligatory (*al-ḍaḥiyya sunnatun wa-laysa bi wājiba*).

Kitāb al-dhabāʾiḥ (ch. 24, pp. 488–90)

1. A prophetical tradition on consecration of the victim by reciting the name of God over it.

2. Same subject: a confirming tradition from ʿAbdallāh b. Abī Rabīʿa.

3. A prophetical tradition on the validity of ritual sacrifice after the natural death of the victim, the permitted instrument being a pointed stick (*shaẓāẓ*).

4. Same subject: also a prophetical tradition, the instrument being a sharp stone.

5. A tradition from ʿAbdallāh b. ʿAbbās approving consumption of sacrifices performed by Christian Arabs, but with citation of Q. 5: 51 'And whoever of your number joins them, is one of them'.[1]

6. A tradition from ʿAbdallāh b. ʿAbbās approving consumption of any victim sacrificed by cutting the jugular vein (*wadaj*). And from Saʿīd b. al-Musayyab: in cases of necessity.

7. Conflicting traditions from Abū Hurayra and from Zayd b. Thābit, defining the moment of death: in terms of spasm and flow of blood. Mālik: flow of blood and movement of the eyes.

8. A tradition from ʿAbdallāh b. ʿUmar on the conditions for valid ritual sacrifice of the unborn foetus.

9. Same subject: a confirming tradition from Saʿīd b. al-Musayyab.

Kitāb al-ṣayd (ch. 25, pp. 491–9)

1. A tradition from ʿAbdallāh b. ʿUmar on the invalidity of ritual slaughter (*dhakā*) if the victim dies first of natural causes.

2. A tradition from Al-Qāsim b. Muḥammad disapproving a victim slain by lance (*miʿrāḍ*) or catapult (*bunduqa*).

3. Same subject: a similar tradition from Saʿīd b. al-Musayyab. Mālik: approval subject to instant death (*balagha 'l-maqātil*), and citing Q. 5: 94 'O you who believe, God will try you with game which you take by hand and spear (*aydīkum wa-rimāḥukum*)'.

4. Mālik had heard traditionists say (*samiʿa ahl al-ʿilm yaqūlūn*) that game was not ritually valid unless it could be proved that it was slain directly by the hunter's weapon, and that it had not been left overnight.

5. A tradition from ʿAbdallāh b. ʿUmar approving the use of trained dogs.

6. Mālik heard (*samiʿa*) a variant of the preceding.

7. A tradition from Saʿd b. Abī Waqqāṣ confirming the preceding.

8. Mālik had heard traditionists (*ahl al-ʿilm*) say that falconry was also ritually valid, on condition that the training was similar to that for dogs and provided

[1] Cf. F. Nau, 'Lettre du bienheureux patriarche Athanase: qu'aucun chrétien ne doit manger (une partie) des sacrifices des Arabes qui dominent maintenant', *ROC* xiv (1909) 128–30.

that the name of God was uttered at dispatch (*irsāl*). Mālik: And the best I have heard (*wa-aḥsanu mā samiʿtu*) is that death by that means must be immediate, otherwise consumption is prohibited. Further, any opportunity (before natural death or killing) for ritual slaughter must be taken, otherwise consumption is prohibited. Finally, it is in our opinion agreed (*al-amr al-mujtamaʿ ʿalayhi ʿindanā*) that Muslim use of a pagan (*majūsī*) weapon/instrument for hunt or slaughter is permitted, though the converse is prohibited.

9. A tradition from ʿAbdallāh b. ʿUmar prohibiting consumption of seafood, but the decision was reversed (*inqalaba*) upon appeal to scripture (*sic*: *muṣḥaf*): Q. 5: 96 'Lawful for you is the pursuit and consumption of (products from) the sea'.

10. A tradition from ʿAbdallāh b. ʿUmar approving consumption of carrion from the sea. Corroboration from ʿAbdallāh b. Amr b. al-ʿĀṣ.

11. A tradition from Abū Hurayra and Zayd b. Thābit approving consumption of seafood.

12. Same subject and tradents in modified circumstances. A prophetical tradition on the purificatory character of the sea.

13. A prophetical tradition prohibiting consumption of anything killed by beasts of prey (*sibāʿ*).

14. Same subject and tradent. Mālik: And that is so in our opinion (*wa-huwa 'l-amr ʿindanā*).

15. The best Mālik had heard (*aḥsanu mā samiʿa*) on beasts of burden was that they were not to be consumed: because (*sic*) of Q. 16: 7 'And the horse and the mule and the ass are for riding and for ornament', and Q. 40: 79 'some for riding and some (others) for eating', and Q. 22: 34 'that you mention God's name over every beast we have granted you . . . (36) and eat thereof and give to the needy and the visitor.'

16. A prophetical tradition approving the use of carrion for other than food (e.g. hides, etc.).

17. A prophetical tradition on the purificatory character of tanning.

18. Same subject: a prophetical tradition.

19. Mālik: And the best I have heard (*wa-aḥsanu mā samiʿtu*): on the consumption of carrion in cases of dire necessity (to avoid theft, etc.), but also on the temptations arising out of such practice.

Kitāb al-ʿaqīqa (ch. 26, pp. 500–2)

1. A prophetical tradition permitting sacrifice for the new-born child.

2. A tradition from Muḥammad al-Bāqir on Fāṭima's having weighed the shorn hair (*ʿaqīqa*) of Ḥasan and Ḥusayn and given alms (*taṣaddaqa*) in silver to that amount.

3. Same subject: corroboration from Muḥammad b. ʿAlī b. Ḥusayn.

4. A tradition from ʿAbdallāh b. ʿUmar on his habitual performance of *ʿaqīqa*: one sheep for all children, male or female.

5. A tradition from Muḥammad b. Ibrāhīm al-Taymī recommending that sacrifice, if only to the amount of one sparrow.

6. Mālik had heard (*annahu balaghahu*) that *'aqīqa* had been performed in the case of Ḥasan and Ḥusayn.

7. A tradition from Hishām b. 'Urwa that his father had performed the sacrifice for all his children, male and female, to the amount of one sheep. Mālik: In our opinion (*al-amr 'indanā*) the *'aqīqa* sacrifice is not obligatory, but if it is to be performed, then for both male and female children, to the amount of one sheep, and according to the conditions obtaining for all propitiatory and ritual sacrifice (*al-nusuk wal-ḍaḥāyā*).

Each of the forty-eight paragraphs in these four chapters contains a report of precedent or of comment on precedent, of which sixteen are traced to the prophet Muhammad himself. Mālik's own commentary is expressed almost exclusively as the transmission and alignment of such dicta: 'the best I have heard', 'I have heard traditionists say', 'the agreed opinion (consensus?) is'. Even the locution 'and that is so in our opinion' is acknowledgement of a received view, approved because included in this collection. Naturally, the juxtaposition of particular reports and their arrangement under particular rubrics exhibit the judgement of Mālik, which might indeed have been arrived at by way of analogy (*ka-dhālika*) or other modes of independent reasoning. It is, however, significant that the articulation of such views is always the report of earlier utterance and/or action. In this style the term 'knowledge' (*'ilm*) refers expressly to those reports, and the phrase 'men of knowledge' (*ahl al-'ilm*) to the authorities responsible for their transmission.

Reference to scripture in those paragraphs is minimal:[1] *K. al-ḍaḥāyā* (none), *K. al-dhabā'iḥ* no. 5, *K. al-ṣayd* nos. 3, 9, 15, *K. al-'aqīqa* (none), and always expressed by Mālik as a tradition neither more nor less binding than those from other sources. Only in *K. al-ṣayd* no. 9 is the scriptural (*muṣḥaf*) verse (Q. 5: 96) adduced as grounds for the reversal of a decision based upon a non-scriptural tradition. The concept of *exemplum* is thus 'precedent', apostolic: first, in the sense of paradigmatic behaviour reported of the Prophet, or of his associates (Companions); second, in the sense of pronouncements on paradigmatic behaviour by competent authorities (traditionists). Numerically, these constitute an élite, but symbolically they are identical with the early community, and their names synonymous in this context with that of the Apostle, none of whose utterances in these chapters of the *Muwaṭṭa'* is linked with a scriptural citation. The exegetical bias of halakhic terminology had thus not yet been formulated.

It may be asserted, without undue injustice, that the earliest halakhic literature exhibits not so much a commentary upon scripture as a refinement of salvation history. There the basic literary unit was the pericope

[1] Cf. *QS*, 171–2.

(*qiṣṣa*), here it is the tradition (*ḥadīth*). A formal property of what I have called the midrashic styles was the presence of material found also in the text of scripture. In the paradigmatic style the word of God is rather less in evidence than the words of men. However, from the point of view of substance, *qiṣṣa* and *ḥadīth* exhibit a shared concern with the figure of the Arabian prophet, the former with his role as recipient of revelation, the latter with his oracular function. Tension between the two might be characterized as a reflex of the soteriological dichotomy history v. law, corresponding roughly to the difference between mythic and normative content. Evolution from one to the other may be observed in the three recensions of the '‘Ā'isha scandal' (*ḥadīth al-ifk*), an elaborate *mise en scène* for the revelation of Q. 24: 11–12 and subsequently a *topos* of Christian polemic against Islam.[1]

The basic narrative is that of Ibn Isḥāq (*Sīra* ii, 297–307), where the episode is dated 6 A.H. during the prophet's return to Medina from the expedition against B. Muṣṭaliq, and includes broadly the following components:

1. Drawing of lots to see which of Muhammad's wives would accompany him on campaign.
2. The meagre diet of women and their near 'weightlessness'.
3. Nocturnal halt of the army near Medina.
4. ‘Ā'isha's removal from the camp and her lost necklace.
5. Departure of the caravan without her.
6. Her discovery by Ṣafwān b. Mu‘aṭṭal, and subsequent return in his company.
7. Her illness in Medina and the indifference of Muhammad.
8. Her removal to her parents' home.
9. ‘Ā'isha informed of the scandal by Umm Misṭaḥ.
10. Muhammad's public address on the subject.
11. Muhammad's sounding of opinion on ‘Ā'isha's character.
12. Altercation between B. Aws and B. Khazraj.
13. Muhammad demands repentance from ‘Ā'isha.
14. Revelation of Q. 24: 11–12, 15, 22.
15. Muhammad's punishment of the calumniators.
16. Muhammad's award of compensation to Ḥassān b. Thābit.

In the recension of Wāqidī (*Maghāzī*, 426–40), like that of Ibn Isḥāq based on the testimony of ‘Ā'isha herself, the following modifications may be noted:

1. The introductory theme is not the revelation of Q. 24: 11–12, but of *Āyat al-tayammum* (Q. 4: 43/5: 6), viz. the problem of ablutions in the desert (426–7, 435).

[1] Abel, 'Le Chapitre CI', 7; C. H. Becker, 'Christliche Polemik und islamische Dogmenbildung', *Islamstudien* i–ii, Hildesheim, 1967 (1924), i, 438.

2. Muhammad was accompanied not by one but two of his wives.

3. The Umm Misṭaḥ motif precedes, rather than follows, ʿĀ'isha's removal to her parents' home, and hence necessitates an earlier confrontation with Muhammad.

4. Muhammad's sounding of public opinion on the character of ʿĀ'isha is expanded.

5. The Aws-Khazraj altercation is related specifically to the Jāhiliyya (Yawm al-Buʿāth) with explicit reference to cancellation of the perennial hostility by the advent of Islam.

6. The decisive revelation is limited to Q. 24: 11–12, and ʿĀ'isha is described as both married (*muḥṣana*) and as 'mother of the faithful' (*umm al-mu'minīn*).

7. The account of Muhammad's reconciliation of Aws and Khazraj is elaborated.

8. The account of Muhammad's compensation for Ḥassān is similarly elaborated.

9. Concluding excursus on the inadvisability (Muhammad's judgement) of visiting women at night without warning.

In the recension of Bukhārī[1] (*Kitāb al-shahādāt, bāb* 15), also based on the testimony of ʿĀ'isha, the narrative is reduced to what might be called its parabolic nucleus:

1. The rubric is 'justification of women by one another' (*taʿdīl al-nisā' baʿḍihinna baʿḍan*).

2. The order of the Umm Misṭaḥ motif is as in Wāqidī, but here reported by indirect speech, thus obviating an initial encounter between ʿĀ'isha and Muhammad.

3. Muhammad's sounding of public opinion is limited, after ʿAlī and Usāma b. Zayd, to Zaynab, the last of which is placed after, rather than before, revelation of Q. 24: 11–12.

4. ʿAbdallāh b. Ubayy is made responsible for the entire episode, and there is no mention of Ḥassān.

Now, the development from loosely structured narrative to concise *exemplum* seems to me fairly obvious.[2] Bukhārī's purpose is exclusively (and expectedly) paradigmatic, though some trace of the original narrative

[1] Bukhārī, *Al-Ṣaḥīḥ*, ed. L. Krehl, Leiden, 1868, ii, 153–7; the two other long versions of *Ḥadīth al-ifk* found in Bukhārī, i.e. K. Maghāzī, bāb 34 (iii, 103–10) and K. Tafsīr, bāb 6 (iii, 292–7), are structurally and substantively the same, save for addition of Ḥassān b. Thābit's role in the affair; references in K. Shahādāt, bāb 2 (ii, 126–7) and K. Iʿtiṣām, bāb 28 (iv, 444), are to the testimony of Usāma, ʿAlī, and Burayra; and in K. Tawḥīd, bābs 35 (iv, 480) and 52 (iv, 496) to the revelation of a 'qur'ān' on this occasion.

[2] But cf. Widengren, 'Oral tradition', 256–8; I cannot agree that Bukhārī's version represents the most polished narrative: his purpose was not in the least haggadic. Ṭabarī (*Annales*, 1/1517–28) is rightly described as a nearly verbatim rendering of Ibn Isḥāq (less the editorial comments of Ibn Hishām and a few verses from Ḥassān). More appropriately, see W. S. Towner, 'Form-criticism of Rabbinic literature', *JJS* xxiv (1973) 101–18.

phraseology has been preserved. Wāqidī's account exhibits an intermediate position: a refinement of the *Sīra* version but without the reductive character of that compiled by Bukhārī. Subsumption of the entire episode under the rubric *Tayammum* may be compared with its similar position in Mālik's *Muwaṭṭa'* (53–6: *K. al-ṭahāra*), where the narrative is even less in evidence than in Bukhārī. The movement from *narratio* to *exemplum* illustrates perfectly the stylistic difference between *Sīra* and Sunna, between the mythic and normative preoccupations (*Geistesbeschäftigungen*) of early Muslim literature.

The two literary types were naturally not mutually exclusive. For the concept of authority, which is here my primary concern, a realistic, didactic, and entertaining portrait of the prophet could never be regarded as superfluous. Authority was after all *paradosis/traditio*, as must be clear from its articulation in the *Muwaṭṭa'*, but what was preserved and transmitted was not merely a set of prescriptions, but also the account of a historical event.[1] In that respect, as in all or most others, Islam exhibits a perpetuation of the Judaeo-Christian legacy. The very notion of 'apostolic' authority presupposes historical continuity resting upon intelligible and above all verifiable data. That the instrument of verification was itself *paradosis* (authentication by the fact of transmission) is additional proof of my thesis, namely, that the source of authority in the Muslim community was not scripture (uncreated, hence ahistorical) but the *exemplum* of its founder. Related, and in many respects essential, to this argument, are three problems, to which brief allusion has been made:

1. The exegetical character of Muslim halakhot.
2. The status respectively of scripture and Sunna.
3. The role of a scholarly/clerical élite.

Common to all three versions of *Ḥadīth al-ifk* was the assumption that problems could be solved by recourse to divine revelation. Its exclusive instrument was the apostle, its basic qualification liturgical, i.e. 'that which was recited at prayer' (*qur'ān yaqra'uhu 'l-nās fī ṣalātihim*), or 'recited in the mosques and used at prayer' (*qur'ān yuqra'u bihi fil-masājid wa-yuṣalla bihi*). Being urged here is the specifically textual character of revelation, in contrast to other forms of divine inspiration (here: 'vision' (*ru'ya*) or 'decision' (*khabar*)) which might from time to time be granted. It was of course the use of 'scriptural' revelation in the particular circumstances of Muhammad's domestic life that provided ammunition for the Christian polemicists. But in the Muslim argument there is a convenient ambiguity: the epithet 'qur'ān' might signify public recitation, but only upon the authority of the apostle. 'Ā'isha's own careful distinction between her obligations respectively to God and to Muhammad, even in the face of

[1] Bultmann, *Theology* ii, 119–27; D. Daube, *The New Testament and Rabbinic Judaism*, London, 1956, 67–89 ('Precept and Example').

her parents' insistence that she apologize to the latter, could be interpreted as a reflex of 'scripturalist' opposed to 'apostolic' authority. And evidence of support for the latter position, that is, stress not upon the liturgical function but upon the recipient of revelation, might be seen in Bukhārī's version, where for the locutions cited above the simple designation 'revelation' (*waḥy*) was substituted, admittedly equated with 'qur'ān' but without explicit reference to the cult.

The first two of the aforementioned problems represent aspects of the same issue: the derivation of halakhah from scripture requires priority of the latter and, conversely, acknowledgement of a different source for halakhah permits at least some latitude in assessing the communal function of scripture. To show that a prescriptive ruling can have had its source in other than scripture is difficult but not impossible: an example I have treated elsewhere was that involving the *muḥāribūn* penalties and Q. 5: 33.[1] To show that a scriptural verse may have had its source in an earlier prescriptive ruling is even more difficult: an example is Burton's demonstration of the origins of the 'stoning verse' in the penalties for adultery.[2] A related exercise, but with the opposite purpose of proving the exegetical origins of *ḥadīth*, is Van Ess's study of early Muslim dogma on the predestination controversy.[3] There, it is difficult to escape the impression that the priority of scripture is assumed rather than demonstrated, and for one example (pp. 32–9) the author concedes that the exegetical link was a secondary development. But the problem in such contexts is to distinguish between actual exegesis and merely introduction of a scriptural prop (cf. Rabbinic *asmakhtā*), after rather than accessory to the fact. The notion of 'Sunna as personalized exegesis' (p. 185) could on the basis of accessible data easily be inverted. It may be tempting, though surely not compelling, to suppose that Muslim scripture was the source of dogmatic theology (*kalām*) as well as of jurisprudence (*fiqh*). But precisely why the maxim 'Act, for each it will be made easy according to his nature' must be interpreted as derived from, and hence posterior to, Q. 92: 5–7 (For him who is generous and pious and believes in the best, We will make it easy) is not at all clear, at least to me (pp. 39–47). Stylistically, the evolution *sanuyassir* (we will make easy) from *muyassar* (made easy) is rather more illuminating. I should, in other words, read the Quranic formulation as a monotheistic recasting of a popular and religiously neutral aphorism. It may be thought that selection of priorities in such contexts is at the very best arbitrary.

A fresh and constructive approach to precisely this problem is Neusner's study of the Mishnaic law of purities.[4] There, for the tractates *Kelim* and

[1] *QS*, 185–8. [2] *QS*, 194–6; Burton, 'Cranes', 246–65; id., *Collection*, 89–104.

[3] J. van Ess, *Zwischen Ḥadīṯ und Theologie: Studien zum Entstehen prädestinatianischer Überlieferung*, Berlin, 1975, 1–55, 185; cf. *BSOAS* xxxix (1976) 442–3.

[4] J. Neusner, *Early Rabbinic Judaism*, Leiden, 1975, 3–33; cf. *BSOAS* xxxix (1976) 438–9; Gerhardsson, *Memory and Manuscript*, 82–3.

Ohalot, the relation between written and oral Torah is shown to be not exegetical, but rather, conceptual, metaphysical, and, eventually, complementary. Neusner's argument is that *miqrā* and *mishnah*, at least for those tractates, exhibit distinct and contrasting cultural backgrounds, what I have here referred to as *Geistesbeschäftigungen* or 'motives'. That these could be connected and interpreted as mutually corroborative by express reference to scripture did not entail exegetical derivation of oral from written Torah.[1] In much the same way I am inclined to read Mālik's prescriptions pertinent to ritual sacrifice (as also those relating to Holy War): the relation to scripture is both posterior and incidental to their original formulation. Whether one might, with Neusner, take the next step to propose that in many instances *mishnah* was chronologically prior to *miqrā*, is problematic. For the evolution of 'normative' Islam the time-span is considerably shorter than for that of Pharisaic–Rabbinic Judaism and, while the polemical character of much of Muslim scripture can hardly be denied, to show that a verse of the Quranic canon owed its formulation to a particular halakhic dispute would not be easy. Burton's interpretation of the 'stoning verse' is of course an example of such, but that verse is not now, and may never have been, included in the canon.

The third of the problems mentioned above, defining the communal function of a scholarly élite, concerns both the expression and transmission of apostolic authority. Initially, the identity of that élite must be extrapolated from the literary device known as ascription (*isnād*), itself the primary component of what I have here proposed was the Islamic concept of authority.[2] From the more or less consistent practice of naming tradents two kinds of information can be inferred: evidential (relating to the authenticity of tradition) and sociological (relating to the membership of circles responsible for transmission). I am concerned here with the latter, though one observation in respect of the former point could be useful: the dichotomy 'written' v. 'oral' law cannot be supposed, in Islam or in Rabbinic Judaism, to represent more than a convention designed to emphasize the dual character of revelation, viz. that which is preserved and transmitted as scripture and that which is preserved and transmitted as other than scripture. The latter, designated Sunna/*mathnāt*/*mishnah*, might also be characterized as Wisdom (*ḥikma*) and thus acknowledged as divine revelation.[3] A vestige of opposition to that practical but generous definition of 'revelation' may be seen in the story of Suwayd b. Ṣāmit and the 'Wisdom scroll'

[1] But cf. Albeck, *Mischna*, 4–55 on the antiquity of the 'oral law' (*mündliche Lehre*).

[2] Neusner, op. cit. 126–36; J. Horovitz, 'Alter und Ursprung des Isnād', *Der Islam* viii (1918) 39–47, 299; id., 'Noch einmal die Herkunft des Isnād', ibid. xi (1921) 264–5 (v. *GdQ* ii, 128–9).

[3] Goldziher, *Studien* ii, 194–202; id., 'Kämpfe um die Stellung des Ḥadīṯ im Islam', *ZDMG* lxi (1907) 860–72 (*GS* v, 86–98); cf. Neusner, op. cit. 73–99 (Rabbinic 'Torah-myth'); Maier, *Geschichte*, 66–71, 84–91 and references.

(*majallat Luqmān*), retailed by Ibn Isḥāq (*Sīra* i, 425–7), in which was stressed the superiority of Muhammad's revelation.

The naming of tradents, like the collecting of 'first' occurrences (*awā'il*), generated an important and extensive branch of Islamic literature (*'ilm al-rijāl: ṭabaqāt/jarḥ wa-ta'dīl*), concerned mostly with questions of chronology and probity, viz. could the members of a chain of transmission have met and were they reliable? Now, analysis of these chains is tedious, and seldom productive of more than pseudo-historical projections of halakhic dispute. What does emerge from their scrutiny is a distinct impression that the bearers of Islamic tradition were very few in number, and further, that transmission (*taḥammul al-'ilm*) was based extensively upon written materials.[1] As for Mālik, so for all traditionists the object of transmission was *'ilm*, that is, documentation of *exempla* from the past. Underlying that concept of 'knowledge' was a conviction that movement in time was practically irrelevant, and that models of conduct ought ideally to persist unchanged. Custody of these was the primary task of scholarship: innovation was accommodated only to the extent that it could be expressed as in fact an earlier established practice. Whether Sunna, once supplied with a chain of tradents, might be represented as 'living tradition' seems doubtful, at least from the point of view of its custodians.[2] For the Muslim traditionists 'history' consisted of ascertainable 'facts', recoverable and verifiable by recourse to presumably unprejudiced witness. Guarantee of that witness lay in continuity, in what could be described as 'apostolic succession'. Whether that succession could be traced to the prophet Muhammad or only to the immediately following generations (Companions or Successors) appears to me of less significance than the assumption that appeal to precedent in general constituted the only valid basis for prescription.[3]

Reference to the organization of techniques, what one might call the mechanics of formulation and dissemination of Sunna, is for the early period meagre. Allusions to regional centres (Ḥijāz, Syria, Iraq, Egypt) and to court patronage (Umayyad, 'Abbāsid) are no substitute for the kind of information available on, say, the Rabbinic academies.[4] Tuition appears

[1] N. Abbott, *SALP* ii: *Qur'ānic Commentary and Tradition*, Chicago, 1967, 5–83 esp. 64–83; F. Sezgin, *Geschichte des arabischen Schrifttums* i (Leiden, 1967) 53–84.

[2] Cf. Schacht, *Origins*, 58–81; on the antiquity of the locution *sunnat al-nabī* see M. Bravmann, *The Spiritual Background of Early Islam*, Leiden, 1972, 123–98, taking issue with J. Schacht, 'Sur l'expression "Sunna du Prophète" ', in *Mélanges d'orientalisme offerts à Henri Massé*, Teheran, 1963, 361–5; both appear to accept at face value the witness of comparatively late sources, and though Bravmann's identification of *sīra* and *sunna* as technical terms for 'procedure' has much merit, each did after all (also!) designate a distinct literary type, or so it seems to me.

[3] Cf. Gerhardsson, *Memory and Manuscript*, 171–89 (Rabbinic *exempla*), 324–35 (Christian *exempla*).

[4] Goldziher, *Studien* ii, 175–93; Sezgin, *GAS* i, 58–60; cf. Gerhardsson, op. cit. 113–70; J. Neusner, *Talmudic Judaism in Sasanian Babylonia*, Leiden, 1976, esp. 46–77; D. M. Goodblatt, *Rabbinic Instruction in Sasanian Babylonia*, Leiden, 1975, esp. 263–85

to have been, if not quite informal, essentially private and dispersed, reflected in the many accounts of long and arduous journeys undertaken by students in search of expertise (*ṭalab al-ʿilm*), as well as of individual libraries and the separate activities of scribes and booksellers. Systematic efforts towards coordination and demarcation of centres of learning appear, retrospectively, in the acknowledgement of eponymous 'legal schools' (*madhāhib*).

The literary formulation of Muslim *paradosis*, the *ḥadīth*, has recently been subjected to some very astute form-critical analysis, in Stetter's study of *topoi* and schemata.[1] Whether the extensive use of formulaic language and mnemonic structures in that literature might indicate oral composition and transmission, as well as oral delivery, is of course a much-disputed problem. It is probably safer to distinguish the three processes from one another and from yet a further procedure, that of preservation, in which written records of some kind undoubtedly played a part. The presence of formulae and schemata can be detected by recourse to standard rhetorical analysis (e.g. figures and tropes), and from the employment of such artifice it is hardly possible to infer oral composition.[2] It is, on the other hand, equally obvious that all or most literary forms reflect something of the spoken word. The criteria applied by Stetter to *ḥadīth* had earlier been, as is well known, even more extensively and successfully used in examination of Jewish and Christian literature, and in particular to the relation between these and the Hellenistic schools of rhetoric. Following upon the research of such scholars as Lieberman, Tcherikover, and Hengel, as well as of Davies, Daube, and Neusner, the Hellenistic penetration of Palestinian Judaism may safely be acknowledged.[3] The specific precipitate of that cultural symbiosis is attested (accidentally perhaps, but such is a recognized hazard of historical research) in the literature of Rabbinic Judaism and of Oriental Christianity. The sociological implication of this fact, namely, an élite schooled in the principles and techniques of Hellenistic rhetoric, must be presumed to apply also to the early period of Islamic formation. By that time, of course, 'Hellenism' had become the property of the church, of the synagogue, and of the virtually infinite spectrum of sectarian expression. The Hellenistic *Vorlagen* of Islamic literary forms may be located not only in Greek, but in Hebrew, Aramaic, and Syriac, modified indeed but none the less recognizable.[4]

[1] Stetter, *Topoi und Schemata*; cf. *QS*, 182–3.

[2] Cf. *QS*, 47–8; *BSOAS* xxxix (1976) 438–9; Stetter, op. cit. 50.

[3] Some impression of the depth and extent of this argument may be gained from the notes and bibliographical references in these two works: M. Hengel, *Judaism and Hellenism: Studies in their Encounter in Palestine during the Early Hellenistic Period* i–ii, London, 1974; H. A. Fischel, *Rabbinic Literature and Greco-Roman Philosophy*, Leiden, 1973.

[4] F. Rosenthal, *Das Fortleben der Antike im Islam*, Zürich, 1965; G. E. von Grunebaum, *Islam and Medieval Hellenism: Social and Cultural Perspectives*, London, 1976; cf. Schacht, *Origins*, 99–100; id., 'Droit byzantin et droit musulman' in *Convegno Volta XII: Oriente ed Occidente nel Medio Evo*, Lincei/Roma, 1957, 197–218.

In Mālik's *Muwaṭṭa'*, the *Kitāb al-Jāmi'* (ch. 45, pp. 884–97) contains twenty-six paragraphs, of which twenty-one are concerned explicitly with the city of the prophet and five with the territory of Syria and Palestine. Both positively and negatively these represent sanctuary traditions in favour primarily of Medina, secondarily of the Ḥijāz, and require to be assessed as such. Those traditions are set out in the following order:

1. A prophetical tradition asking God's blessings upon the people of Medina for their just weights and measures.

2. *Narratio*: a prophetical tradition praising Medina for its produce, comparing Muhammad's role in Medina with that of Abraham in Mecca, and bestowal of fresh fruit upon the youngest member of his entourage.

3. *Narratio*: a prophetical tradition discouraging emigration from Medina.

4. *Narratio*: an encounter between Muhammad and a bedouin wishing to emigrate, after which Medina likened to the bellows of a purifying fire.

5. A prophetical tradition likening Medina to an omnivorous purifying fire.

6. A prophetical tradition attesting divine compensation for loss to Medina by emigration.

7. A prophetical tradition discouraging emigration from Medina following upon the Arab conquests.

8. A prophetical tradition forecasting the desertion of Medina.

9. An anecdote relating the sadness of 'Umar b. 'Abd al-'Azīz upon leaving Medina.

10. A prophetical tradition on making a sanctuary (*ḥaram*) of Medina, as Abraham had done in Mecca.

11. A prophetical tradition on Medina as sanctuary for game.

12. Same subject: a confirming tradition from Abū Ayyūb al-Anṣārī.

13. Same subject: a confirming tradition from Zayd b. Thābit.

14. *Narratio*: a tradition from 'Ā'isha on the illness of Abū Bakr and Bilāl following Muhammad's *hijra* to Medina, and the prophet's prayer that Medina be made as salubrious as Mecca.

15. A tradition from 'Ā'isha adding to the preceding.

16. A prophetical tradition on the preservation of Medina from plague and from the anti-christ (*dajjāl*).

17. A prophetical tradition on the expulsion of Jews and Christians from the Ḥijāz.

18. A variant (prophetical) of the preceding, and 'Umar's decree of expulsion (*ijlā*), of Jews from Khaybar.

19. The conditions of 'Umar's expulsion of the Jews from (Najrān), Fadak, and Khaybar, following the treaty stipulations of the prophet.

20. A prophetical tradition worded as no. 10 above, but without reference to Abraham and Mecca.

21. *Narratio*: ʿUmar's predilection for *nabīdh* and for Medina rather than Mecca.

22. *Narratio*: a tradition from ʿAbdallāh b. ʿAbbās on ʿUmar's expedition to Syria, his hearing of the plague there, his consulting in turn the Muhājirūn, the Anṣār, and Quraysh, and his decision, on the basis of a prophetical tradition, not to enter Syria.

23. A prophetical tradition confirming the preceding.

24. A prophetical tradition confirming the preceding.

25. ʿUmar's action in compliance with the preceding.

26. A tradition from ʿUmar attesting his preference for the Ḥijāz over Syria, because of its architecture (?).

A characteristic specimen of the paradigmatic style, the chapter contains no scriptural reference, and all but seven of the traditions are traced to an action or utterance of the prophet. The genre is panegyric, specifically a celebration of virtue and excellence (*faḍā'il*), and is related to, if not directly derived from the Classical *genos epideiktikon*.[1] Of the five components in Quintilian's schema (founder/antiquity/achievements/situation/inhabitants), only the first (paras. 2, 10–13, 17–19, 20), third (paras. 1, 2, 4, 5, 6, 21), and fourth (paras. 22–6) can reasonably be argued, and the latter only by acknowledging its antithetical relation to paras. 3, 4, 6–9, 14–16, in which is stressed the unhealthy climate of Medina. The Classical model is thus not attested formally, but enough of its substance to make likely the supposition of a literary tradition. Such is also corroborated by the presence of schematic formulation, e.g. triadic structure and litany (paras. 1, 2, 4, 7, 14, 22), paraenesis (paras. 3, 4, 5, 6, 7), parallelism (23, 24, 25). The imagery throughout is derived from the concept 'sanctuary' (*ḥaram/bayt*), emphasized on the one hand in contrast to the priority of Mecca (explicitly Abraham), and on the other to Syria (implicitly Muʿāwiya).

Stylistically, these paragraphs exhibit the types found by Stetter to conform to Rabbinic and Synoptic forms, though the problem of diffusion and/or polygenesis is admittedly not thereby solved.[2] The predominance of dialogue over circumstantial description in the narrative sequences reflects very clearly what I have called the 'apostolic' concept of authority, as contrasted with one based on scriptural citation. The literary forms: blessing, admonition, maxim, ruling, prediction, prayer, and interrogation, might be characterized as *apophthegmata*, that is, authoritative sayings embedded in a narrative context.[3] That 'context' may be no more than a

[1] E. A. Gruber, *Verdienst und Rang: die Faḍā'il als literarisches und gesellschaftliches Problem im Islam*, Freiburg, 1975, 49–82, esp. 57–9; cf. *BSOAS* xxxix (1976) 506–7; Noth, *Quellenkritische Studien*, 51–3; Grunebaum, 'Observations on city panegyrics in Arabic prose', *JAOS* lxiv (1944) 61–5 (*Islam and Medieval Hellenism*, ch. XX); H. Lausberg, *Handbuch der literarischen Rhetorik*, München, 1960, para. 247.

[2] Stetter, *Topoi und Schemata*, 48–51, 62, 66, 72, 83, 95–8.

[3] Neusner, *Early Rabbinic Judaism*, 115–26 (following Bultmann).

simple reference to posture (para. 3), or to gesture (para. 2). It could, on the other hand, be expanded to what might almost be described as a dramatic *mise en scène* (e.g. paras. 14, 21, 22), of which the climax is represented by the saying itself or a symbolic action. Absent from the narrative context are specifically historical data, that is, situational references from which a sense of continuity, if not causality, could be inferred. That much at least was achieved in the *sīra–maghāzī* literature, by both midrashic and non-midrashic styles. The impression of movement conveyed there is lacking in the much more extensive corpus of *ḥadīth*. Since the substance of the two literatures is essentially the same it is clear that the difference between them must lie in a formal property of some kind. That could be something as obvious, and as mechanical, as the distribution of reference to tradents (the *isnād*), much more frequent in the *ḥadīth* than in the *sīra–maghāzī*. Certainly the effect is disrupting, but does not, I think, quite account for the peculiarly static quality of the paradigmatic style. Action, if it may be so called, in the *ḥadīth* is exclusively symbolic, isolated, stylized, and ritualistic. That could be to some extent illustrated by comparing the three versions of *Ḥadīth al-ifk*, in which may be seen the distillation of an *exemplum* from a collection of discrete and contingent episodes. Similarly, Mālik's recital of Medinese sanctuary traditions exhibits a symbolic reorganization of originally discrete and contingent materials, given new meaning by the mere fact of a different context.

. . . . .

If from the witness of Islamic salvation history the early community could be described as 'scripturalist', it seems to me that the evidence of the Sunna might be adduced in support of another rubric from my proposed typology, namely, 'ritualist'. Preoccupation with the Law as a corpus of *exempla* (invariably 'apostolic') applicable to every aspect of community life can hardly be derived either from the formulation of salvation history, which was polemic, or from that of scripture, which was liturgical. The distinction is both structural and conceptual, and may be expressed by reference to a modified notion of communal authority. That notion, and its modification, can be traced in the several uses of the term *umma*. In the *sīra–maghāzī* literature the basic sense—faction/community/nation—occurs as an element of the foundation syndrome: documented by the 'constitution' of Medina (*Sīra* i, 501–4), by express reference to the dissolution of tribal bonds in favour of confessional allegiance, and by the role of what I have described as 'institutional' traditions adapted from Biblical salvation history (e.g. sanctuary, calendar, apostle). All the material there, whether mythic or normative, contributed to a portrait of the religious polity called into being amongst members of an ethnic group until then without a divine dispensation of its own. The Jewish and Christian options were thus explicitly rejected in favour of something approaching 'national' solidarity.[1] The historical *umma* was seen to have both a pedigree and a destiny.

I have referred above to another aspect: in the account (*Sīra* i, 222–32) of the *ḥanīf* Zayd b. ʿAmr an allusion to Abraham as progenitor of God's people was contained in Muhammad's observation with regard to Zayd that he by himself constituted an *umma* (cf. Q. 16: 120, Genesis 12: 2, but also Q. 2: 124 and the equivalence *umma*:*imām*).[2] In respect of Zayd *umma* can only have signified *imām* (*exemplum*), of which the semantic field included prophetical Sunna, scriptural canon, celestial register, and community leadership. An essential characteristic of the *imām* in sectarian theology was impeccability/infallibility (*ʿiṣma*), and that feature was, not unexpectedly, applied also to the *umma*. The context was not theological but juridical, and the purpose to guarantee that the 'community could not agree in an error'. The specific problem was the nature of consensus (*ijmāʿ*), and the primary agent in the semantic transfer from *consensus doctorum* to *communis opinio* was the jurist Shāfiʿī (d. 204/820), a student of Mālik. That transfer was consistent with, indeed a consequence of, Shāfiʿī's argument for the unique validity of the prophetical Sunna, whose faithful transmission could be insured only by the community at large (*tawātur*). It was also that community whose consensus, in contrast to that of a scholarly élite, could be considered binding.[3] The polemic was clear: Shāfiʿī's quarrel was with the regional legal schools, his objective was uniformity, his achievement was to create a mystique round the Sunna of the prophet and the infallibility of his community. Juxtaposed thus to the historical *umma* was a metaphysical one.

The process was rather more complex than is here necessary to depict, but that it owed something to sectarian (Shīʿī) theories of the imamate is a reasonable assumption. Incorporation of the historical *umma* into the vocabulary of theology, by way of credal statements, exhibits a concession to the metaphysical concept of *umma*.[4] For Mālik the *ahl al-ʿilm* had represented an élite, one which for Shāfiʿī came gradually to be identified with the whole community the more its function was confined to transmitting the prophetical Sunna. There, too, the historical quality of *traditio/paradosis* was gradually usurped by a metaphysical concept: once fixed the paradigm did not, indeed could not, alter. The term 'ritualist' descriptive of a confessional orientation is thus for the early Muslim community

[1] Grunebaum, 'Arab unity before Islam', 5–23.

[2] *QS*, 54, 162 n. 4.

[3] Schacht, *Origins*, 82–97, esp. 92–4; id., *An Introduction to Islamic Law*, Oxford, 1964, 30–1, 47, 59, 202; cf. G. Hourani, 'The basis of authority of consensus in Sunnite Islam', *Studia Islamica* xxi (1964) 13–60, esp. 19–38; F. Rahman, *Islamic Methodology in History*, Karachi, 1965, 1–26.

[4] A. J. Wensinck, *The Muslim Creed*, Cambridge, 1932, 104, 112, 269–70.

doubly apt: first, because the prophetical Sunna was concerned largely with matters of ritual; second, because it was thought to be immutable.

Now, it may be supposed that between scripturalist and ritualist notions of authority there could be very little practical difference. Similarly revealed and equally canonical, the two sources exhibit variations upon a single theme which, for want of a better term, I have called precedent. That theme may be traced from the *sīra–maghāzī* literature, where it was historically articulated, to the *sunna–ḥadīth* literature, where it was idealized and hence shorn of its historical dimension. Instrumental in that evolution were the dogmatically defined properties of scripture (theophany), itself made ahistorical by relation to the concept of celestial register. Precedent became prescription (*sharīʿa*): law in the sense of a unique and binding expression of ideal conduct, and applicable to every condition of social and political life. It was also meant to, and to some extent did, provide the pattern for salvation, the existential task imposed upon every believer by his membership of the community.

. . . . .

The articulation of soteriological categories, an acute issue in modern Muslim theology,[1] is not as such attested in early Islamic literature. The scriptural theodicy was essentially covenantal, a characteristic fundamental also to the literary forms of both *Sīra* and Sunna, in which is stressed the oracular and paradigmatic role of the agent of covenant renewal. Oracle and paradigm were prescriptive and became, through the application of halakhic procedure, legislative. This apostolic concept of authority was paralleled, illustrated, and buttressed by a portrait of its inception containing the basic ingredients of salvation history: teleological, nomothetic, and kerygmatic. The intention of that history was a *praeparatio evangelica* with, I have suggested, very little or no reference to eschatological time. The historical framework was, however, essential to the Islamic kerygma, not only in haggadah but also in halakhah, signalled by the preservation and transmission of dissenting opinions (*ikhtilāf al-fuqahā'*).[2] The soteriological or redemptive function of the community as portrayed in its earliest literature might be described as 'covenantal nomism':[3] acknowledgement of the prophet entailed membership of his congregation (*umma*). Reflection upon the significance of membership and the direction of the *umma* was a theological exercise hardly adumbrated in *Sīra* and Sunna,

[1] e.g. R. Wielandt, *Offenbarung und Geschichte im Denken moderner Muslime*, Wiesbaden, 1971.

[2] Cf. E. E. Urbach, 'Halakhah and History', in R. Hamerton-Kelly and R. Scroggs (eds.), *Jews, Greeks and Christians: Religious Cultures in Late Antiquity* (Essays in Honour of W. D. Davies), Leiden, 1976, 112–28; cf. *BSOAS* xl (1977) 603–4.

[3] E. P. Sanders, 'The Covenant as a soteriological category', in *Jews, Greeks and Christians*, 11–44, esp. 41–2.

but none the less implicit in the data of the Islamic theodicy: that is, whether the role of the prophet was messianic or that of the community eschatological.

The literary deposit of that theodicy, available from the end of the second/eighth century, may be set out schematically:

(A) History (kerygma)
(B) Scripture (covenant)
(C) Paradigm (*paradosis*).

Each exhibits a separate development, hardly self-contained but discernible in the major themes of later Islamic literature, itself an elaboration of the theodicy:

(*a*) Eschatology
(*b*) Prognosis
(*c*) Messianism.

Those themes represent soteriological modes or categories and may, in my opinion at least, be more or less directly derived from the three varieties of literature containing the initial theodicy.

The evolution postulated for (A) requires assent to the kerygmatic quality of its normative (documentary) as well as of its mythic (midrashic) components. The community depicted there is the instrument of a dispensation *de novo* although familiar from the history of its rejection and/or distortion by earlier and contemporary beneficiaries. The familiarity of the dispensation, evident especially in its 'scripturalism', makes Islamic history a part of world history, traced from its origins in divine creation. Once inserted into the framework of universal history its direction and resolution were also provided, namely, in the eschaton of monotheist theology. In the *Sīra* that historical process is naturally open-ended, but emerges clearly enough from repeated reference to the author of creation. Allusion to the eschaton itself is found in the midrashic styles, and in the text of scripture in many places but concentrated in *Sūras* 55–6, 75, 81–4. The imagery is not unexpected, is derived entirely from the Judaeo-Christian lexicon, and has been the object of several linguistic and theological analyses.[1] The context of that imagery is invariably paraenesis: while it undoubtedly furnished some at least of the material of later Muslim apocalyptic, its scriptural employment is exclusively liturgical. In Sunna, as in *Sīra*, reference to the eschaton is sparse.[2] Central in both, on the other hand, is the *umma*: its origin, its function, its destiny. It is there, if anywhere, that the earliest Islamic eschatology is located. Before

[1] Andrae, *Origines*, 145–61, 175–80; T. O'Shaughnessy, *Muhammad's Thoughts on Death: a Thematic Study of the Qur'ānic Data*, Leiden, 1969; cf. *BSOAS* xxxiii (1970) 613–15.

[2] A. J. Wensinck, *A Handbook of Early Muhammadan Tradition*, Leiden, 1960 (1927), s.vv. Dadjdjāl, Fitan, Resurrection.

adducing my evidence for that argument I should like to trace the remaining strands of the theodicy.

For (B) the evolution from covenant to community (*umma*) required the interpretative device called in the Qumran literature *pesher* and defined as prognostic exegesis.[1] In salvation history the role of scripture, I have suggested, was polemical. In the community it was originally liturgical, and could hardly have been employed outside the cult. It was by recourse to a series of exegetical devices that Muslim scripture was adapted to the several needs of a new confessional community. Of those devices haggadic exegesis employed the greatest number whose function could be described as 'prognostic', that is, designed to adapt the *topoi* of Biblical salvation history to the mission of the Arabian prophet. The procedure is manifest in the Qur'ān itself, a feature which I have described as its 'referential' style.[2] The actualization of earlier history (e.g. the retribution pericopes) may be envisaged as a cultic practice: again, paraenetic. Selection of the same and similar *topoi* as components of Muslim community history exhibits an extension of the material beyond the boundaries of cult. By way of exegesis the text of scripture was thought to document the origins of the *umma* and thus, to some extent, the purpose for which it had been founded.

For (C) it is proposed that in Islamic literature messianic imagery was generated by the initial *paradosis*, itself secular, ritualist, and paradigmatic. The *exemplum* was that of the leader (*imām*) of the community (*umma*), two concepts etymologically and exegetically linked.[3] The relation of prescriptive character to paradigmatic function was facilitated by identifying law with scripture, regulation with revelation. The recipient of that revelation might be a prophet (*nabī*), must be an apostle (*rasūl*), could be, if not proved otherwise, a king (*malik*). Such were the standard features of charisma in Biblical salvation history and hence in its Islamic adaptation (*sīra–maghāzī*). Of genuinely messianic *topoi* there are, however, none in *Sīra* or in Sunna. Messiology, like eschatology, was elaborated in the rather later genre of apocalyptic. To that imagery sectarian views of the imamate contributed significantly.

Now, it must from the foregoing observations be clear that the earliest expression of Islamic soteriology consisted in membership of the *umma*. I have alluded to the evolution of that concept: from historical to metaphysical to theological. Some, unfortunately ambiguous, information about its earliest (historical) form is found in the documents comprising the 'constitution' of Medina (*Sīra* i, 501–4). There membership and affiliation

[1] O. Betz, *Offenbarung und Schriftforschung in der Qumransekte*, Tübingen, 1960, 36–50, 73–88; Wieder, *Judean Scrolls*, 199–213; id., 'The Dead Sea Scrolls type of Biblical exegesis among the Karaites', in A. Altmann (ed.), *Between East and West: Essays Dedicated to the Memory of Bela Horovitz*, London, 1958, 75–106; cf. *QS*, 50, 245–6; Seeligmann, 'Midraschexegese', 167–76.

[2] *QS*, 1, 40–3, 47–8, 51–2, 57–8.

[3] *QS*, 54.

are not clearly distinguished, and 'apostolic' authority is defined as (merely?) court of appeal (*maradd*). Sanction consists in expulsion and the wrath of God on the Day of Judgement, the latter one of the few references to God (He is also *maradd*) lending a semblance of divine purpose to the organization. Such it was indeed intended to be, and serves thus in the literary tradition as point of departure for community history. Explicit reference to the Day of Judgement/Resurrection may surely be understood eschatologically, as may all similar references in the *Sīra*, though about most there is a formulaic character that suggests an absence of theological significance. Put in the simplest possible way: was the concept of eschaton more than a merely formal factor in the composition of salvation history? Primitive martyrologies, such as those of Yazīd b. Ḥāṭib and Quzmān, might be thought to indicate an affirmative reply, while the imagery associated with Abū Lahab and Umm Jamīl would suggest the opposite.

For a concept of 'realized' eschatology there is no explicit evidence.[1] Emphasis upon the commonalty, upon the minutiae of ritual, and upon the divine imperative (*fī sabīl allāh*), especially in Sunna, might seem to supply an eschatological context, but that could be misleading. It is precisely the cultic setting of the *umma* which is so difficult to assess: of ascetic preparation, sacramental participation, and the presence of the Spirit there is no trace. About ritual prayer and sacrifice there is no sense of immediacy or impending judgement. Fellowship is indeed stressed, but neither as a 'regathering of the peoples' nor as restitution of a primal and pure state in anticipation of the messianic drama. And yet, the principle of *pesher* as fulfilled prognosis went some way towards defining a *praeparatio evangelica* and alignment of the *umma* with peoples eligible for salvation. The circumstances of the community might be described not as redemptive but as elective. That is substantiated by the description of its founder. The 'emblems of prophethood' are essentially Mosaic, elaborated upon the *topoi* commander, legislator, and thaumaturge.[2] Of the later aretalogy (*dalā'il al-nubuwwa*) derived from *theios aner* and eschatological motifs there is little or nothing in *Sīra* and Sunna. Royal imagery of the kind associated with Moses by Philo, Rabbinic, and Samaritan sources, and the gospel of John is, on the other hand, the object of considerable dispute in the Muslim tradition, and may be thought in fact to reflect a rejection of Jewish messianic *topoi*, as well as of the more extreme Samaritan and Christian imagery.[3] Such were not altogether discarded, but appear in sectarian (Shīʿī) doctrine.

[1] D. E. Aune, *The Cultic Setting of Realized Eschatology in Early Christianity*, Leiden, 1972, 1–28, 45–135; W. D. Davies, *Paul and Rabbinic Judaism*, London, 1970, 285–320; Bultmann, *Theology* ii, 95–202.

[2] *QS*, 35–8, 55–6, 65–73, 78, 83, 99.

[3] W. A. Meeks, *The Prophet-King: Moses Traditions and the Johannine Christology*, Leiden, 1967, 1–31, 216–57, 103–7, 137–42; Andrae, *Person Muhammeds*, 290–390.

Islamic soteriology was thus originally, and remained in its normative (Sunnī) expression, a historical event. In common with the mainstream of Judaeo-Christian tradition, for which ahistorical concepts of salvation and/or redemption crystallized as heterodox or heretical, the Muslim dispensation was an act in history, temporally and spatially defined.[1] An important exception to this rational view of divinity was the dogma of the uncreated Qur'ān, which entailed several comparatively irrational notions of authority within the community. In so far as scripture was a putative source, law was diametrically opposed to the notion of development implicit in a historical view of salvation. Such is only partly true of the second substantive source of the law: tradition (Sunna), however bound to the prophetical paradigm, exhibited an essential flexibility in the very fact of recorded dispute (*ikhtilāf*). In jurisprudence (*fiqh*) scripture might be interpreted to conform with tradition; in dogmatic theology (*kalām*) scripture served as witness to divinity, with which it was ontologically identified.[2] That the latter exhibits a secondary phenomenon seems to be clear from the literature of salvation history, according to which the word of God was uttered in response to local circumstances. The doctrinal dilemma may be formulated as a choice between regarding the historical environment of the theophany as irrelevant or making of that environment a permanent criterion for assessing inevitable change. Paradoxically, either choice entails abandoning a historical interpretation of Islam.

During the classical and medieval periods the options were for the most part left open. The present intellectual predicament of Islam is not under discussion in these pages, though it could be remarked that the abandonment of historical interpretation has not gone unnoticed.[3] Much of the difficulty must lie, and must always have lain, in the failure to distinguish between history as narrative and history as process. The clerical élite responsible for production of the literary types so far examined was undoubtedly concerned with the former, but provides oblique witness to the latter. What I have described as the paradigmatic style was very seldom a vehicle for transmitting agreed prescription, but rather, for recording divergent opinions. In that style chronology is implicit only and narrative sequence altogether absent, but not, I think, every trace of historical preoccupation. My last specimen of the style contains some allusion to early expressions of soteriology: Mālik's *Kitāb al-Jihād* (*Muwaṭṭa'*, ch. 21, pp. 443–71) includes sixty-eight literary units arranged in twenty-one chapters

[1] Cf. H. Lazarus-Yafeh, 'Is there a concept of redemption in Islam?', in Z. Werblowsky and C. J. Bleeker, *Types of Redemption*, Leiden, 1970, 168–80; D. Flusser, 'Salvation present and future', ibid. 46–61.

[2] *QS*, 77–84.

[3] G. E. von Grunebaum, *Modern Islam: the Search for Cultural Identity*, Berkeley, 1962, 47; J. Berque, cited ibid. 186 n. 23; Y. Moubarac, cited *QS*, 21 n. 5.

related to four themes: enjoining Holy War, conduct in Holy War, division of spoils, martyrdom and its reward.[1]

1. A prophetical tradition equating him (*mujāhid*) who wages Holy War with one who fasts and prays without ceasing.

2. A prophetical tradition on God's reward for the *mujāhid*: heaven or booty.

3. A prophetical tradition on the relation of a horse to its owner: it may be the occasion of reward (*ajr*), serve him as protection (*sitr*), or become a burden (*wizr*). When asked whether the same applied to asses, he cited Q. 99: 7–8 promising recompense for all good deeds, retribution for all evil.

4. A prophetical tradition placing the abstemious and pious man after the *mujāhid* in rank.

5. A tradition from ʿUbāda b. al-Ṣāmit on the necessity of unquestioning obedience to authority.

6. A tradition from Zayd b. Aslam recounting ʿUmar's exhortation to perseverance and trust in God in the face of adversity, and his citing Q. 3: 200 to that effect.

7. A prophetical tradition prohibiting taking the Qur'ān into hostile territory. To which Mālik added: for fear that it would fall into the hands of the enemy.

8. A prophetical tradition prohibiting the slaying of women and children (*scil.* in battle).

9. A prophetical tradition on same subject (probably prior to and referred to in the preceding).

10. A tradition from Yaḥyā b. Saʿīd on Abū Bakr's list of virtues recommended for Holy War (e.g. sparing non-participants, crops, buildings, livestock, yield neither to deceit nor cowardice).

11. A prophetical tradition on exemplary conduct in Holy War, enjoined upon all field commanders.

12. A Kufan tradition against treachery in the issue of a safe conduct. To which Mālik added: this tradition is neither agreed nor authoritative (*laysa hādhā 'l-ḥadīth bil-mujtamaʿ ʿalayhi wa-laysa ʿalayhi 'l-ʿamal*).

12ᵇ. Mālik, when consulted about the respective value of sign and word in the issue of a safe conduct (*amān*), stated that they were in his opinion of equal validity, and added that ʿAbdallāh b. ʿAbbās had predicted divine vengeance for anyone breaking a treaty (*ʿahd*).

13. A tradition from ʿAbdallāh b. ʿUmar on the rightful possession of a donation to the cause of Holy War after a certain stage of the expedition had been reached.

14. Same subject: a tradition from Saʿīd b. al-Musayyab specifying the stage as starting-point of the expedition.

14ᵇ. Mālik, when consulted about a man who had vowed both to participate and to donate but was prevented by his parents from doing so, stated that

[1] *QS*, 171–2.

he should obey them and wait a year with his donation, or convert his donation into something useful for the campaign he is allowed to make.

15. A prophetical tradition on the division of spoils: to the effect a portion (*sahm*) represented equal division and that *nafal* was allocation above and beyond the rightful share.

16. A tradition from Sa'īd b. al-Musayyab that in the division of spoils a camel was the equivalent of ten sheep.

16[b]. Mālik stated that to a combatant who was a freeman one portion was allocated, and that in his opinion (*wa-arā*) there would otherwise be no division at all.

16[c]. Mālik stated that in cases of shipwreck (i.e. *lex naufragii*) only the *imām* might determine the allocation of spoils.

16[d]. Mālik stated that in his opinion Muslim troops in enemy territory might eat what they wished without its being reckoned in the division of spoils (*maqāsim*).

16[e]. Mālik stated that in his opinion camel, cattle, and sheep were to be reckoned food, but that such must in fact be consumed, not taken home as plunder.

16[f]. Mālik, when consulted about a man who had more than he could consume, stated that if he sold it when still in the field the money must go to all the Muslims, but if he took it home he might consume it there, provided it were only a small amount.

17. A tradition from Mālik about a runaway slave and horse belonging to 'Abdallāh b. 'Umar captured by the enemy (*mushrikūn*): if it fell to the Muslims it must be returned to Ibn 'Umar without being subject to the division of spoils.

17[b]. Same subject: Mālik was heard to say that such obtained only if it happened before the division took place; otherwise it was reckoned part of the spoils.

17[c]. Mālik, when consulted about a slave in such circumstances, stated that so long as the division had not yet taken place the owner had prior claim without payment of any kind (*thaman/qīma/ghurm*), but if the division had taken place the former master had first refusal but had to pay.

17[d]. Mālik stated, in the case of a slave who had borne a child to her master (*umm walad*) in such circumstances (i.e. capture by the enemy, recapture by the Muslims), that if the division had taken place the *imām* should redeem her for her former master, and that if he did not do so then her former master should. In any case she could not be re-enslaved.

17[e]. Mālik, when consulted about slaves or freemen acquired in enemy territory by redemption, purchase, or gift, stated that the freeman had only to repay whatever amount had changed hands in order to effect his release, and that in the case of the slave his original owner had first refusal but also the obligation to repay whatever money had changed hands.

18. A prophetical tradition on the rightful acquisition of plunder (*salab*) from the body of one slain in combat: to the slayer if he leaves some proof or has a witness.

19. A tradition from Ibn ʿAbbās, faced by a very persistent questioner, to the effect that both horses and personal property (*salab*) were to be reckoned as *nafal*.

19^b. Mālik, when consulted about the claim to *salab*, stated that allocation lay exclusively with the discretion (*ʿalā wajh al-ijtihād*) of the *imām*, and that the prophet's ruling (no. 18 above) applied only to the Battle of Ḥunayn.

20. A tradition from Saʿīd b. al-Musayyab to the effect that the army had been given *nafal* out of the fifth (*khums*). To which Mālik added: that is the best I have heard on this matter (*wa-dhālika aḥsanu mā samiʿtu ilayya fī dhālika*).

20^b. Mālik, when consulted about *nafal*, stated that he knew of no fixed ruling (*wa-laysa ʿindanā fī dhālika amr maʿrūf mawqūf*), and that it lay entirely with the discretion of the *imām/sulṭān* (*sic*) (*ʿalā wajh al-ijtihād min al-imām/ ijtihād al-sulṭān*). The prophet had allocated *nafal* only at the Battle of Ḥunayn.

21. A tradition from Mālik to the effect that ʿUmar b. ʿAbd al-ʿAzīz had said: two portions (*sahmān*) for the horse, one for the rider. To which Mālik added: that is what I have always heard (*wa-lam azal asmaʿ dhālika*).

21^b. Mālik, when consulted about portions for a combatant who had brought many horses, stated that he had not heard that (*lam asmaʿ bi-dhālika*) but that in his opinion the man should be given a portion only for the horse on which he had fought.

21^c. Mālik stated that in his opinion pack animals (*barādhīn*) and camels (*hujun*) were in this respect to be reckoned as horses, if the field commander (*wālī*) said so. He cited Q. 16: 8 and 8: 60, as well as the opinion of Saʿīd b. al-Musayyab, in support of this ruling.

22. A prophetical tradition prescribing generosity in the division of spoils regardless of their value (great or small), since such would be accounted on the Day of Judgement/Resurrection, save for the fifth (*khums*) which belonged anyway to the community.

23. A prophetical tradition on last rites for one slain in battle but found to have cheated in the matter of spoils.

24. A prophetical tradition emphasizing the stigma attached to cheating (*ghulūl*) in the matter of spoils.

25. A prophetical tradition predicting the fires of hell for one found to have cheated in the matter of spoils.

26. A tradition from Ibn ʿAbbās predicting divine vengeance (retribution) for several kinds of immorality, of which one is defeat in war for violation of a treaty (as in no. 12^b above).

27. A prophetical tradition in which is expressed a desire for repeated martyrdom (triad).

28. A prophetical tradition on divine reward for martyrs.

29. A prophetical tradition on the same subject.

30. A tradition from Zayd b. Aslam on 'Umar's prayer not to be slain by a Muslim (? *rajul ṣallā laka sajda wāḥida*), who could offer that in his defence on the Day of Judgement.

31. A prophetical tradition to the effect that for a martyr in Holy War all transgressions would be forgiven, save for financial obligations (*dayn*). Thus he had been told by Gabriel.

32. A prophetical tradition bearing witness to the martyrs in the battle of Uḥud, and expressing uncertainty about the future of his community after his death.

33. A prophetical tradition stressing the incomparability of martyrdom, and his repeated preference (triad) for burial in Medina.

34. A tradition from Zayd b. Aslam recounting 'Umar's wish for martyrdom in Medina (*wafāt bi-balad rasūlika*).

35. A tradition from Yaḥyā b. Sa'īd recounting 'Umar's preference for martyrdom over other deaths.

36. A tradition from 'Abdallāh b. 'Umar that 'Umar had been washed and wrapped in a shroud and was (in fact) a martyr.

37. A tradition from Mālik anonymously authenticated (*'an ahl al-'ilm*) to the effect that martyrs were neither washed nor prayed over, and that they were buried in the garments in which they had been slain. To which Mālik added: this is the practice (*sunna*) regarding those killed on the battlefield not found until after death. But those found before dying are washed and prayed over, as was done in the case of 'Umar.

38. A tradition from Yaḥyā b. Sa'īd on 'Umar's vicarious participation in Holy War.

39. A prophetical tradition recounting his dream about and prayer for the martyrdom of Umm Ḥarām bt. Milḥān after his death (transmitted with variants and confirmation that it had in fact taken place during the reign of Mu'āwiya).

40. A prophetical tradition expressing concern for his community (*umma*) after his death and a desire for repeated martyrdom (triad; see above, no. 27).

41. A prophetical tradition recounting the admonition of Sa'd b. al-Rabī' that no man ought by rights to survive the apostle of God.

42. A prophetical tradition on enjoining participation in Holy War.

43. A tradition from Mu'ādh b. Jabal on the necessity of pure intention during a campaign (*ghazw*).

44. A prophetical tradition on the benefit of horses (*scil.* employed in Holy War) accruing to their users on the Day of Judgement.

45. A prophetical tradition on the training of horses (*scil.* for employment in Holy War).

46. A tradition from Sa'īd b. al-Musayyab on the legality of horse racing so long as it is not conducted as gambling.

47. A prophetical tradition recommending the care of horses.

48. A prophetical tradition, with reference to the siege of Khaybar, specifying the necessity of prior warning.

49. A prophetical tradition equating the salvation of the *mujāhid* with other forms of piety (see above, nos. 1–4).

49[b]. Mālik, when consulted about converts to Islam among conquered peoples, admitted that it was a matter of dispute (*dhālika yakhtalif*): those conquered by treaty (*ṣulḥ*) who became Muslims might retain their property; those conquered by force (*'anwa*) who became Muslims must forfeit (as *fay'*) their property to the Muslims.

50. A tradition from Ibn Abī Ṣa'ṣa' recounting the story of two members of the Anṣār killed at the Battle of Uḥud whose bodies were discovered incorrupt after forty-six years.

50[b]. Mālik stated that, when such was necessary and the tallest aligned with the direction of prayer (*qibla*), there was nothing wrong with two or even three men being buried in one grave.

51. A tradition from Ibn Abī 'Abd al-Raḥmān on the payment (after his death) of the prophet's debts by Abū Bakr.

Of these 68 items 29 are based on the authority of the prophet, 22 on other sources, and 17 contain Mālik's commentary (plus observations included in the texts of nos. 7 and 37). The role of scriptural authority is minimal, vague and almost irrelevant in nos. 3 and 6 (respectively, prophetical and non-prophetical), only just to the point in Mālik's comment in no. 21[c]. Of rather more significance is the fact that, with the exception of nos. 7 and 49, Mālik's rulings relate exclusively to non-prophetical material, from which it may be supposed that he acknowledged readily the authority of the prophet, that is, apostolic dicta were not questioned.[1] The total number of tradents is limited, possibly standardized, Abū Hurayra and 'Abdallāh b. 'Umar cited nine and five times respectively, while Yaḥyā b. Sa'īd appears eighteen times, in eight of which he is the sole tradent.

From the point of view of structural integrity, priority of composition would seem to belong to the prophetical collection (nos. 1–4, 7–9, 11, 15, 18, 22–5, 27–9, 31–3, 39–42, 44–5, and 47–9), which exhibits a degree of thematic and lexical consistency. For example, nos. 1–4 represent an *inclusio* (*taḍmīn*) tracing the definition of *mujāhid* as warrior—as pious believer—as warrior, to which may be related no. 49, where *jihād* is enumerated as one of several forms of piety. Again, nos. 8–9 constitute a unit, but probably in reverse order, while nos. 22–5 stress eschatological sanction for deceit and treachery, transgressions which, however skilfully concealed, will not remain hidden from God. The three blocks 27–9, 31–3, and 39–42 contain materials of disparate provenance (i.e. propaganda, concern for

[1] But cf. Schacht, *Origins*, 70–1 (Mālik's restrictive interpretation of Ḥunayn: i.e. in para. 19[b]).

posterity, and a sanctuary tradition) but linked here by the common theme martyrdom, the earliest form of soteriological reflexion in Islamic literature. Nos. 41–5 and 47 share a preoccupation (care and training of horses for warfare) with the homily in no. 3.

In the second collection (nos. 5–6, 10, 12–14, 16–17, 19–21, 26, 30, 34–8, 43, 46, 50–1) three primary themes may be isolated: paraenesis (nos. 5–6, 10, 12, 26, and 43), proper division of spoils (nos. 16–17 and 19–21), and the vexed problem of whether ʿUmar's assassination made him eligible for martyrdom (nos. 30 and 34–8). With the exception of those concerning ʿUmar, there is less thematic contiguity than in the prophetical collection, which might possibly indicate a secondary composition. Nos. 46, 50, and 51 are comparatively independent.

Mālik's commentary is, as has been remarked, devoted almost exclusively to the second collection, the two exceptions (in the texts of nos. 7 and 37) contributing very little to the argument. The same can be said of no. 50^{b}, which might be thought to reveal some embarrassment. It is in the blocks 16^{b-f} and 17^{b-e} that the record of dissent is most graphically recorded, with regard respectively to the consumption of plunder and the assignment of recaptured Muslim property. Of particular interest is Mālik's appeal to the discretion of the *imām* (*taʿzīr*, the term is not employed) in nos. 16^{c}, 19^{b}, 20^{b}, and 21^{c}. In the last it is admittedly the field commander (*wālī*, presumably delegated by the *imām*) to whose decision recourse is had, and that appears to take precedence over the scriptural citations (Q. 16: 8 and 8: 60), which become thus props rather than sources. Mālik's primary concern is with technicalities, only secondarily with the ethos of Holy War, or that much at least may be inferred from his own observations.

On the other hand, the major part of his material is contained in the prophetical collection, the purpose of which is not elucidation of juridical difficulties, but rather, paraenesis (*targhīb fil-jihād*). The role of the prophet as source of these utterances, abstract and fragmentary, is a principal feature of the paradigmatic style. Even the single, reiterated historical reference, Ḥunayn (nos. 18, 19^{b}, 22, 23), is symbolic, employed by Mālik to illustrate an exception to the rule. Historical allusion is, however, not absent: the prophet's concern for the future of his community (nos. 39–40) and Mālik's discussion of the status of converts (no. 49^{b}) reveal a concept of projected development as clearly as do the records of juridical dispute. For the problem of authority the paradigmatic composition is fundamental: inclusion here of pious legend (no. 50) as well as of dogma (no. 7: 'Qur'ān' can only be codex/*muṣḥaf*, which makes of the utterance at the very least an anachronism) is evidence of concern for community instruction in such basic matters as divine recompense and revelation. The historical process envisaged was contemporary and futurist, but could of course only be illustrated by *exempla* from the past.

III

IDENTITY

CHARACTERISTIC of the sectarian milieu was the proliferation of hardly distinguishable confessional groups. Structural and typological similarity might be concealed only by an eponym or toponym or virtually insignificant doctrinal nicety. The process is abundantly documented in the literature of heresiology, topically oriented and composed from positions conventionally defined as normative, e.g. Patristic, Rabbinic, Sunnī. The genre was productive, separate sects being generated by points of doctrine and often quite arbitrarily related to eponyms/toponyms, a procedure which might be described as historicization of dogma. An underlying motive (*Geistesbeschäftigung*) was establishment of a norm by which 'orthodoxy' could be distinguished from 'heterodoxy' and the latter identified as the heresy of a specific group. In the interests of both narrative and doctrinal tidiness the sequence orthodoxy → heterodoxy was seen as not merely logical but also temporal. The priorities of *historia ecclesiastica* are unmistakable. The sectarian designations thus produced may of course allude to historical realia, but could just as easily be drawn from a traditional stock of epithets symbolic of separatism, that is, from the *topoi* of confessional polemic.

However persuasive the style of heresiography, the historical priority of orthodoxy in the development of sectarianism is anything but clear. In several areas of the Judaeo-Christian tradition modern scholarship has revealed the role played by 'history' in the service of orthodoxy: witness to the original truth in relation to which various kinds of error became from time to time manifest. An alternative to this view of progressive fragmentation is to posit orthodoxy as the end, rather than the beginning, of the process of doctrinal formulation, and to admit the possibility of local and temporal variation in the nature of communal authority. The concept of *ecclesia* as universal, tolerant and inclusive presupposes at least in practice a conjuncture of social, political, and economic circumstances more extensive than those characteristic of sectarian communities. The difference between 'church' and 'sect' is not merely quantitative but also qualitative, and evolution from the one to the other, if it takes place at all, requires among other things time. Even without that evolution sectarian communities may persist (e.g. Karaite, Mandaean, Samaritan), and it is precisely their persistence as phenomena peripheral to 'ecclesial' authority which facilitates the study of confessional origins.

Emergence within or from the sectarian milieu of a dominant expression (*Grosskirche*) may be the consequence of inherent superiority in, say, organizational techniques, or of historical developments outside the orbit of confessional activities, and hence inexplicable in terms of these. Two major events in the Judaeo-Christian tradition, the appearance of Roman Catholicism and of Rabbinic Judaism, have been interpreted as the result now of one, now of the other of the two processes.[1] Whatever the interpretation the pre-history of eventually 'normative' structures must be sought in the confused accounts of competing 'heterodoxies'. And it is there of course that difficulties arise. These may be the product of uncertain or inventive nomenclature (e.g. Cerinthian, Symmachian, Ebionite), of doctrinal distinctions (e.g. Dosithean, Marcionite), of regional tensions (e.g. Melkite, Nestorian, Jacobite). Often 'heresy' was nothing more than the persistence of views at one time regarded as orthodox or representative at least of majority opinion.[2] Unravelling the many strands leading to the formulation of a normative structure requires a good deal of imaginative reconstruction which may, but also may not, correspond to the actual historical development. For Islam, as for the Roman and Rabbinic 'orthodoxies', the choice between internal organization and external circumstances is to some extent arbitrary.[3] Both the quantity and quality of source materials would seem to support the proposition that the elaboration of Islam was not contemporary with but posterior to the Arab occupation of the Fertile Crescent and beyond. To account for the intervening 150 years or so would thus be the task set historians. Hypothetically, the dislocation of concepts and terms in the composition of salvation history as well as in the exegetical and juridical descriptions of authority indicates a confessional development separate from that of the secular community. The elaboration of Islam might be envisaged either as within and tolerated by the Arab polity or outside and opposed to it. Evidence of hostility, or at least of tension, between secular authority and the ethical demands of a pious minority is ample, and symbolically enshrined in the term *fitna*.

Fundamental to the documentation of confessional identity was selection of appropriate insignia from the monotheist compendium of symbols, *topoi*, and theologoumena. What could be called the 'sectarian syndrome' exhibits a lingua franca composed of such elements, whose sole condition of employment is adaptability. These may be adduced as nomenclature (tags, eponyms, toponyms), as emblems (initiation rites, ritual acts), as creeds (membership rules), as catechisms (dogmatic formulae), and

[1] W. Bauer, *Rechtgläubigkeit und Ketzerei im ältesten Christentum*, (2nd edn. G. Strecker), Tübingen, 1964, 115–33, 231–42; Neusner, *Early Rabbinic Judaism*, 34–49.

[2] Klijn–Reinink, *Patristic Evidence*, 3–43, 52–4, 67–8; Strecker, *apud* Bauer, *Rechtgläubigkeit*, 245–87, esp. 274–87; S. J. Isser, *The Dositheans: a Samaritan Sect in Late Antiquity*, Leiden, 1976, 151–64; cf. *BSOAS* xl, 1977, 604–5.

[3] *QS*, 43–52, 82–3, 88–93, 145–8, 201–2.

correspond functionally to the several stages of confessional elaboration: identity (polemic), consolidation (proselytism), orthodoxy (instruction). Progression from one stage to another is usually uneven and often incomplete, since some symbols may never achieve 'orthodox' status, but rather, persist as sectarian or 'heterodox' insignia.

Selection from the compendium was often, perhaps inevitably, arbitrary, and hardly the result of careful deliberation. In the Islamic version of monotheism the adopted symbol might be a calque superimposed upon an existing doctrinal concept, e.g. for angelology (*karūbiyyūn*: *muqarrabūn*) and resurrection (*qiyāma*:*qāma*).[1] It might, on the other hand, become a structural component of the final (and 'orthodox') edifice, e.g. what I have elsewhere described as 'schemata of revelation': retribution pericope (*umam khāliya*), sign/miracle (*āyāt*), exile (*hijra*), and covenant (*'ahd/mīthāq*).[2] Like some of the polemical *topoi* described in my first chapter and all of the theologoumena discussed in the second, the schemata exhibit a basic symbolism, integral to doctrinal development. It is that kind of symbolism which I am concerned here to analyse, though it may be worth mentioning that within the Islamic lexicon such eccentricities as the virgin birth and the messiah epithet of Jesus are also found. Originally quite alien to the formulation of doctrine, these eventually generated a kind of subsidiary imagery to discussions respectively of divine attributes and apocalyptic.

For Islam the initial range of basic symbols is contained in what I have called the 'apostolic catechism' recited by Ja'far b. Abī Ṭālib for the Ethiopian Najāshī (*umūr al-islām*): acknowledgement of one prophet, of one God, of dietary laws, of sexual abstemiousness, of family responsibilities, of treaties, of moral probity, and of cultic obligations.[3] Elements of these were subsequently codified as the (five) 'pillars of observance' (*arkān al-islām*): witness, prayer, almsgiving, fasting, and pilgrimage, to which could be added the duty to wage Holy War: literally, to propagate the religion, and in the extended sense of self-discipline (*scil.* all action evaluated *sub specie aeternitatis*). Save for the Meccan pilgrimage no item in these lists falls outside the standard monotheist vocabulary, and is thus of little use in the description of origins. The same may be said of the polemical *topoi*, except that these exhibit a marked Jewish/Judaeo-Christian character, in contrast with a Christian or Gnostic environment. Symbols eventually incorporated as insignia included also epithets for the community (*umma/milla/jamā'a*), its leader (*imām/rasūl/khalīfa*), its testimonial (*kitāb/qur'ān*), its intention (guidance: *hidāya*, cf. *sabīl/ṣirāt/ṭarīq*), and for proselytes (*ḥanīf/ṣābi'/muhājir/anṣār*).

Occasionally perceptible is literary development related to the phenomenon described above as exemplification, e.g. in the *Sīra* accounts of the

[1] *QS*, 30–3. [2] *QS*, 2–12. [3] *QS*, 38–43.

first and second meetings at 'Aqaba, where the terms of stipulation between Muhammad and his followers evolve from a simple non-Quranic catechism (i, 433–4: *bay'at al-nisā'*) to an elaborate scriptural theodicy (i, 446–8, 454, 467–8: *bay'at al-ḥarb*, derived from Q. 22: 39 and 2: 193).[1] The actual procedure for conversion was uniformly uncomplicated: a stylized set of formulae was employed for Ṭufayl b. 'Amr (*Sīra* i, 384), Sa'd b. Mu'ādh (i, 436), and Usayd b. Ḥuḍayr (i, 437), viz. ablution (*ightisāl*), purification (*taṭahhur*), purification of clothing (*taṭhīr al-thawb*), witness to the truth (*shahādat al-ḥaqq*), ritual prayer (two *rak'as*). Equally stylized is description of the circumstances preceding conversion: scepticism, resistance, conviction while the rudiments were set out (i, 383, 436: *fa-'arada 'l-islām/fa-kallamahu bil-islām*) and the invitation articulated (*wa-talā 'l-qur'ān/wa-qara'a 'alayhi 'l-qur'ān*).[2] A celebrated exception was the conversion of Ka'b al-Aḥbār, whose metanoia could only be justified, in the interests of polemic, as response to the discovery of Jewish perfidy (scriptural forgeries and the prognosis of Muhammad).[3] Another equally celebrated instance, this time of a miscarried attempt at conversion, was that of the poet A'shā b. Qays (*Sīra* i, 386–8), in the course of which the Islamic prohibitions of fornication, gambling, wine, and usury were adduced.[4]

But the original Islamic kerygma was depicted as guidance. Within the framework of Jāhilī mythology the demise of the (pagan) oracle (*inqiṭā' al-kahāna*) was linked with confusion in the celestial order, the traditional means of temporal and spatial orientation (*Sīra* i, 204–7, esp. 206: paraphrase of Q. 6: 97). Divine revelation by means of a prophet signified supersession of the natural order by guidance (*rushd/hudā/ṭarīq mustaqīm*) of a supernatural order. Several designations of 'proselyte' might be thought reflexes of this basic concept of guidance, of movement along an approved course. Among, for example, the several disputed etymologies of *ḥanīf*, the standard Arabic one is 'he who turns from (any) false religion to the true one' (*al-mā'il 'an kull dīn bāṭil ilā dīn al-ḥaqq*). The notion of proselyte, as opposed to a specific sectarian designation, is symbolized by the Quranic link between *ḥanīf* and Abraham, a reflex of the Judaeo-Christian tradition from Philo to Paul.[5] Similarly, the Quranic *ṣābi'*, whatever its 'baptist'

[1] Cf. Schoeps, *Judenchristentum*, 259–61, 303 (*Aposteldekret*).

[2] For *qur'ān* as *da'wa* cf. Kosmala, *Hebräer*, 67 and 73–4 n. 36: Qumranic Heb. *qeru'ei* (*qeri'ei*) *El*; and R. Murray, *Symbols of Church and Kingdom: a Study in Early Syriac Tradition*, Cambridge, 1975, 291: Syr. *qeryānā d-'ammē*.

[3] M. Perlmann, 'A legendary story of Ka'b al-Aḥbār's conversion to Islam', in *Joshua Starr Memorial Volume*, New York, 1953, 85–99; id., 'Another Ka'b al-Aḥbār story', *JQR* xiv (1954) 48–58; cf. *QS*, 189.

[4] Cf. Ma'arrī, *Risālat al-ghufrān*, Cairo, 1950, 167–73.

[5] Zamakhsharī, *Al-Kashshāf 'an ḥaqā'iq al-tanzīl*, Beirut, 1967, i, 194 *ad* Q. 2: 135; cf. Y. Moubarac, *Abraham dans le Coran*, Paris, 1958, 151–61; Rabin, *Qumran*, 117–18; Sanders, 'Covenant', 29; *QS*, 21, 54.

connotations may be worth, is glossed in the exegetical tradition 'he who separates himself from the religion' (*al-khārij min al-dīn*), a sense confirmed, or at least not contradicted, by reference in the *Sīra* (i, 344) to Muhammad as 'this *ṣābi'* who destroyed the authority of Quraysh' (*hādhā 'l-ṣābi' 'lladhī farraqa amr quraysh*).[1] Comparable usage is found in Wāqidī (*Maghāzī*, 32: *hādhā Muḥammad wal-ṣubāt ma'ahu*), where, moreover, the conversion of 'Umayr b. Wahb is described as *ṣaba'a* in a context which hardly requires the meaning 'baptized' (*Maghāzi*, 127). The iconoclasm characteristic of a break with tradition underlying both *ḥanīf* and *ṣābi'* was of course a fixed component of the midrashic embellishment of Genesis: Abraham was the archetype.[2] It is also Abraham who provided a third figure of the proselyte: the *muhājir*, whose exile (*hijra*) signified conversion.[3]

Now, the process exemplified here is not one of lexical calque but rather, of symbolic transfer. The migration of symbols may be either productive or reductive: as so often in the Islamic adaptation of Biblical motifs, the examples enumerated above belong to the second category. Assimilation of heterogeneous elements of this nature is an acknowledged feature of syncretism, but the crucial process is after all one of assimilation. However derivative the components, however disparate their original symbolic values and underlying mythologies, their retention in a fresh configuration entails a successful semantic shift.[4] I have alluded to the monotheist transposition of Alexander the Great. A related, but not quite identical, process may be seen in the figure of St. George, an example of symbolic re-creation, not from historical realia but rather from the equally malleable stuff of mythology.[5] Even the most sacred symbols of a religious tradition, those which, like the tabernacle menorah, belong to the earliest stages of cultic expression, are susceptible of such analysis (here: *arbor* and *lumen*).[6] Similarly, the ecclesiological imagery of Aphrahat and Ephrem exhibits the successful, if occasionally strained, adaptation of a quite extraordinary range of motifs whose original symbolic value for the authority of the

[1] Zamakhsharī, *Kashshāf* i, 146 *ad* Q. 2: 62; J. Horovitz, *Koranische Untersuchungen*, Berlin–Leipzig, 1926, 121–2; R. Paret, *Der Koran: Kommentar und Konkordanz*, Stuttgart, 1971, 20–1; G. Widengren, *Muhammad, the Apostle of God, and his Ascension*, Uppsala–Wiesbaden, 1955, 133–9.

[2] H. Schützinger, *Ursprung und Entwicklung der arabischen Abraham-Nimrod Legende*, Bonn, 1961, 138–200; R. Mach, *Der Zaddik in Talmud und Midrasch*, Leiden, 1957, 53–166.

[3] *QS*, 7–8; P. Crone and M. Cook, *Hagarism: the Making of the Islamic World*, Cambridge, 1977, 1–38; cf. *BSOAS* xli (1978) 155–6; D. Corcos, *Studies in the History of the Jews of Morocco*, Jerusalem, 1976, 61 n. 64; cf. *The Maghreb Review*, 1977, no. 4, p. 23.

[4] Cf. Neusner, *Early Rabbinic Judaism*, 209–15 (on Goodenough).

[5] Pfister, *Alexander der Große*, esp. 24–35; Jolles, *Einfache Formen*, 46–50.

[6] M. Smith, 'The image of God: notes on the Hellenization of Judaism, with especial reference to Goodenough's work on Jewish symbols', *BJRL* xl (1957–8) 473–512; C. Meyers, *The Tabernacle Menorah: a Synthetic Study of a Symbol from the Biblical Cult*, Missoula, Montana, 1976; cf. *BSOAS* xxxix (1976) 644–5: rev. M. Metzger, *La haggada enluminée* i, Leiden, 1973.

Church was anything but obvious. The manner in which these motifs evolve from alien status via individually inspired juxtaposition to established communal imagery is the substance of religious iconography. Attention to 'testimonia' and 'typologies' may account for much of the transmission history of symbols, but probably not for the way in which these were finally accepted as community emblems, that is, as the undisputed evidence of a distinct confessional identity.[1] In any case, the transfer of concepts presupposes a prior, or simultaneous, linguistic contact, or what could be described as terminological transfer and distinguished from the more general (because necessarily imprecise) problem of thematic adaptation. Location of the linguistic contact is a problem of literary history and one more readily solved where source materials are abundant.

. . . . .

For the origins of Islamic terminology the paucity of unambiguous witness is notorious. My point of departure in these studies has been that the earliest formulation of Muslim identity is contained in the *sīra–maghāzī* literature. Contemporary materials for comparative analysis include scripture and Sunna. All three genres represent a linguistic initiation in religious imagery: that is, there is no earlier documentation in Arabic of the language employed to expound the Islamic kerygma. Such putative allusions to formal religion as may be found in the corpus of Jāhilī poetry are of virtually no value in ascertaining the origins of what became the religious vocabulary of Islam.[2] Now the conceptual motive (*Geistesbeschäftigung*) in the production of those three genres was polemic, and it seems reasonable to suppose that the gradual refinement of religious terminology was the consequence, and cause, of further, increasingly sophisticated polemic. The way in which this might have taken place was indicated many years ago by C. H. Becker, but has been since then more cogently put by H. A. Wolfson.[3] I should like here to illustrate the process with two examples.

The passage *Sīra* i, 573–84 contains a primitive exposition of Christology. The setting is one of several delegations from Najrān (possibly composite) reported to have reached Muhammad, at Mecca as well as at Medina, and customarily the venue for public dispute. I have alluded above to the stereotyped imagery of these reports:[4] here it is the doctrinal descriptions which deserve notice. Besides the tripartite allocation of authority within the community (*scil.* between *'āqib*, *sayyid*, and *usquf*) and an eastern *qibla*, the delegation is characterized, not in their own words

[1] Murray, *Symbols of Church and Kingdom*, esp. 279–347.

[2] *QS*, 94–8.

[3] Becker, 'Christliche Polemik', esp. 441; H. A. Wolfson, *The Philosophy of the Kalam*, Harvard University Press, 1976, esp. 70–1; cf. *BSOAS* xli (1978) 156–7.

[4] Schmucker, 'Christliche Minderheit', esp. 263–78.

but in those of Ibn Isḥāq, as ineligible for Islam (*sic*) because they attribute progeny to God, worship the cross, and eat pork. Of these, the only disqualification analysed in this passage is the nature of Jesus: he is God, the son of God, and the third of three. The first allegation is supported by reference to his miracles, the second by reference to the virgin birth, and the third by reference to the scriptural employment of *pluralis majestatis* (the trinity in question included God and Maryam). The level of discourse can thus only be described as colloquial, and a reflex not of the current state of trinitarian doctrine, but rather, of the register of that expression in the Arabic language. The brief exposition is here followed by a selection of Quranic verses (Q. 3: 1–8, 18–21, 26–7, 31–7, 42–64), in the course of which the miracles of Jesus are explained as having been authorized by God (*bi-idhn allāh*), his birth as having been no more wondrous than that of Adam (*scil. min turāb*), and the use of a plural pronoun irrelevant in the light of explicit assertion of God's unicity (*tawḥīd*). The Quranic passages are adduced exegetically, and are of paraenetic rather than doctrinal value. Further, they do not include the trinitarian charge (cf. Q. 5: 73), adoration of the cross (4: 157), or the prohibition of pork (5: 3). Juxtaposition of scripture and historical report must here be considered secondary to the independent origin of each.

Now, comparison of Ibn Isḥāq's exposition with that contained in a report of the Nestorian patriarch Timothy, approximately a generation later, is instructive. Though the level of discourse might still be described as popular, the argument is rather more sophisticated and the lexicon considerably expanded. Whether these qualities may be attributed to the simple fact of a translation into Arabic from Syriac is of course something of a problem. And there are others: the authenticity of the treatise is not undisputed; whether of the two versions preserved the Arabic is in fact a translation of the Syriac has not been demonstrated; the reported dialogue, if it ever took place, must have been in Arabic.[1] If one could postulate (and it is anything but certain) an uninterrupted progression of terminological development, Timothy's report must fall somewhere between the formulation of Christological doctrine in the *Sīra* and the subtle philosophical argument of Theodore Abū Qurra, the Melkite bishop of Ḥarrān (d. *c.* 825).[2] What could be, again hypothetically, a link between *Sīra* and Timothy may be seen in the anonymous tract from Sinai on the trinity,

[1] Syriac: Mingana, *Timothy's Apology*; Arabic: Cheikho, *Al-Muḥāwara al-dīniyya*; G. Graf, *Geschichte der christlichen arabischen Literatur*, Studi e Testi, Citta del Vaticano, 1944–53, ii, 114–18; cf. Browne, 'The Patriarch Timothy', 38–45; Fritsch, *Islam und Christentum*, 2.

[2] Arabic: C. Bāshā, *Mayāmir Thāudūrus Abī Qurra*, Beirut, 1904; Graf, *Die arabischen Schriften des Theodor Abū Qurra, Bischofs von Harran*, Forschungen zur christlichen Literatur- und Dogmengeschichte, Band X, 3–4, Paderborn, 1910; id., *GCAL* ii, 7–26; I. Dick, 'Theodore Abu Qurra, évêque melkite de Harran: la personne et son milieu', *Proche-Orient Chrétien* xii (1962) 209–23, 319–32; xiii (1963) 114–29.

entitled by its editor *Fī Tathlīth Allāh al-Wāḥid.*[1] Related in content and expression to the latter is the Heidelberg papyrus PSR 438, also anonymous and undated as well as very poorly preserved.[2] With such scanty materials a reconstruction of trinitarian terminology in Arabic hardly invites confidence, but the quite extraordinary difference between the doctrinal discussions in Ibn Isḥāq and Abū Qurra does require explanation.

The most remarkable feature of the Sinai document, a Christian apologia, is its 'Quranic' language. Explicit reference to Muslim scripture is meagre (eight instances) but the frequency and distribution of what has come to be regarded as distinctively Quranic phraseology are impressive. I refer to such locutions as: *ilayka 'l-maṣīr*, *'alā 'l-'arsh istawā*, *'alā kull shay' qadīr*, *sharaḥa ṣadrahu* (read so), *ma'ādh allāh*, *fi'l-hudā wa-dīni 'l-ḥaqq*, *in sha' allāh*, *wa-hum yastahzūna* (sic) *bihi*, *fa-kallamahu 'llāh taklīman*, *fi kull umma wa-kull qawm*, *yawm al-qiyāma*, *al-ḥamdu lillāhi 'lladhī . . .*, *'adhāb alīm*, *fanẓur kayfa . . .*, *'adhāb al-jaḥīm*, as well as such slight variations as *ahlu baytihi*, *ahlu 'l-kitāb*, *aḥbār al-yahūd*, and designations like *iblīs*, *ḥawāriyyūn*, *karūbiyyūn*, *ṣiddīq*, *kanīsa* for synagogue, *madīna* for city, *masjid* for Temple, etc. The only argument adduced is that the messiah promised by the Biblical prophets was divine, the son of God, and hence, Jesus, whose incarnation could not, however, be interpreted as compromising the unicity of God. These unsophisticated assertions exhibit a counterpoint to the Quranic testimonia of the *Sīra* exposition, and moreover, in the same language. For that writer at least, despite a good deal of what can be described as Middle Arabic admixture, the only standard available was the literary language of the Muslim community.[3] The extent to which that was so may be seen in his rendering of Luke 1: 34 in the Annunciation scene: always (edition pp. 83, 90, 93, 100) by a (faintly colloquial) reproduction of Q. 3: 47 (or 19: 20), that is, with *massa* in the metaphorical sense of 'to know carnally'. The linguistic, literary, and cultural problems evoked by the Sinai Christian Arabic (originally Palestinian) material are well known.[4] Were it not for explicit (and more or less correctly given) reference to the canonical Quranic text, it might just be possible to argue that the 'Muslim' diction of this particular trinitarian treatise contains vestiges of a pre-Islamic liturgical language, adopted later by the Muslim community for its own liturgy and, ultimately, scripture. The alternative, and

[1] M. D. Gibson, 'On the Triune nature of God', *Studia Sinaitica* vii (London, 1899) 74–107 (text), 2–36 (trans.); Graf, *GCAL* ii, 27–8.

[2] Graf, 'Disputation zwischen Muslimen und Christen', 1–24; id., *GCAL* ii, 26.

[3] J. Blau, *A Grammar of Christian Arabic, based mainly on South Palestinian Texts from the First Millennium*, CSCO Subsidia 27–9, Louvain, 1966–7 (*ASP*), esp. 36–58; cf. *BSOAS* xxxi (1968) 610–13.

[4] e.g. A. Baumstark, 'Das Problem eines vorislamischen christlich-kirchlichen Schrifttums in arabischer Sprache', *Islamica* iv (1931) 562–75; Blau, 'Reste arabischer Bibelübersetzungen', 67–72; id., *ASP*, 22 (para. 1.4.1.4), 52 n. 61.

undoubtedly sounder, explanation is to suppose that the language of polemic, at least at a popular level, did not initially extend beyond the register established in the *Sīra*, and that when it eventually did, that progress was the result of an infusion from Syriac or Greek or both.

Possible witness to that evolution is the Arabic version of Timothy's dispute with the caliph al-Mahdī, though the fragments of a similar dialogue contained in PSR 438 exhibit some terminological improvement upon the Sinai document (e.g. *uqnūm*, *lāhūt*, *nāsūt*). The trinitarian material in Timothy's report (edition pp. 359–65) is, like the Sinai document, essentially a messianic proclamation. But unlike the latter, the argument here is derived not from scriptural testimonia but from an analogy with the sun, whose heat and light are distinct and yet inseparable from their source. That analogy was merely mentioned in the Sinai document (76 top): for Timothy it is the foundation of the trinitarian dogma, which depends upon a distinction (*tamyīz*) between simple (*basīṭ*) and compound (*murakkab*), and between substance (*jawhar*) and hypostasis (*uqnūm*, pl. *aqānīm*). In addition to the sun analogy, procession of Word (*kalima*) and Spirit (*rūḥ*) from the Lord is compared with the scent and taste (distinct sensory experiences) of an apple, and with the issue of a written decree (intellect: command: paper) by the king. In neither case has the emanation meaning apart from its source. Citation of scripture is minimal: nothing of Qur'ān, four verses from the Psalter, one from Isaiah, four from the Gospel of John, and one from Matthew. The argument exhibits thus a rationalization of this fundamental problem in Muslim–Christian polemic: the caliph's questions are merely a foil for the patriarch's insistent logic, nowhere more obvious than in discussion of the virgin birth, a point accepted after all by both sides. My interest here is in the appearance of technical terms in Arabic, e.g. *tashbīh* (analogy), *ṣifāt* (attributes), *azaliyy* (eternal), *zamaniyy* (temporal), *ṭabīʿa* (nature), *mawjūd* (existent), *maʿdūm* (non-existent), and *burhān* (proof), in addition to those above mentioned. These represent extrapolation from the data of revelation, a movement away from the often blunt assertions characteristic of a theodicy and towards the standard of general concept. The source of the new and abstract terminology is not thereby detected, but such a discovery is of less significance than the fact of a fresh level of discourse. The Quranic vocabulary, which informs the *Sīra* and Sinai document, is superseded in Timothy's report. Dating the process is quite another matter: a conservative guess would be the end of the second Islamic century (200/815).

The writings of Theodore Abū Qurra are thought to have been composed during the period 780–820. They exhibit a considerable refinement of polemical expression, at least for those preserved in Arabic (14 tracts). Those preserved in Greek (43 tracts) represent of course a much older doctrinal lexicon, which may be accepted as the substratum of Abū

Qurra's own intellectual formation, probably adapted to Syriac.[1] Whether the latter or Arabic was the author's native language is uncertain; the literary Arabic preserved in his name is of a high standard. But it is the quality of his argument that I wish here to stress, not perhaps unexpected from the translator into Arabic of the *Prior Analytics*.[2] For a scholar with those technical proficiencies terminological coinage must have been a familiar necessity. The actual selection of calques or loan-translations was complex and demanded a grasp of varying contexts, as Walzer has shown for Abū Qurra's rendering of *doxa*.[3] In his trinitarian treatise the author's exposition is appropriately tripartite:[4] a preface on faith and epistemology (pp. 23–7), a section of scriptural testimonia supporting the proposition that, despite His several manifestations, God is One (pp. 27–33), and finally, a carefully constructed philosophical argument in favour of the same proposition (pp. 33–47). The burden of the opening section is that faith, after all, is an essential component of all experience, e.g. seeking medical advice, travel at sea, and thus not to be discounted in the acquisition of knowledge. The messianic testimonia include Psalter, Hosea, Genesis, Exodus, and the gospels of John and Matthew. In the third section the point of departure is the fundamental distinction between 'nature' (*ṭabīʿa*) and manifestation or 'aspect' (*wajh*): while the latter can be both named and numbered the former can be only named, thus, John is a man but mankind is not John. The categories so established might appear to correspond to genus and species. By way of illustration, such alleged analogies as the light from several sources, recitations in unison of a single poem, collective designation of such material substances as gold, the designation of agency in human speech (voice v. man), vision (eye v. man) labour (hand v. man), as well as the now familiar relation between the sun and its rays, are adduced in sequence. The point seems to be that hypostasis (*uqnūm*) is not the equivalent of 'nature' (*ṭabīʿa*) or substance (*jawhar*) or compound (*muḍāf* and *muḍāf ilayhi*), but rather, of manifestation or 'aspect' (*wajh*).The coexistence of three such manifestations of deity (*ab/ibn/rūḥ al-qudus*), representing aspects of agency, may not be seen to contradict the essential/substantial unity of God. The argument is thus an elaboration of the elements found in Timothy's dispute with the caliph, the terminology somewhat expanded by inclusion of several words for analogy (*qiyās/naẓīr/ashbāh*), the use of *tabʿīḍ* and *iḍāfa* in addition to *tarkib* for compound, of *hayūlā* for matter, and abstract formations like *ghayriyya* (otherness), *qunūmiyya* (hypostasis), and *jawhariyya* (substance).

[1] Graf, *Die arabischen Schriften*, 20–5; Dick, 'Theodore Abu Qurra', 218–22.

[2] R. Walzer, *Greek into Arabic: Essays on Islamic Philosophy*, Oxford, 1962, 68, 84–97 (accepting the conjecture of P. Kraus).

[3] Ibid. 94–7.

[4] Bāshā, *Mayāmir*, 23–47; Graf, op. cit., 133–60 (III).

Now, if the biographical data so far assembled for Abū Qurra are even approximately exact and the works ascribed to him more or less authentic (a critical edition of the Arabic treatises has yet to be made) then we are dealing with material contemporary with the earliest formulation of a technical vocabulary in Arabic. The enigmatic nature of that process has been often remarked, and some progress made towards isolating the several strands of transmission.[1] It is also in the (Greek) writings of Abū Qurra that a proper basis for polemical dispute is defined as 'concepts shared and agreed' by all participants, that is, argument not from private visions but from rational and verifiable foundations.[2] The course of trinitarian dispute in the literature posterior to Abū Qurra is well known.[3] For the earlier stages Wolfson has demonstrated the Neoplatonic component in the development of the Muslim doctrine of attributes out of the trinitarian concept of hypostasis.[4] The problem of terminological calques is there aided by identifying *kharakteristikon* and *ṣifa*. It seems to me that it was precisely by means of the expansion of the Arabic lexicon that the rudimentary scriptural imagery employed by Ibn Isḥāq for his exposition of Christology could be gradually, perhaps even imperceptibly, superseded by the vocabulary (and concepts) found in the writings of the philosopher Kindī (d. 259/873) and his successors.[5] The notion of conceptual expansion by means of lexical innovation is an epistemological axiom which can be made to account for most forms of intellectual progress. But the residue of earlier positions is never quite obliterated: the epithet *masīḥ* (messiah) remained in Muslim Arabic a proper name, that of 'Isā ibn Maryam, just as the so-called 'docetic' interpretation of his crucifixion was inconsistent with Muslim anti-trinitarian doctrine.[6] The source of both utterances was of course Muslim scripture (Q. 4: 157), the verbatim text of which continued to occupy exegetes long after it had ceased to be the major source of speculative theology.

The elaboration of polemical *topoi* by lexical addition is thus not difficult to document, though the very nature and quantity of pertinent source

[1] e.g. F. W. Zimmermann, 'Some observations on Al-Farabi and Logical Tradition', in *Islamic Philosophy and the Classical Tradition* (Essays presented . . . to Richard Walzer), Oxford, 1972, 517–46, esp. 529–36.

[2] e.g. Migne, *PG*, 97, 1551, cited by Becker, 'Christliche Polemik', 445; cf. Dick, 'Théodore Abu Qurra', 320.

[3] Fritsch, *Islam und Christentum*, 102–27; Eichner, 'Nachrichten über den Islam', 197–202.

[4] Wolfson, *Kalam*, 112–32, 304–54.

[5] Ibid. 318–36, 70–1, 114 ('ideas riding on the back of terms'); some polemicists were of course unaffected: cf. C. Pellat, 'Christologie ǧāḥiẓienne', *Studia Islamica* xxxi (1970) 219–32.

[6] Graf, 'Wie ist das Wort Al-Masīḥ zu übersetzen?', *ZDMG* civ (1954) 119–23; Fritsch, *Islam und Christentum*, 66; K. Ahrens, 'Christliches im Qoran', *ZDMG* lxxxiv (1930) 154; but cf. also C. K. Barrett, 'Jews and Judaizers in the Epistles of Ignatius', in *Jews, Greeks and Christians*, 220–44, esp. 224 ff.

materials do not permit a historical reconstruction (*wie es eigentlich gewesen*). My second example is taken from the passage *Sīra* i, 530–72 in which, as I have indicated above, is retailed a series of public altercations between Muslims and members of a Jewish community in Medina. The identity of that community is anything but clear and the polemic heavily stereotyped. One *topos* emerges as dominant: the Muslim charge of scriptural falsification (*taḥrīf*) and its corollary, supersession (*naskh*) by Islam of the Biblical dispensation granted to Israel. Ibn Isḥāq's version is not unexpectedly primitive. The imagery is basically scriptural and turns upon the three concepts *kitmān* (concealment, e.g. 534 *ad* Q. 2: 42), *tabdīl* (substitution, e.g. 535 *ad* Q. 2: 58), and *taḥrīf* (alteration, e.g. 536–7 *ad* Q. 2: 75). The accusation is usually made *in foro externo* in circumstances calculated to reveal Jewish perfidy in failing to preserve the original of their own scriptures, because these had (!) contained prognosis of the Arabian prophet. Similarly, the faithlessness of both Jew and Christian could be demonstrated by their refusal (*sic*) to acknowledge the evidence of their scriptures respectively for Jesus and Moses (549). It was specifically *kitmān* when the Jews would not allow Muhammad access to their scriptures (551, 553) or, in the celebrated instance of the 'stoning verse', both *kitmān* and *taḥrīf* (564–6). Jewish perfidy was revealed in their insistence on the one hand that there could be no scripture after Moses (*sic*, 562–4), and on the other that Muhammad must produce as credential a scriptural revelation (570–1). The use and abuse of 'scripture' was thus a polemical concept, adduced in support of the Muslim claim that God's salvific design had been achieved only with the revelation granted Muhammad.

In that context *naskh*, a term not in fact employed by Ibn Isḥāq, could only refer to 'abrogation' as supersession of one scripture by another. And it was in that sense that *naskh* informed the later development of polemical literature, that is, as part of a discussion of the textual integrity of scripture, seen not merely as unchanging but as properly immutable.[1] The charge of falsification and/or alteration was flexible, and might refer not to the transmission but to the exegesis of the scriptural text. Adopted into the lexicon of hermeneutics, the concept of *naskh* as abrogation became infinitely more complex, generated a number of subdivisions (*takhṣīṣ*, *tafsīr*, *taḥwīl*, etc.), and was seen to be the instrument whereby scriptural props for ordinances whose source was anything but scriptural could be recruited.[2] Abrogation in the sense of supersession had of course, and much earlier, been a weapon in the arsenal of Christian polemic with Jews. In Muslim polemic Christians did not escape the charge of having distorted

[1] *QS*, 63, 70–1, 76, 188–90, 199–201; M. Steinschneider, *Polemische und apologetische Literatur in arabischer Sprache*, Leipzig, 1877, 320–5; M. Schreiner, 'Zur Geschichte der Polemik zwischen Juden und Muhammedanern', *ZDMG* xlii (1888) esp. 603–39.

[2] *QS*, 190–200; Burton, *Collection*, index s.v. *naskh*.

maliciously the legacy of their founder, but it was largely the Jews upon whom the role of opposition was thrust. Thus, in the work of Ibn Ḥazm (d. 456/1064) it was with a Jewish adversary, Shmuel Ha-Nagid, that he disputed the integrity of Hebrew and Muslim scripture.[1] And it was a Jewish renegade, Samaw'al al-Maghribī (d. *c.* 570/1175), who argued the cause of Islamic *naskh* against his former coreligionists.[2] And finally, it was the Jew Ibn Kammūna (d. 683/1284) who rejected most vehemently the Muslim allegation of scriptural abrogation.[3]

Whether understood as superseding dispensation or as halakhic hermeneutics, or as a blend of both, the concept of abrogation became a symbol of confessional authority, and its defence or rejection the primary expression of Judaeo-Muslim polemic. From one point of view, the argument was merely about the respective merits of two specific documents of revelation. Both sides agreed after all that the source of authority was indeed scripture. That this shared point of departure was itself spurious may or may not have been known to the polemicists: certainly the exegetical techniques employed in Rabbinic Judaism and Sunnī Islam were identical.[4] None the less, the principle of scriptural authority provided an enduring topic for dispute. Its earliest record after the *Sīra* is a curious document retailing an exchange of views between the Muʿtazilī theologian Ibrāhīm al-Naẓẓām (*c.* 230/845) and an otherwise unknown Jew called Yassā b. Ṣāliḥ (*sic*). It reads as follows:[5]

It has been asserted that Ibrāhīm al-Naẓẓām met the Jew Yassā b. Ṣāliḥ who asked him: When God decrees a law (*sharīʿa*) is it not so that He would not have done it had it not been an (expression of divine) wisdom? Ibrāhīm replied: That is so. Yassā continued: And is it not according to your view permitted that God decree a law which is observed for a time, and then that He decree its abrogration (*tabṭīl*) entirely and observance of something else; does it not seem that in prohibiting its observance He has in fact prohibited an act of (divine) wisdom? Ibrāhīm replied: Wisdom is of two kinds: (first) wisdom as such, non-contingent (*lā li-ʿilla*), such as justice, faith, honesty and charity, which it is inconceivable that God should ever prohibit; (second) wisdom which becomes such contingent upon its very decree (*li-ʿillat al-amr bihā*), such as ritual, prayer, and fasting; now what God decrees of these is good and His authority is good, and should He then rescind and decree something else, that is both good and (of His divine) wisdom; for wisdom in such case is obedience

[1] E. García Gómez, 'Polemica religiosa entre Ibn Ḥazm e Ibn Al-Nagrila', *Andalus* iv (1936–9) 1–28; Arabic text in I. Abbas (ed.), *Al-Radd ʿalā Ibn Al-Naghrīla Al-Yahūdī wa-rasā'il ukhrā*, Cairo, 1960, 45–81.

[2] M. Perlmann (ed.), *Samau'al Al-Maghribī: Ifḥām Al-Yahūd*, *PAAJR* xxxii (New York, 1964) esp. 6–10, 16–23.

[3] M. Perlmann (ed.), *Ibn Kammūna: Tanqīḥ al-abḥāth lil-milal al-thalāth*, Berkeley–Los Angeles, 1967, esp. 45–7.

[4] *QS*, 199–201.

[5] L. Cheikho, *Vingt traités théologiques (d'auteurs arabes chrétiens)*, Beirut, 1920, 68–70: *nubdha thāniya fī naskh al-sharā'iʿ*.

to God and abiding by His decree, since it is a good event (*waqʿ*) both decreeing it and obeying it constitutes wisdom, (and similarly) rescinding it, decreeing something else, and obeying that is also wisdom; but that is not at all like honesty (*ṣidq*) which is always good and whose opposite is always evil.

Yassā then said: And thus it is not denied that the law Moses decreed is good and that its abrogation (*naskh*) is impossible (*ghayr jāʾiz*)? Ibrāhīm replied: That is not so, for if the law were good as such (*li-aʿyāniha*) men would know its goodness, whether or not it had been revealed through a prophet, such as charity, avoidance of evil, and the pursuit of honesty are known to the good man; but as for such contingent matters (*al-ashyāʾ al-muqayyada bil-ʿilal*) as prayer and fasting, were it not that a prophet had taught us that prayer is obligatory and that it is forbidden not to fast at the appointed time, and were it not that Moses had said that work on the Sabbath is forbidden, we would not know that this was so or that there was even a difference between the Sabbath and Sunday; and since we cannot know these prescriptions except by tradition (*samʿ*) and were it not that a prophet had imposed them upon men they would not know them, your view that the Mosaic law is good as such is thus invalid.

Yassā then said: Is it conceivable that God should impose a law upon men by the agency of Moses saying 'this is imposed upon you for ever and he who does not observe it shall be sentenced to death' and then rescind it? Ibrāhīm replied: Yes, that is conceivable, for Moses compelled its acceptance by means of signs and miracles and thus imposed the laws upon men, informing them that their source was God; so anyone who like Moses can provide signs and miracles can compel acceptance of his word just as Moses had done; and if it were conceivable that the Messiah had lied, despite the signs which he manifested, then it is just possible that Moses also lied, but if that possibility is rejected for both of them it follows that both were telling the truth; now if Moses said 'it is imposed upon you for ever' it is recognized from an exegetical point of view (*min jihat al-taʾwīl*) that he only meant by 'for ever' a long time and/or a specified period (*mudda maʿlūma*); so now whoever came after Moses did not abrogate (*taʿṭīl*: *sic*) those things which God had made good in their very nature (*li-aʿyāni-hā*), but rather, abrogated (*naskh*) that whose performance was good contingent upon decree or prohibition (*li-ʿilla fiʾl-amr wal-nahy*); and the prophet Jeremiah wrote: 'The Lord says I will make a new covenant (*ʿahd jadīd*) with Israel and the house of Judah, not like the covenant which I made with them when I brought them out of Egypt' (31: 31–2), and thus stated that it is possible for God to decree a law and then later to decree something different.

Then Ibrāhīm said to Yassā the Jew: Would you agree that God's ordering Abraham to sacrifice his son was wisdom, or was it folly? Yassā replied: Wisdom, undoubtedly. Ibrāhīm continued: And did Abraham not take the knife and rope and firewood and ascend the mountain with his son in order to sacrifice him, and then, when he had laid the knife upon his throat, God forbade him to do it (Genesis 22: 1–19)? Yassā replied: Yes. And Ibrāhīm said: Thus God forbade him wisdom, however you regard it? Yassā replied: God ordered Abraham to sacrifice his son in order to test him, to see whether he could do it or not, then

He tested him to see whether he could abstain from doing it. Ibrāhīm said: You are quite right, there is thus no dispute between us in this matter; merely that we say that both the decree and its rescission constitute wisdom, because for us there is good in every decree, while you deny that.

Here, as for Timothy and the caliph, the dialogue form is merely a convention: Yassā (Jesse) is a foil for Ibrāhīm's theory of 'natural' as opposed to 'revealed' law. God's knowledge/wisdom (*ḥikma*) is not arbitrary: certain manifestations are non-contingent and hence irreversible, that is, once articulated they achieve a kind of semantic independence. There is of course a measure of agreement between the disputants: for Yassā the Mosaic law is also irreversible, not intrinsically, but because God has so decreed. A distinction between its contingent and non-contingent elements is not admitted by the Jew, while the Muslim insists that every decree of God's must be good. It is the latter, after all, who adduces in support of his argument both Jeremiah 31 and Genesis 22. The fictive character of the dialogue emerges quite clearly in the light of any collection of Rabbinic *middot*, the purpose of which was to allow continuing modification of the law. But here Yassā's position symbolizes Jewish intransigence in the face of the Muslim kerygma, and is thus irrelevant to the question of hermeneutical method. It is precisely this ambiguity which characterizes all Judaeo-Muslim polemic: its value here is as foil to the Muʿtazilī's exposition, first, of God's necessary justice, second, of His being in fact circumscribed by certain non-contingent categories (e.g. the definitions of good and evil). A third, almost equally significant, point is the relegation of prophetical authority to matters of contingent knowledge, thus susceptible of modification, even of reversal. It was of course not merely Mosaic authority which was being sacrificed upon the altar of reason, though Moses was the obvious symbol of prophethood for Jew and Muslim. The historicity of this document is irrelevant: what does matter is that the Mosaic law should serve as paradigm of a superseded dispensation, superseded not merely by being chronologically overtaken but also by virtue of its explicitly contingent nature.

For Saadya Gaon (d. 330/942) the eternal, non-contingent quality of the Mosaic law had at all cost to be defended.[1] The structure of his argument is as follows: functional identification of law and community (132: *innamā hiya umma bi-sharāʾiʿihā*); contingencies (*ʿilla*) explicit in prescriptions do not constitute abrogation (*naskh*: 132–3); abrogation is not analogous (*qiyās*) to supplementary prescriptions brought about by changed circumstances (133–5); the basis for acceptance/rejection of Moses, and any other prophet, is not signs/miracles but rather, the reasonableness of

[1] Y. Qāfeḥ (ed.), *R. Saadya ben Yūsuf Al-Fayyūmī: Sefer ha-emūnōt weha-deʿōt*, Jerusalem, 1970, 131–49, esp. 139–42; cf. *QS*, 200 and Schreiner, 'Zur Geschichte der Polemik', 603–6.

his/their claim (*da'wa jā'iza*: 136–7); there are no inconsistencies in scripture (137–9); there is no abrogation in scripture (139–42); the commandments of scripture are corroborated by both reason (*'aql*) and tradition (*naql*), the first prior to, the second posterior to, the utterance of revelation (143–9). It is clearly a question of defining terms: for Saadya if abrogation is not absolutely explicit there can be no question of its taking, or having taken, place. Arguments from contingency (*'illa*) or necessity (*ḍarūra*) may be interpreted not as abrogation, but rather, as licence or special indulgence (*'udhr*, understood as *rukhṣa*) not affecting the character of divine legislation. Moreover, scriptural testimonia like Genesis 22 and Jeremiah 31 may not be read as abrogation, but rather, as evidence of God's original design being revealed as planned: Abraham was only meant to prepare the sacrifice of his son; and the new covenant (*'ahd jadīd*) was only the old one restored.

Abrogation is here, and elsewhere in Jewish polemic, regarded as threatening the historical foundation of God's covenant with Israel, and is thus duly rejected. To the kind of argument adduced by Ibrāhīm al-Naẓẓām, Saadya's reply would be that a true prophet could only decree what accords with non-contingent hence eternal truth. This is of course terminological sleight-of-hand and hardly unexpected in polemical discourse. It is in polemic that the Islamic doctrine of *naskh* had its origins: from the charge of scriptural falsification, the forensic demonstration of true prophethood, and finally, the argument about supersession. The material was traditional, e.g. retention of the Law argued in the gospel of Matthew 5: 17–19, and the respective merits of Abraham and Moses exhibited in Luke 16: 19–31.[1] The specifically Islamic contribution to the tradition was a highly differentiated exegetical lexicon, of which some elements appear in the tract ascribed to al-Naẓẓām and in Saadya's chapter on *naskh*. That the former should be identified as an exponent of *naskh* is not surprising: his critical views on the mechanics of transmission (*tawātur*/*ijmā'*/*ṣaḥāba*, etc.) were recorded elsewhere.[2] His adversary in the abrogation dispute was appropriately a Jew, whose symbolic value depended upon the ambiguity of Arabic *naskh*: supersession and/or hermeneutics. Al-Naẓẓām's contribution was to distinguish between contingent and non-contingent categories of authority, and hence to effect a rationalization of confessional polemic. Thus, the significance of the abrogation discussions is comparable to those of the trinitarian attributes: the extrapolation of concepts from empirical data. For documentation of that process confessional affiliation of the disputants is less important than the evidence

[1] Schoeps, *Judenchristentum*, 156, 372–3; Strecker, *apud* Bauer, *Rechtgläubigkeit* 265–6; Widengren, *Religionsphänomenologie*, 450.

[2] J. van Ess, 'Ein unbekanntes Fragment des Naẓẓām', in *Der Orient in der Forschung* (Festschrift für O. Spies), Wiesbaden, 1967, 170–201; id., *Das Kitāb an-Nakṯ des Naẓẓām und seine Rezeption im Kitāb al-Futyā des Ǧāḥiẓ*, Göttingen, 1972.

of a shared vocabulary. Of some interest in this respect are those locutions containing the term *ʿilla* and employed in what seems to be a sense of 'contingent' (e.g. *liʿilla/li-ʿillat al-amr bihā/al-ashyā' al-muqayyada bil-ʿilal/* and in Saadya: *muʿillan bi-ʿilla*). In Saadya's usage those decrees labelled contingent are not susceptible of abrogation, precisely because their obsolescence is calculated (132–3). For Ibrāhīm it is only those called contingent which may be abrogated. The difference of opinion is terminological, not substantive: in the Arabic philosophical lexicon *ʿilla* may be *causa* or *ratio*, even rule or pretext, and approximately 'occasion' (as indeed, Ar. *sabab*: both 'cause' and 'occasion').[1] Both writers admit that certain prescriptions express, or are the expression of, spatial and temporal limits: whether the extension or abolition of those limits might be described as abrogation is almost a matter of philosophical style. For the further problem of the nature of prophetical authority, Saadya's more rational position reflects a polemical situation different from that of al-Naẓẓām, who was for most of his scholarly life engaged in dispute with (in his opinion) undisciplined exponents of the prophetical Sunna.

From these two areas of contention, trinity and abrogation, the early Muslim community acquired, perhaps accidentally, two symbols of permanent value for its confessional image: the doctrine of divine attributes (*ṣifāt*) and the concept of scriptural authority (*kalām allāh*). The first provided a point of departure for speculative theology, the second a rubric under which several quite disparate notions of authority could be accommodated. A third important area, that of the predestinarian controversy, would undoubtedly yield a comparable symbolism. The studies so far published by van Ess demonstrate the evolution of theological concepts from the often primitive material of traditions (*ḥadīth*).[2] For that development, depicted by van Ess as internal to the Muslim community, it seems not unlikely that extramural polemic contributed something.[3] The result in any case provided a means of tempering the remoteness of an absolutely transcendent deity by making His immediate decision the formative component of every individual human act. The religious anthropology of Islam is an elaboration of that quite extraordinary proximity of God to His creation.

. . . . .

Most of the material analysed in the immediately preceding pages belongs to a recognizable literary type: the dialogue. It is to some extent that

[1] e.g. Tahānawī, *Kitāb Kashshāf iṣṭilāḥāt al-funūn*, Calcutta, 1862, 1036–44, esp. 1038–9; cf. *QS*, 168, and also (?) Van Ess, 'Fragment des Naẓẓām', 171, 186, 193.

[2] *Zwischen Ḥadīṯ und Theologie;* cf. *BSOAS* xxxix (1976) 442–3.

[3] e.g. the Arabic terminology in Abū Qurra's treatise on free-will: Bāshā, *Mayāmir*, 9–22; cf. Graf, *Die arabischen Schriften*, 46–53, 223–38 (IX); Becker, 'Christliche Polemik', 441.

formal criterion which permits description of these sources as polemic, certainly for the examples of public dispute but also for the attenuated epistolary specimens, characterized by the contrapuntal structure 'If you say . . . then I reply . . .'.[1] Of what must be the original form, the '*dialogue devant le prince*', there are several examples in Islamic salvation history, e.g. depicting delegations to the rulers of Byzantium and Ethiopia. The antiquity of the motif is well established, and its employment as vehicle for doctrinal assertions easily documented.[2] The motives (*Geistesbeschäftigungen*) which contributed both to its literary development and to its repeated application were several: to curry imperial/royal favour, to secure court patronage, to advance a cause by the display of wit and erudition. Evolution of the form may be traced from public debate via the symposium to the fictive or epistolary dialogue, though the *Sitz im Leben* of each may well, at different times and in different places, be found in another sequence. The documentary or 'historical' value of such stereotyped materials will always be problematic, but appearance of this particular type in the half-century after establishment of the ʿAbbāsid caliphate (132/750) is appropriate to circumstances attending the transfer of authority and introduction of new procedures for access to that authority.

A second type of polemical literature, less obvious perhaps but only because less explicit than the dialogue, is apocalyptic. Its literary origins are well known, and might be described as the 'Danielic paradigm'. From that model is generated a fairly stable sequence of 'kingdoms' designed to demonstrate first: that political change is historically significant; second: that a world conqueror must be seen as a divine instrument; and third: that conquest so wrought must be interpreted as an episode in the messianic drama.[3] The intellectual pre-conditions of such argument are not merely historical but also, and emphatically, theological, though perhaps not necessarily, or at least originally, monotheist. Its *Sitz im Leben* can probably be identified as the oracle, from which could be traced the *vaticinatio ex eventu/post eventum*, 'prognostic exegesis' (*pesher*), culminating in predictions of cosmic disaster and the irreversible dislocation of the universe, of time, etc. The primary impulse in this kind of literature is

[1] Grunebaum, 'Islam and Hellenism', *Scientia* xliv (Como, 1950) 23 n. 1 (*Islam and Medieval Hellenism*, ch. I).

[2] *EI*, s.v. Ḳayṣar; *QS*, 38–43; cf. Pfister, *Alexander der Große*, 24–35 (Alexander and the Jewish high priest), Isser, *Dositheans*, 5–10 (Ptolemy and the Samaritans), 63–9 (Eulogius and the Samaritans); Dick, 'Théodore Abu Qurra', 324–5, 126–8 (AQ and Ashod), 330–2, 128–9 (AQ and Ma'mūn).

[3] A. Szörenyi, 'Das Buch Daniel, ein kanonisierter Pescher?' *Vetus Testamentum*, Suppl. xv (1966) 278–94; A. Abel, 'Changements politiques et littérature eschatologique dans le monde musulman', *Studia Islamica* ii (1954) 23–43; id., 'L'Apocalypse de Baḥîra et la notion islamique de Mahdî', in *Annuaire de l'Institut de Philologie et Histoire orientale* (Bruxelles) iii (1935) 1–12; D. Flusser, 'The Four empires in the Fourth Sibyl and in the Book of Daniel', *IOS* ii (1972) 148–75; Russell, *Apocalyptic*, 104–39, 178–234.

exegetical and teleological: the interpretation of events as movement towards an identifiable conclusion. That such historiography is outspokenly *heilsgeschichtlich* need hardly be mentioned: its documentary value is not necessarily diminished but certainly altered. Like the polemical dialogue, with its origins in public oratory, the literature of apocalyptic also served a polemical purpose: occasionally tribute to the victorious, usually consolation for the oppressed. Also like the dialogue, the contents of apocalyptic are fairly rigidly stylized.

A third distinct but related literary type is heresiography, of which the formative element is systematic: to the enumeration of errors must correspond a catalogue of their authors. Exposition in the classical Islamic treatises is seldom or never historical, e.g. those of Ashʿarī, Baghdādī, Ibn Ḥazm, and Shahrastānī. It tends, instead, to be schematic and based upon a variety of propositions: (1) numerical (to make up the celebrated total of '73 sects'),[1] (2) *ad hominem* ('schools' generated from the names of individuals by means of a *nisba* suffix), (3) doctrinal (divergent attitudes to specific problems). These organizing principles are usually found in combination, particularly in works like those of Ashʿarī and Shahrastānī, which may be described as descriptive and normative, but not stridently polemical like those of Baghdādī and Ibn Ḥazm. In Shahrastānī, foı example, the 'sects' are described in terms of deviation from four fixed dogmas; in Baghdādī, on the other hand, according to their proximity to the Islamic community.[2] The absence of a historical framework and the proliferation of nominal splinter groups diminish the documentary value of this literature, that is, for historical reconstruction, but not of course for the study of the reductive techniques employed by polemicists to neutralize their opposition. To that end no device could be more effective than the identification of 'heterodoxy' with eccentric, peripheral, and eventually isolated individuals. The evolution of doctrine is there reduced in effect to a series of discrete biographies.

My purpose in adducing this recital of familiar fact is to underline the apologetic character of *historia ecclesiastica*. That several attempts to elucidate the 'origins of Islam' have drawn almost exclusively upon these traditional literary types is well known, and it seems to me that here a serious methodological problem is often ignored.[3] As succinctly as possible: can

[1] Goldziher, 'Le Dénombrement des sectes mohamêtanes', *RHR* xxvi (1892) 129–37 (*GS* ii, 406–14; cf. ii, 345, i, 266–7, 348–50); Isser, *Dositheans*, 11–16, 38, 41, 51, 58–64, 103 for the numbering of Jewish sects.

[2] D. Sourdel, 'La Classification des sectes islamiques dans "Le Kitāb al-Milal" d'al-Šahrastānī', *Studia Islamica* xxxi (1970) 239–47; H. Laoust, 'La Classification des sectes dans "Le Farq" d'al-Baghdadi', *REI* xxix (1961) 19–59; id., 'La Classification des sectes dans l'hérésiographie ashʿarite', Studies . . . Gibb, 377–86.

[3] e.g. F. Nau, *Les Arabes chrétiens de Mésopotamie et de Syrie*, Paris, 1933; Rabin, *Qumran Studies*, 112–30; C. Cahen, 'Note sur l'accueil des chrétiens d'Orient à l'Islam', *RHR* clxvi (1964) 51–8; Crone-Cook, *Hagarism*, esp. 1–38; cf. *BSOAS* xli (1978) 155–6.

a vocabulary of motives be freely extrapolated from a discrete collection of literary stereotypes composed by alien and mostly hostile observers, and thereupon employed to describe, even interpret, not merely the overt behaviour but also the intellectual and spiritual development of helpless and mostly innocent actors? It is one thing, for example, to attempt identification of formulaic and symbolic references in Jewish apocalyptic by recourse to the data of Muslim sources, though such efforts are always incomplete and usually impressionistic.[1] It is, however, quite another to invert that procedure, that is, to supplement and/or modify the data of Muslim sources by recourse to the formulaic and symbolic references found in Jewish apocalyptic.[2] That the Arab expansion of the seventh century should be depicted in contemporary (or later?) Christian apocalyptic (Ps.-Methodios) as a component of the messianic drama is hardly surprising.[3] Similarly, whatever the literary and linguistic (terminological) value of the type '*dialogue devant le prince*', its worth for historical reconstruction is not direct but oblique. That, for example, a Christian or Judaeo-Christian confessional dispute about messianic identity (divine or human) and foundation of the law (whether or not scripture) should be represented as having taken place between a Monophysite patriarch and an Arab governor might well exhibit an effort (Jacobite?) to forestall Melkite advances to the new rulers of Syria.[4] In neither case, it seems to me, are conclusions about the religious views of the conquerors justified.

Material of this sort might be described as the property of a 'minority historiography': the sum of stereotyped literary reactions to political change, to the presence of a new and alien authority. Nor are such apparently neutral accounts as those found in the 'chronicles' of the anonymous Nestorian and the Armenian Sebeos entirely free of that imagery. Allusion in the latter to an alliance between Muhammad and the Jews (here disaffected by eviction from Edessa), and in the former to Arab worship at an Abrahamic sanctuary (here Midian/Medina) do not really admit of historical conclusions.[5] Both *topoi*, Jewish complicity in an unwelcome (!) change of political sovereignty and Abraham as prototypal founder of sanctuaries, belong to the standard ingredients of *historia ecclesiastica*. Their employment in what I have called minority historiography is the more or

[1] e.g. B. Lewis, 'An apocalyptic vision of Islamic history', *BSOAS* xiii (1950) 308–38; id., 'On that day: a Jewish apocalyptic poem on the Arab conquests', in *Mélanges d'Islamologie* (Festschrift A. Abel), Leiden, 1974, 197–200.

[2] Cf. the judicious observations of M. Steinschneider, 'Apocalypsen mit polemischer Tendenz', *ZDMG* xxviii (1874) 627–59; xxix (1875) 162–7.

[3] Crone-Cook, op. cit. 22; cf. Abel, 'Changements politiques', 26–32.

[4] Crone-Cook, op. cit. 11, 14; cf. M. Morony, 'Religious communities in late Sasanian and early Muslim Iraq', *JESHO* xvii (1974) 113–35.

[5] Respectively: Cahen, 'Note sur l'accueil', 52–3 and 53–4; Crone-Cook, op. cit. 4, 24–5, and 6–8.

less arbitrary consequence of confessional distribution. Apart from the difficulty of dating such material (arguments tend to be of an *e silentio* variety) are the more general problems of its bias, its purpose, its public (i.e. *Sitz im Leben*). Most (if not quite all) convey the fact of Arab hegemony in the Fertile Crescent but virtually nothing of the confessional community eventually called Islam. Those few comments which might seem to do so are in fact confessionally indifferent or, at least, not sufficiently distinctive to permit identification of that community: e.g. recognition of the exclusive authority of the Pentateuch, reference to the commandments of Abraham, to Jesus as messiah, and assertions of docetic doctrine. Indeed, the appearance of an army of conquest and of a new ruling class was described in formulaic and symbolic language.

Now, it is precisely the polemical character of these source materials, whether Jewish, Christian, or Muslim, which has consistently stimulated interpretation of the Arab conquest as religiously inspired and the resulting socio-political structure as religiously directed. That this interpretation is entirely the product of 'formulaic and symbolic language' may be an exaggerated claim, but it does describe the quality of available sources. In one sector only, that exhibited in the earliest Arabic chancery papyri, is the religious orientation absent, or at least considerably diminished.[1] The style of those papyri is of course neither descriptive nor literary, and their coexistence with linguistic records of different register and provenance does not pose much of a problem. It might, however, be thought that in the Middle East of late antiquity the only available medium of historical description was the language of salvation history. Every incident of *histoire événementielle* was reported as the expression of a theodicy. Historical reconstruction based upon such reports is probably fruitless. Their interpretation demands a degree of what in another context has been called 'literary competence'.[2] Here, as there, it is the acknowledgement and mastery of a technique, employed in the act of reading as in the act of writing and derived from a set of established conventions. Discovering these is not difficult. Drawing the obvious conclusion from them, that historiography is primarily a form of literature, is a step seldom and then only very reluctantly taken in the field of Islamic studies. For historical discourse the major convention is the stipulated existence of an external referent ('event'), about which an empirical observation can be made: where, when, how, even why 'it happened'. The postulated 'event' does not of course alter the linguistic/literary medium: the language of a historical report is also the language of fiction. The difference between the two is a psychological assumption shared by writer and reader, and it is

[1] Cf. *QS*, 90–3.

[2] J. Culler, *Structuralist Poetics: Structuralism, Linguistics and the Study of Literature*, London, 1975, esp. 113–30.

from that assumption that the historical report acquires significance, is deemed worthy of preservation and transmission.[1]

A number of shared assumptions, not only about the 'event' but also about its interpretation, characterizes the source materials for a history of the 'origins of Islam'. From the foregoing sketch of literary types it ought to be clear that there can be no question of a neutral or 'objective' source. Each witness, regardless of its confessional alignment, exhibits a similar, if not altogether identical, concern to understand the theodicy. Here, of course, the reductive properties of analogy must be taken into consideration, and the (apparent) uniformity of 'events' seen as a consequence of the uniform language of their interpretation.[2] As evidence of linguistic and literary continuity, of the adaptation of stylistic convention and symbolic mode, these materials may indeed be regarded as 'sources'. As witness to event they are more than a little suspect. What they do not, and cannot, provide is an account of the 'Islamic' community during the 150 years or so between the first Arab conquests and the appearance, with the *sīra–maghāzī* narratives, of the earliest Islamic literature.

. . . . .

In Muslim terminology the word *fitna* comprehends a fairly extensive semantic field generally reducible to the notion of communal fragmentation/disintegration/dissolution. Its scriptural employment in the sense of 'ordeal' as well as its use in apocalyptic to designate an aspect of the eschaton would seem to be reflexes of the primary significance. From the several traditions relating the events of the classical *fitna* ('Alī and Mu'āwiya) it is clear that the issue was one of political authority, not religious doctrine. Such sparse mention as the latter achieved (none of the extant traditions can be dated to less than a century after the events) is limited to depicting intervention of the *qurrā'* and the role of *qur'ān* as arbiter in the dispute.[3] As preserved and transmitted, the account might be read as a dispute about sources (*uṣūl*) of authority, though that interpretation must be conceded to reflect its period of composition (late second/eighth century). A similar dislocation, of a kind which could be attributed to interpolation, may be seen in the accounts of most early 'heresiarchs'. The dislocation is one between the substance of dispute, invariably about the office of *imām*, and the terms in which the quarrel was reported, often of an emphatically doctrinal character. In the well-known letter of 'Abdallāh b. Ibāḍ (*c.* 81/700) to the caliph 'Abdalmalik the argument for rejection of Umayyad authority turns upon a moral assessment of the incumbent,

[1] R. Barthes, 'Historical discourse', in M. Lane, *Structuralism: a Reader*, London, 1970, 145–55.
[2] Von Rad, *Theology* i, 105–28, esp. 107 n. 3 (citing Troeltsch), ii, 99–125.
[3] E. Petersen, ''Ali and Mu'āwiyah: the rise of the Umayyad caliphate 656–661', *Acta Orientalia* xxiii (1959) 157–96.

illustrated by the contrast between on the one hand Muhammad, Abū Bakr, and ʿUmar, and on the other ʿUthmān, Muʿāwiya, and Yazīd. That the whole is introduced by an assertion of scripture as the basis of right conduct might be understood as evidence of an *uṣūl* controversy.[1] Approximately the same argument was employed for the inverse proposition in the *Kitāb al-Irjā'* of Ḥasan b. Muḥammad b. al-Ḥanafiyya (*c.* 100/719): there the scriptural theophany becomes the basis for rejection of extremist (Saba'-iyya) claims for a Shīʿī *imām* and for reserving judgement on the caliphates of Abū Bakr and ʿUmar. In both documents *fitna* signifies a crisis in the concept of authority; in both explicit appeal is made to the text of revelation.[2]

Related to that process of depicting political controversy by reference to theological doctrine is the use made of such figures as Maʿbad al-Juhanī (d. 83/702), Ghaylān al-Dimashqī (d. 125/743), and Jahm b. Ṣafwān (d. 128/746): their historiographical manipulation in the interests of a tidy catalogue of errors has been demonstrated by van Ess in a series of remarkable studies.[3] Political rebellion of variable and often uncertain origin is retailed in terms of doctrinal conflict: theological positions later found untenable were thus relegated to 'original' heterodoxy by identification or at least association with known insurgents. That kind of analysis may go some way towards dispelling the widespread view that in Islamic history political and religious expression are indistinguishable. Concern for survival of the community (*umma*) may indeed have acquired a 'religious' connotation, but probably not the complexities of dogmatic theology. It was a conscious historiographical metaphor that made heretics of rebels.

Definition of the community whose survival these sources disclose as imperative is problematic. Such material as can be culled from the preislamic past reveals a vague concept of *dīn al-ʿarab* derived from a common socio-economic experience (nomadism), a shared folklore (*ayyām al-'arab*), and a lingua franca (*ʿarabiyya*). Political and geographical factors appear to have been very unstable indeed: one sociologist has proposed the epithet *Kulturnation*, as contrasted with *Staatsnation* (a stage achieved only with the advent of Islam).[4] However plausible, the sources for such a hypothesis are entirely Islamic and belong to the traditional material of salvation history. There is a further consideration: whether this particular societal

[1] R. Rubinacci, 'Il califfo ʿAbd al-Malik b. Marwān e gli Ibāḍiti', *Annali Istituto Universitario Orientali di Napoli* v (1953) 99–121.

[2] Van Ess, 'Das *Kitāb Al-Irǧā'* des Ḥasan B. Muḥammad B. Al-Ḥanafiyya', *Arabica* xxi (1974) 20–52.

[3] Van Ess, 'Maʿbad Al-Ǧuhanī', in *Islamwissenschaftliche Abhandlungen* (Festschrift F. Meier), Wiesbaden, 1974, 49–77; id., 'Les Qadarites et la Ġailānīya de Yazīd III', *Studia Islamica* xxxi (1970) 269–86; id., 'Ḍirār b. ʿAmr und die "Cahmīya": Biographie einer vergessenen Schule', *Der Islam* xliii (1967) 241–79, and xliv (1968) 1–70, 318–20.

[4] Grunebaum, 'Arab unity before Islam', 5–23, esp. 18 ff.; Bravmann, *Spiritual Background*, 39–122 ('Heroic motives').

evolution can be envisaged as one from a limited and voluntary association (*Interessengemeinschaft*) towards an unlimited and involuntary society (*Lebensgemeinschaft*) or vice versa.[1] The former is what might be called the standard view and corresponds more or less to the Muslim historiographical tradition. The latter is a hypothetical alternative adduced here in support of the following proposition: that the emergence of sectarian (voluntary) associations, clerical (and other) élites, and eventually a representative ('orthodox') majority, might be seen as secondary and posterior to the Arab conquests. What must of course be explained is the transition from a concept of 'community' as (primarily) ethnic, social, and political to one of 'community' as confessional, eschatological, even metaphysical. The exercise is largely lexical and, as I have suggested, involves locating the intervention of sectarian symbols in otherwise neutral or profane historical accounts. I should define that transition as one from nation-state (*Staatsnation*) to culture-group (*Kulturnation*), thus inverting the process alluded to above.

Reference to 'community' as *umma* can only be Islamic usage, and owing to the chronology of available sources it is impossible to assess the gradual impingement of that concept upon such comparatively neutral terms as *qawm*, *nās*, *ahl*, and *jamā'a*. Some differences in the use of *umma* itself are discernible but hardly datable.[2] The term appears always to designate the community in the sense of permanent congregation, even of sacred sodality, but unlike *jamā'a* (which may indicate all three), never in the sense of *ad hoc* assembly.[3] Such usage could suggest a terminological calque, but it is worth recalling that the *imām* presided not only over the *umma* but in the assembly for ritual prayer. A direct link between *umma* and the sacral 'congregation' imagery of the Judaeo-Christian tradition cannot be established, and it seems not unreasonable to suppose that the earliest connotation of the term was secular.[4] Functional designations of community, abundantly attested in the sectarian vocabulary of Islam (e.g. Khawārij/Mu'tazila/Munāfiqūn/Anṣār/Muhājirūn), survived the separation of 'orthodoxy' from 'heterodoxy' only in the form of Muslimūn and Mu'minūn. Selection of these, in every likelihood also in origin sectarian or partisan epithets, may be attributed to that antonomastic process by which *umma* designates, from any and every vantage point, the entire

[1] Cf. Widengren, *Religionsphänomenologie*, 594–634.

[2] Cf., however, W. Watt, *Muhammad at Medina*, Oxford, 1956, 238–49.

[3] Goldziher, 'Beiträge zur Literaturgeschichte der Šī'a und der sunnitischen Polemik', *SKAW* lxxviii (1874) 446–7 (*GS* i, 268–9); cf. Rabin, *Qumran Studies*, 37–52 (*'edah* and *qahalā* as contrasted with *moshav*).

[4] Cf. D. Flusser, 'The Dead Sea Sect and pre-Pauline Christianity', *Scripta Hiero.* iv, 227–36 (extension of Temple imagery); Kosmala, *Hebräer*, 44–75, 117–34, 277–81, 345–85 (messianic and eschatological imagery); J. Barr, *The Semantics of Biblical Language* Oxford, 1961, 119–29 (*qahal* and *ekklesia* compared and contrasted).

community.[1] Such a process may be envisaged as taking place in either one of two ways: (1) from specific (*nomen proprium*) to generic appellative, as in the post-Biblical Hebrew adaptation of Apiqoros (Epicurus) for 'heretic' (*min*);[2] (2) from generic (*nomen adjectivum*) to personal or proper name, as in the emergence of an eponym Ebion from Hebrew *ebionim* ('poor', cf. *ptokos*) as designation of one or more Judaeo-Christian sects.[3] In Muslim heresiography the first of these devices is well documented by the proliferation, noticed above, of 'sects' derived from personal names plus the *nisba* suffix. Though I am unable to adduce instances of eponyms generated by functional designations, it is clear that these exhibit a process of centripetal concentration, in the course of which general characteristics (political, social, or confessional) widespread in the community were attached to specific groups. That procedure for describing, and eventually naming, confessional associations is illustrated by the epithets Essene and Therapeutes.[4] The inherently arbitrary character of such naming cannot of course be overlooked: it is seldom that epithets so derived provide adequate descriptions of the group. It is more often one attribute, say, an initiation rite, a liturgical expression, or a public posture of some sort which is stressed at the expense of other equally, or more, important qualities. The *locus classicus* for such problems is identification of the Qumran community: from the evidence of its halakhic stringency and of its practice of prognostic scriptural exegesis, two rather different images are generated, neither of which provides, incidentally, unambiguous corroboration of the sources which describe Essenes and Therapeutae.[5] Similarly, such community designations as Qumranic Benei Berit and Syriac Christian Benai Qyama, if they were general epithets, might be thought to fall somewhat short of conveying the entire aim of their respective confessions.[6]

Whether *umma* might represent a functionally specific epithet generalized, either by extension or by elimination, to comprehend the whole community is certainly arguable: its *nisba* form in Muslim scripture (Q. 2: 78, 3: 20, 3: 75, 7: 157–8, 62: 2) connotes an exclusivist or separatist position of some kind (if only as *laikos/gentilis*).[7] To what extent its relation

[1] e.g. Ṭabarī, *Annales*, 1/3336 on the separate designation of *muslimūn* and *mu'minūn* among the supporters of both 'Alī and Mu'āwiya during the *fitna*.

[2] Fischel, *Rabbinic Literature*, 4 n. 48, 10 nn. 82–92, 14 n. 113, 40 n. 52.

[3] Klijn-Reinink, *Patristic Evidence*, 19–43; cf. A. Paul, *Écrits de Qumran et sectes juives aux premiers siècles de l'Islam*, Paris, 1969, 117–19.

[4] G. Vermes, *Post-Biblical Jewish Studies*, Leiden, 1975, 8–36; cf. *BSOAS* xxxix (1976) 436–8.

[5] L. Schiffman, *The Halakhah at Qumran*, Leiden, 1975, esp. 1–21, 134–6; cf. *BSOAS* xl (1977) 137–9; and Vermes, op. cit. 37–49.

[6] Murray, *Symbols of Church and Kingdom*, 13–17; cf. Islamic *ahl al-sunna* (*wa'l-jamā'a*), *ahl al-qibla*.

[7] *QS*, 53–4, 63; cf. Isser, *Dositheans*, 85, 87, 108–9.

to *'ammei ha-aretz* is symbolic or etymological or both need only be mentioned: the pariah concept of that locution may never have attained the status of a sectarian designation, but did none the less convey the fact of liturgical and social exclusion.[1] The employment of *umma* in the 'constitution of Medina' (*Sīra* i, 501–4) might be thought to indicate just such an act of separation from Ḥijāzī tribal society (that is, an exclusive rather than inclusive notion).

That a term of obloquy (cf. 'gentiles') could become a confessional designation employed by the sectaries themselves hardly requires demonstration. On the other hand, the very use of *umma* (as contrasted with, say, *qawm*, *nās*, or *ahl*) might suggest separation not from a tribal background but rather, from an environment dominated by one or more ecclesiastical organizations. It was the task of Islamic salvation history to depict the former: thus, survival of the community must depend upon suppression of those traditional forces, tribal and pagan (polytheist) which threatened it. That those forces should eventually be labelled not merely hostile but 'heterodox' required formulating the community 'foundation event' as a theophany. The result was primitive but effective, as my analysis of the *sīra–maghāzī* literature was intended to reveal. To gain acceptance for that theophany was the burden of the earliest polemic: first, as the next and natural stage in the evolution of monotheist salvation history; second, as the logical reply to demands for legitimation of civil authority. Elaboration of the 'foundation event' followed traditional (archetypal) patterns in conformity with the only linguistic/literary medium available for such expression: the language of *historia ecclesiastica*. The final product of that elaboration was the *umma*, a concept sufficiently amorphous to endure the vicissitudes of long and bitter dispute. The definitive guarantee of its survival was the Sunnī interpretation of 'community' not as *Staatsnation* but as *Kulturnation*, not as an exercise in practical politics (*Lebensgemeinschaft*) but as an articulation of exemplary ethics (*Interessengemeinschaft*). Of this articulation the instrument was not, in my opinion, the existence (undoubted) of an autocratic but comparatively inefficient political and military establishment, but rather, the persistence of pious and scholarly individuals exposed to the several ideologies of what I have called the sectarian milieu. It was by the membership of this clerical élite (*'ulamā'*/*fuqahā'*) that the Islamic version of salvation history was composed, the prophetical Sunna compiled, Muslim scripture edited, and dogmatic theology expounded. It would not, in fact, be an exaggeration to speak of a professional monopoly of those various agencies responsible for the expression of 'normative' Islam.

[1] A. Oppenheimer, *The 'Am Ha-Aretz: a Study in the Social History of the Jewish People in the Hellenistic–Roman Period*, Leiden, 1977, esp. 67–117; cf. *BSOAS* xli (1978) 150–1.

The operation of an élite is reflected in, and very probably answerable for, the structure of the *uṣūl* controversies, reducible for the most part to the binary terms *riwāya* (*traditio*) and *dirāya* (*ratio*).[1] I have referred in my second chapter to the role of this élite in transmission of the prophetical Sunna, its monopoly of literacy and other techniques for the dissemination of learning. Of its socio-political function as midwife to the *umma* the sources bear unanimous witness, being themselves the product of that élite. Evidence for the evolution I have proposed is thus unavoidably tendentious: literary remains attest the activity of a literate class. It might not be superfluous to add that from these remains it is logically impossible to infer more about 'Islam' than is or could be characteristic of a minority phenomenon. Now, that may be (and is generally and tacitly interpreted as) an accident of historical preservation. It may, on the other hand, be one of the few 'facts' of early Islamic history: namely, that the religious movement later identified with the state began as the sectarian expression of a scholarly élite.

One, perhaps the only, advantage of that proposition is that it can be used to explain the curious doctrinal precipitate from the Judaeo-Christian tradition which became the theological superstructure of the movement. That dogmatic theology is anyway the property not of popular worship but of scholarship must of course be acknowledged. For Muslim theology, however, that concession is inadequate: its content, its very name (*kalām*), its literary format, are typically the products of symposium, seminar, and academy.[2] That argument is the subject of my final chapter, but one observation will be appropriate here: the theology of Islam is likely to have been formulated in a pluralist and cosmopolitan society, uninhibited by the presence of an authoritarian establishment. By way of illustration one need only recall the coexistence of several halakhic 'schools' (*madhāhib*), the degrees of tolerated divergence in such dogmas as those concerning the divine attributes, predestination, and the eternity of the Quranic text, the recognized variation in epistemological hierarchies or in the qualifications for the imamate. What has been described by Weber (more or less accurately) as the 'patrimonial structure' of Islamic society did not preclude a considerable margin for disagreement on basic intellectual issues.[3] Now, this image of a tolerant, pluralist society corresponds to the transmitted portrait of the early ʿAbbāsid period, but there is no valid reason to suppose that circumstances were tangibly different for the preceding 150 years. It was naturally the aim of Muslim salvation history to depict the appearance of 'heresy' as fragmentation of an earlier and

[1] *QS*, 154, 227.

[2] For a recent description: van Ess, 'The beginnings of Islamic theology', in *The Cultural Context of Medieval Learning* (eds. Murdoch–Sylla), Dordrecht, 1975, 87–111.

[3] Turner, *Weber and Islam*, 75–92, 171–84.

absolutely monolithic unity. In so doing it merely conformed to type. Equally, if not more, plausible is a model illustrating 'orthodoxy' as the convergence of several quite disparate sources of theological and ideological inspiration.

Such a model was employed by Bauer in his description of Christian origins.[1] There particular attention is drawn to the claim of polemicists (especially Eusebius) to have drawn their doctrinal interpretations from writings preserved from Apostolic times and transmitted without interruption 'up to the present'. To students of early Islamic history the allegation is familiar (*scil.* proliferation of the *isnād*): it was by means of that device (*scil. tawātur/ittiṣāl*) that the legitimation of time could be won for views currently held. Orthodoxy was served by the mechanism of retrojection ('ancient writings').[2] The illusion of antiquity, and hence of authority, is thus easily generated, and like pseudepigraphy, consciously linked with key figures from the past. An example is the figure of Paul, whose 'apostolic authority' could be, and was, pressed into the service of such diametrically opposed views of ecclesiastical organization as those of Marcion and Ignatius of Antioch.[3] For the latter emphasis upon the necessity of 'ecclesia' (episcopal hierarchy) not only as the vessel of tradition but as the framework of daily worship is remarkably similar to stress upon survival of the *umma* found in every form of Muslim polemic.[4] A common concern for continuity is thus symbolically expressed in the semantic evolution of 'community': from voluntary association to a gradual identification with the political 'establishment'. For the Christian community the agent in that evolution was of course Rome, by that time the traditional paradigm of centralized and rationalized authority. The transfer of means and methods characteristic of civil authority to ecclesiastical authority (e.g. interventions in Corinth and Antioch) was neither difficult nor unexpected.[5] These were both spiritual and material and exhibit a self-consciousness in political affairs which from the second century determined the course of Roman Catholicism:

'Es ist ja eigentlich ein merkwürdiges Spiel der Geschichte, dass das abendländische Rom dazu ausersehen war, gleich zu Beginn den bestimmenden Einfluss auf eine Religion, deren Wiege im Orient gestanden, auszuüben, um ihr diejenige Gestalt zu geben, in der sie Weltgeltung gewinnen sollte. Aber als weltverachtende Jenseitsreligion und unerbittliche Lebensordnung eines himmelentstammten Übermenschentums oder als komplizierter Mysterienkult für religiöse und geistige Feinschmecker oder als enthusiastischer Überschwang, der heute anschwillt und morgen abebbt, hätte das Christentum eine solche niemals erlangt.'[6]

[1] Bauer, *Rechtgläubigkeit und Ketzerei*, 6–133 (regional analysis), 134–242 (topical analysis); cf. Strecker's second addendum on the reception of Bauer's thesis, 288–306.

[2] Bauer, op. cit. 150–61, 182–7.

[3] Ibid. 215–30.

[4] Ibid. 65–80; cf. also Barrett, 'The Epistles of Ignatius' esp. 221–2, 243–4; Aune, *Cultic Setting*, 136–65.

[5] Bauer, op. cit. 99–133.

[6] Ibid. 242.

Thus Bauer: the argument is Hegelian and can be even more succinctly formulated as Wellhausen's celebrated dictum on the foundation of the Umayyad state: 'dass die Geschichte eine legitimirende Kraft besitzt, dass der Staat seiner eigenen Raison, dem Zweck der Erhaltung und Mehrung seiner Macht folgt, und dass die bestehende Regierung sich schwer von ihm unterscheiden lässt.'[1] According to that view 'orthodoxy' is not a doctrinal but a political emblem, signifying compromise. The 'orthodox' community was simply the one which survived, its spokesmen that clerical élite whose position was least intransigent, its theology the neutralized precipitate of traditional polemic. The utility of Bauer's model for analysis of Islamic origins is twofold: (1) by postulating the *coexistence* of variant and competing confessional expressions, each potentially and, from a local point of view perhaps actually, 'orthodox'; (2) by assuming the *prior existence* of a political structure within which the emergence in fact of one of those expressions as 'orthodox' (viz. survival as compromise) could have meaning. It was primarily a question of technique and of example: Roman statecraft and the imperial tradition provided the framework and the security essential to the development of voluntary confessional associations.

Now, the argument that the Hellenist/Roman/Byzantine legacy was a major formative factor in the development of Islam is a familiar one.[2] Its several articulations, however divergent in other respects, have in common this assumption: that the Arab 'movement' (communal consolidation/military conquest/territorial expansion) was religiously motivated. 'Islam' was thus an Arabian datum later modified by external circumstances: the general historical problem is formulated as an 'encounter' (of peoples, religions, cultures) and solved by recourse to a tabulation (of debts and credits, victories and defeats). Documentation for this argument is found in the Muslim version of monotheist salvation history and in the literature of inter-confessional polemic. There the entire spectrum of sectarian symbols is also found, arranged to suggest that the new 'orthodoxy' represented the natural and logical supersession of earlier dispensations. Whether it is legitimate to extrapolate from this catalogue of traditional symbols principles of priority and sequence seems to me very questionable. But only in that way is it possible to argue that Arabian Islam contained a nucleus of basic tenets later modified by encounter with the outside

[1] J. Wellhausen, *Das arabische Reich und sein Sturz*, Berlin, 1960 (1902), 38–40, assent to which hardly entails acceptance of the author's opening gambit (p. 1): 'Die politische Gemeinschaft des Islam erwuchs aus der religiösen', for which assertion curiously little support is found in the monograph itself.

[2] e.g. Becker, 'Der Islam als Problem' and 'Der Islam im Rahmen einer allgemeinen Kulturgeschichte', *Islamstudien* i, 1–39 (but in fact all of this volume); Grunebaum, 'The convergence of cultural traditions in the Mediterranean area', *Diogenes* lxxi (1970) 1–17, and 'The sources of Islamic civilization', *Der Islam* xlvi (1970) 1–54 (reprinted as chs. VI and VII in id., *Islam and Medieval Hellenism*); cf. *BSOAS* xl (1977) 395; Crone–Cook, *Hagarism*, 41–70 and 73–148 (i.e. pts. II 'Whither Antiquity?' and III 'The Collision').

world. Reconstruction of that nucleus from the sources available is a speculative exercise. An alternative approach to these same sources would be to assume the persistence of Judaeo-Christian sectarianism in the Fertile Crescent under Arab political hegemony, the establishment of a *modus vivendi* between the new authority and the indigenous communities, and the distillation of a doctrinal precipitate (a common denominator) acceptable initially to an academic élite, eventually an emblem of submission (*islām*) to political authority.

My two examples of terminological transfer were adduced in order to illustrate that process of distillation: the neutralizing of Christian trinitarian dogma by its reduction to a general concept of divine attributes, and of Jewish scriptural dogma by its abrogation on the grounds of a malicious forgery. In both cases the substance of the legacy was preserved in forms sufficiently innocuous to be adopted as fresh sectarian insignia. There is, in my opinion, nothing of Islamic dogma (*kalām*) and very little of Islamic doctrine (*fiqh*) whose genesis cannot be described in approximately the same manner. But the most significant factor in any such instance is linguistic: the formulation for the first time in Arabic of dogma and doctrine irrespective of its confessional bias. As much as any other, it was this process of converting into Arabic the traditional content of Judaeo-Christian monotheism that made of that medium the *lingua sacra* of Islam.[1] That Arabic was anyway the language of the political establishment does not really require to be demonstrated. From that position its employment in sectarian dispute was a logical, even necessary, step: how else might confessional minorities gain access to authority? As with the other developments which culminated in the religious definition of Islam, this linguistic operation was the activity of one or more élites. It is tempting to interpret the entire problem of 'Islamic origins' in this light, that is, as a linguistic reformulation (transfer) of tradition. I have elsewhere described the composition of Muslim scripture from collections of prophetical *logia* as an example of linguistic transfer.[2] There, a characteristic of the finished product was its allusive or 'referential' style, which could be understood as evidence of just such linguistic transfer, a kind of procedural 'lag' resulting from impatience, uncertainty, or simply ignorance. The phenomenon is of course a general one: from Hebrew to Greek to Aramaic, etc., of which the Arabic rendering exhibits only a final stage. Because linguistic transfer is always a semantic problem, an exegetical element is inevitable, though I am inclined to read the Arabic material as witness primarily to a *fait accompli*: a reductive process already achieved in Judaeo-Christian polemic.[3]

[1] *QS*, 93–106.

[2] *QS*, 33, 47–52.

[3] Cf. Barr, *Biblical Language*, 25–45 (caveats), 206–62, 282–7 (TWNT); and Fischel, *Rabbinic Literature*, n. 113 (pp. 114–15) on the antonomastic employment of 'Epicurus' in Graeco-Roman rhetorical usage.

Identification of the earliest Islamic community may thus be regarded as the investigation of process rather than of structure. The process in question may be envisaged as twofold: (1) linguistic transfer/adaptation of *topos*/theologoumenon/symbol to produce an instrument of communication and dispute (lingua franca); (2) distribution of these elements as confessional insignia (sectarian syndrome). At the beginning of this chapter I spoke of 'selection' from the monotheist compendium as being in all likelihood arbitrary, hardly deliberate. The extent to which choice was at all a factor in the distribution of confessional insignia is of course problematic: the very existence of a technical lexicon makes its use inevitable. The translation of word, and with it concept, into Arabic exhibits the one, perhaps only, class of 'fact' unambiguously attested in the earliest literature. Some impression of the awkwardness occasioned by such 'facts' can be seen in the Islamic accommodation (or, rather, non-accommodation) of Christological concepts like messiah, virgin birth, and docetism. An instance of successful reception, on the other hand, would be the differentiation of contingent and non-contingent categories of revealed prescription employed in the Islamic elaboration of *naskh*. A compromise, and withal something of a puzzle, is exemplified in the Arabic adaptation of vocabulary pertinent to the problem of *liberum arbitrium*.

An alternative, indeed the traditional, approach to the formation of a theological lexicon in Arabic is the detection of an ancient and indigenous conceptual stock, locally and gradually modified by the revelation of Islam.[1] *Loci probantes* for the alleged pre-islamic usage are also traditional, and too familiar to require further comment. Of more value, however, and a particular merit of Bravmann's researches, are examples of parallel (synchronous) employment of the same expression in secular and theological contexts, e.g. *wajh* as 'soul'/'life' (to be sacrificed in battle)[2] and, as remarked above in the trinitarian treatise of Abū Qurra, synonymous with *uqnūm* (hypostasis). It is, of course, precisely that kind of conceptual link which facilitates the introduction of a neologism, and in this particular instance, extension of a theological vocabulary. It is none the less a move of some distance, if that was in fact the path of the semantic development in question, from *wajh* as 'soul' to *wajh* as 'hypostasis', and I should be most reluctant to dismiss the agency of Christian polemic in this evolution.

Now, the collection of confessional insignia which eventually crystallized as 'Islam' does, despite its clearly heterogenetic origins, exhibit a reasonable degree of internal consistency, but owing almost certainly to the limited scope of Judaeo-Christian polemic. The range was hardly extended by inclusion of those items (e.g. creation, causality, dualism, and rejection

[1] e.g. Bravmann, *Spiritual Background*, esp. 1–198; id., *Studies in Semitic Philology*, Leiden, 1977, 434–64.

[2] Bravmann, *Studies*, 434–54.

of prophecy) later, and no doubt correctly, ascribed in Muslim heresiography to disputes with opponents nominally outside the Judaeo-Christian sphere (e.g. *zanādiqa, dahriyyūn, falāsifa*). It seems thus difficult to argue that the identity of the Islamic community (*umma*) was significantly confessional, despite the accretion of sectarian insignia. These were traditional emblems derived from standard *topoi*. Other, more significant, features could have been ethnic or linguistic, though the community's single most distinctive property was its political autonomy. That of course was the product of territorial conquest, and confessionally indifferent. But its historical description is formulaic, generated by polemic, and designed as a chapter in the monotheist tradition. It is unlikely that it could have been recorded in any other way.

IV

EPISTEMOLOGY

THE literature produced by a confessional community reflects not only historical image and structural insignia, but also the cognitive categories acknowledged, however tacitly, by its members. The fact of having composed a history of its origins, undertaken a recension of its scripture, and compiled an anthology of apostolic dicta, reveals a concept of authority based upon precedent. *Exempla* preserved and transmitted from the 'past' (whether or not fictive) may be the deposit of an antiquarian impulse, but also witness to a concern for present and future. There the impulse is paradigmatic: what was preserved is (thus) what can be known. If it does not logically follow that what could be known has (thus) been preserved, it is none the less true that this proposition characterizes well enough the Muslim emphasis upon precedent. From one point of view that emphasis is not confessionally distinctive, being the common property of all monotheist sects and a major, if not the only, premiss of salvation history. The components of that literary type are well known, and I attempted in my first chapter an exposition of its Islamic form. The evolution from a narrative to a paradigmatic style (second chapter) may be described as ahistorical, formally though not substantively. Entirely ahistorical is the paraenetic/liturgical style of scripture as well as the schematic presentation of heresiography (second and third chapters). Such compositions as are found in polemical literature (e.g. dialogue and apocalyptic) could be called pseudohistorical (also third chapter). Now, despite these qualifications it must be admitted that the primary concern of Islamic literature is with the past. Even the utterly timeless quality of scripture was neutralized by the several varieties of exegesis, each designed to provide a temporal and spatial context for revelation. The concerted achievement of the literary types outlined here was to describe the *umma* as a product of theophany, its course as divinely guided, and its enemies as heretics or infidels. My intention in this final chapter is to examine the epistemological implications of that achievement: to ask about the role of that historically fixed theophany in the organization of communal and individual experience.

The concepts of legitimation and redemption, familiar to every student of comparative religion, are sociologically archetypal and more or less constant in the analysis of monotheist faiths.[1] For the study of Islam their realizations may conveniently be reduced to three types:

(*a*) *nomos*
(*b*) *numen*
(*c*) *ecclesia*.

Under the first rubric (*nomos*) I would interpret legitimation as theodicy based upon a public epiphany eventually deposited as the document of revelation. 'Scripture' is understood to record a single historical act: the transfer by angelic mediation of God's decree from a celestial to a terrestrial register. Acknowledgement of that act, temporally and spatially, entails a commitment to the principal implication of salvation history: the revelation of divine purpose in the affairs of men. The complementary notion of redemption is thus also historically directed: the existential task of the believer is the ritual submission to prescription set out in scripture. Scripture is, however, timeless (though manifested in time), eternal hence immutable: acknowledgement of its prescriptive authority is thus, simply, recognition of (divine) precedent, of a unique expression of God's will. '*Nomos*' exhibits a category of legislation that includes neither the possibility of appeal nor the promise of change: the law may be disobeyed, it may be forgotten, but it cannot be altered. Its 'historical' character is thus severely restricted: assent to the linear progression of time entails assent to the possibility of modification, of repeal, and of further disclosures. A concept of 'history' that does not admit of such movement can hardly be defined as historical, but might rather be described as poetic: the lyrical record of a single encounter, carefully depicted and nostalgically recalled, but not seriously regarded as susceptible of repetition.

Under the second rubric (*numen*) I would subsume legitimation as the product of a private vision, the consequence perhaps of intellectual vigour or of ascetic discipline. There is here no question of historical location: the achievement is personal, timeless in the sense that the precise circumstances of the epiphany do not really matter. In this context the eternity of divine utterance, being always and anywhere available, does not conflict with the alleged historicity of its public manifestation. Redemption may then be interpreted as attainment to absolute wisdom (*gnosis*), historically unmediated and personally vouchsafed. The social expression of this achievement, a more or less private experience, is impossible or at least difficult to assess, and thus incurs (in the biographies of mystics) the charge of ritual laxity or even antinomianism. The existential task of the believer is a posture of contemplative prayer, in solitude or as novice/member of a monastic association, virtually autonomous in matters of

[1] e.g. P. Berger, *The Social Reality of Religion*, London, 1973, esp. 61–87, 177–90; Werblowsky-Bleeker, *Types of Redemption*, esp. 13–25 (V. Maag), 247 (citing H. Schär).

recruitment. '*Numen*' exhibits thus a category of religious activity free of public scrutiny and unaccountable to the demands of public authority. As a category of religious expression it may be described as ahistorical, unconcerned with the temporal and spatial location of deity, though not oblivious to the formal properties (imagery and phonology) of Muslim scripture. In that respect the lyrical record of the theophany is stressed, its quality as historical document virtually ignored.

Under the third rubric (*ecclesia*), finally, I understand legitimation as communal membership, initially an act of voluntary association, eventually a position conferred by birth. The aim of the act is solidarity, and the introduction of a theophany posterior to the social formation. In this instance the historical record is theologically neutral, and the legitimation derived therefrom an expression of anthropological security. If it is permissible to employ the term 'redemption' in this context, that notion consists basically in the acceptance of authority, for individual as well as for social reasons. Within that framework the existential task becomes a matter of cultivating and preserving communal, hence individual, identity, and remains so even after incorporation of the theophany. Here the concept 'precedent' need not be related to a single foundation-event, but may, rather, signify the collective memory of the association. Moreover, its preservation may, but need not, be 'historical', that is, as a sequence of temporally and logically connected events. Reference to the past is paradigmatic and retroflexive, again an expression of nostalgia. However, a sense of duration can be derived from the fact of the community's survival, and hence the possibility of development, of altered circumstances demanding a redefinition of the community. It is here, if anywhere, that the Islamic notion of 'history' may be seen as process, witness to (potentially) constructive change, not merely proof of the corruption of an ideal state (*nomos*).

It is no doubt hazardous to extend this admittedly rough typology beyond the limit of its function as a principle of literary criticism. The varieties of Muslim historiography can certainly be distributed under the proposed rubrics, an exercise stressing morphological rather than thematic qualities. My analysis of the *sīra–maghāzī* literature was indeed undertaken to that end, and may have disclosed the range of stylistic variation in that particular corpus. There the dominant cognitive category was unquestionably '*ecclesia*', though it is also precisely in the composition of that literature that the impingement of '*nomos*' can be located. In the paradigmatic style of the Sunna '*nomos*' is dominant, and the category of '*ecclesia*' restated as an etymon (*umma* : *imām*). Of what I have designated '*numen*' there is in that literature hardly a trace: individual conversion to Islam is depicted as ritual gesture and group conversion as the fruit of diplomatic negotiation. In a much cited report (Waraqa b. Nawfal) even Muhammad's private epiphany was described as reception of the Mosaic Law (*Sīra* i, 238: *al-nāmūs* (!) *al-akbar alladhī jā'a Mūsā*). Altercation with Jews and Christians turned usually upon the form and content of 'scripture' (*scil. nomos*), with polytheists upon their fears of political and social disorder (*scil. ecclesia*). Polemic aimed at unwelcome variations in personal religious experience (*scil. numen*) is restricted in these accounts to the *ḥanīf* phenomena, and then more often than not in terms denoting a breach of communal solidarity.

The important exception to these patterns of Islamic salvation history is of course Ṣūfī literature, in which conventional notions of intellectual and spiritual authority are challenged by a radical gnostic epistemology (*numen*). Standard sectarian expressions, on the other hand, exhibit extreme formulations either of communal (e.g. Khawārij, Shī'a) or of scriptural (e.g. Mu'tazila) authority. This impression is as much the product of heresiographical symbolism as of historical realia, and thus of greater utility in source analysis than for historical reconstruction.[1] That entails acknowledgement of a 'fact' already indicated: we are dealing perforce with a minority phenomenon. It is not unlikely that the religious experience of the majority in the early history of Islam is reflected in the (admittedly later) Ṣūfī literature which, however arcane, includes a great deal of what was by the clerical élite often and disparagingly described as popular piety, superstition, even heresy. Naturally, the cognitive categories in my proposed typology cannot be regarded as mutually exclusive, though the possible (existential) combinations do not affect the (theoretical) structure of Muslim epistemology. Like the concept of salvation history, the hierarchy of knowledge was formulated in confessional polemic, expressed in Arabic terms and communicated by Muslim tradents. Here, as elsewhere, the problem of 'origins' is a literary one.

Direct witness, as opposed to tacit and oblique allusion, to epistemological structure is found in the literatures of *falsafa* and of *kalām*. Their relevance to my purpose here lies in a common concern with the concept of authority. The philosophical implications of revelation (source) and prophethood (mode) have been analysed with exemplary clarity by Fazlur Rahman.[2] Here, as in other monotheist forms, accommodation of intellectual procedure and terminology to the central fact of a scriptural theophany was achieved without enormous sacrifice. This process is well documented: one convenient illustration is Wolfson's 'double-faith' theory, according to which it was a but slightly modified Aristotelian source that permitted employment of the term 'faith' (*pistis*) to the act of assent, whether to

[1] Cf., however, such efforts as those of M. Seale, *Muslim Theology*, London, 1964; and W. Watt, *The Formative Period of Islamic Thought*, Edinburgh, 1973.

[2] F. Rahman, *Prophecy in Islam: Philosophy and Orthodoxy*, London, 1958, esp. 36–45, 54–64, 107.

primary and self-evident data or to secondary and derived propositions. To that theory there are two 'single-faith' alternatives: 'authoritarian' (scriptural truth must be accepted as such) and 'rationalist' (scriptural truth can be logically demonstrated).[1] In the several philosophies of monotheism all three positions are represented, and exhibit the facility with which Greek philosophical procedure could be adapted, and thus a theological parallel to the same process in juridical and exegetical method. Scripture was of course an oracular form with at least one very special property: it was permanently recorded and thus more or less generally accessible. As a source of truth it was protected not merely by its divine origin but by what Rahman called the 'compulsory law of symbolization': that process by which abstract concepts are imagined (made intelligible to the human intellect). To define scripture as a product of externalized imagery was to assist its incorporation into philosophical discussions of epistemology. But the psychological 'law' had socio-political overtones: knowledge of the concept behind the symbol might be restricted to an élite qualified or eligible to understand. Thus, 'symbol' might well indicate the external version of an internal truth but at the same time the absolute limit of truth for popular consumption. From that point of view revelation is interpreted as an alternative to reason, an intellectually less rigorous medium of truth.

The 'symbolic mode' of the philosophers belongs to that cognitive category I elected to call '*nomos*': a tangible (terrestrial) representative of absolute (celestial) truth. Its intention is guidance, formulated within the framework of a community (*milla*) guaranteeing a measure of security and continuity. As the law, so the community is seen to reflect an absolute rational order of being, corresponding to my category '*ecclesia*', though seldom depicted by philosophers as 'historical', that is, as exhibiting a capacity for change. As sources of authority neither category is in fact, or at least may be thought, appropriate to the composition of salvation history. The contribution of both to Islamic historiography was negative: the foundation-event was interpreted as an unattainable ideal and the community itself as at the very best a compromise.

Some notion of change is preserved in the writings of theologians. I have referred above to two manifestations: the concept of flexibility in the very fact of recorded dispute (*ikhtilāf*), and that of development contained in the doctrine of abrogation (*naskh*). A theological version of that latter was Naẓẓām's description of divine knowledge as of two varieties: non-contingent (e.g. justice, honesty, faith) and contingent (e.g. ritual ordinances).[2] With the latter the possibility of change/development/

[1] H. Wolfson, 'The double faith theory in Clement, Saadia, Averroes and St. Thomas, and its origin in Aristotle and the Stoics', *JQR* xxxiii (1942–3) 213–64.

[2] Cheikho, *Vingt traités*, 68–70.

alteration (*badā'*) was implicitly introduced, a possibility accepted also by some philosophers, though the term *badā'* itself became a crux of sectarian dispute.[1] The idea of contingency may (!) underly Naẓẓām's scepticism towards the several modes of transmission employed by Muslim scholars to create a sense of continuity between the original theophany and the current authority of the community. For him the only reliable criteria appear to have been reason and attention to the literal meaning of scripture, both of which exhibit, ironically, an ahistorical notion of authority.[2] A moderate scepticism is displayed in the writings of Naẓẓām's pupil Jāḥiẓ, whose treatment of tradition was articulated as a joke at the expense of bluff and hearty adversaries. His idiosyncratic style may indeed betray a formidable intellect but probably also a good deal of idleness and no little amount of ambition; like his teacher he was too eccentric either to formulate a consistent philosophy or to establish a school.[3] The bases of authority had none the less been challenged, and from a position which stressed the literal content of scripture by sacrificing the exegetical tradition: in other words '*nomos*' required neither development nor interpretation. That is of course an extreme statement, and is unlikely to have been seriously envisaged by anyone but Ibn Ḥazm.[4] From outside the establishment Ibn Rāwandī (*c.* 256/870) could demolish the entire structure of '*nomos*' by insisting, in the name of extreme rationalism (symbolically enshrined in the epithet 'Barāhima'), upon the absurdity of scripture, the superfluity of prophecy, and the unreliability of tradition.[5] A similar, if not the same, path was taken by his colleague Abū 'Isā al-Warrāq (*c.* 247/861), whose rationalist position is evident in, *inter alia*, his treatment of Manichaean mythology.[6] Now, it would be easy but possibly simplistic to attribute this iconoclasm (*scil.* Naẓẓām, Jāḥiẓ, Ibn Rāwandī, Abū 'Isā) to a common Mu'tazilī background. The nature of the iconoclasm does of course help to explain the peculiarly anti-rationalist posture of the 'orthodoxy' which in the event survived.

The necessity of '*nomos*' was also called into question by the Mu'tazilī interpretation of *fiṭra* as 'natural law'. The evolution of that term, from 'innocence' to 'acknowledgement of God', has been several times analysed and its origins traced, correctly in my view, to sectarian (Khawārij)

[1] *QS*, 197–201 (*badā'*); cf. *EI* s.v. and Rahman, op. cit. 54, citing Fārābī.

[2] Van Ess, 'Fragment des Naẓẓām', 171, 186, 193 (I doubt, incidentally, whether '*illa* means here 'explicit *ratio legis*', which anyway seems to be a contradiction in terms).

[3] Jāḥiẓ, *Kitāb al-tarbī' wal-tadwīr*, Leiden, 1903, 90–105; cf. van Ess, 'Fragment des Naẓẓām', 196–200.

[4] Cf. Rahman, op. cit. 93–4.

[5] P. Kraus, 'Beiträge zur islamischen Ketzergeschichte: das *Kitāb az-Zumurrud* des Ibn ar-Rāwandī', *RSO* xiv (1934) 93–129, 335–79, esp. 341–57 on Barāhima, with which may be compared F. Rahman, *EI* s.v.

[6] C. Colpe, 'Anpassung des Manichäismus an den Islam (Abū 'Isā al-Warrāq)' *ZDMG* cix (1959) 82–91.

dispute.[1] Its employment to designate a kind of pre-covenantal (Q. 30: 30 and 7: 172) discernment could be understood to indicate the dispensability of revelation: if salvation could anyway be gained what was the purpose of theophany? That view was also the property of the philosophers, and found its most felicitous expression in the story of Ḥayy b. Yaqẓān.[2] For Ibn Sīnā, Ḥayy was the Active Intellect, external to man, and in fact an instrument of revelation (though not theophanic); for Ibn Ṭufayl, Ḥayy was the Active Intellect personified in man, depicted as autodidacticus. Both versions represent the category I have called '*numen*' and a concomitant supersession of '*nomos*', which in the work of Ibn Ṭufayl is relegated to 'symbolic' status, being that form of truth intelligible to the common man. There, at least implicitly, '*ecclesia*' is also relegated: to the agency by which 'symbols' could be preserved and transmitted for the common (social) good. The philosophers' view found its most extreme formulation in the work of Ibn Rushd, whose 'double-faith' theory was in fact a dichotomy: the rational apprehension of truth and simple faith in it may not overlap. Whether, as Wolfson conjectured, this position reflected political circumstances in twelfth-century Muslim Spain, or, as I suspect, merely the logical conclusion of an ancient Islamic dispute, need not be decided.[3] The cognitive category '*numen*' remained the exclusive property of philosophers and mystics, and exerted little influence upon the composition of salvation history.

. . . . .

In the terrestrial setting of '*ecclesia*' the apprehension of truth might be represented as persuasion conditioned by environmental factors. In a treatise devoted to that subject the Nestorian Ḥunayn b. Isḥāq (d. 260/873) opposed to six grounds for accepting falsehood (coercion/survival/ambition/deceit/ignorance/kinship) four for acknowledging truth (miracle/mystery/rational demonstration/historical record).[4] His own position was justified by eliminating the six and pointing to the example of the Apostles. Within the framework of a confessional minority the polemical note is unmistakable, but the criterion of historical consistency (p. 285, l. 15: *an yakūn ākhir al-amr muwāfiqan li-awwalih*) indicates a pragmatic concern, found occasionally even in the works of philosophers.[5] Assent is here reckoned in terms which made of community history a datum worthy of serious consideration. The same argument was employed by the convert 'Alī b. Rabbān Ṭabarī in favour of Islam,[6] by 'Abd al-Masīḥ

[1] Van Ess, *Zwischen Ḥadīṯ und Theologie*, 101–14; Wensinck, *Creed*, 42–4, 214–16.

[2] A. M. Goichon, *EI* s.v. Ḥayy b. Yakẓān.

[3] Wolfson, 'Double faith theory', 250–1.

[4] L. Cheikho, 'Un traité inédit de Ḥonein', in *Orientalische Studien Theodor Nöldeke . . . gewidmet*, i, 283–91.

[5] Cf. Rahman, *Prophecy*, 58–60, citing Fārābī.

[6] 'Alī Tabarī, *Kitāb al-dīn wal-dawla* (ed. A. Mingana), Cairo, 1923, 50–66; trans. Mingana: *The Book of Religion and Empire*, Manchester, 1922, 57–76; cf. M. Bouyges, 'Nos Informations sur 'Aliy . . . aṭ-Ṭabarī, *MUSJ* xxviii (1949–50) 69–114.

Kindī against,[1] and most of Ḥunayn's criteria were incorporated into an apologia by the Jacobite Yaḥyā b. ʿAdī.[2] *Pro et contra* the argument was easily manipulated: the criterion of success was evidence either of God's design or of effective coercion. But that it should have been adduced at all was of some significance for the composition of salvation history. The material of that record could be seen as its own justification (*legitimirende Kraft*) and the burden of proof shifted from the foundation event (*nomos*) to the subsequent understanding of that event.

Now, in my observations on Islamic soteriology (second chapter) it was precisely as 'event', rather than as historical process, that I interpreted its normative (Sunnī) expression. That such was in part at least related to the dogma of an uncreated Qur'ān (whether as cause or effect is difficult to say) seems likely, and thus it could be supposed that opponents of the dogma might have been willing to concede that revelation was to some extent historically determined/conditioned. Some evidence is found in the later Muʿtazilī ʿAbd al-Jabbār (*c.* 416/1025), who argued precisely from his concept of divine justice that God's speech, including Qur'ān (*sic*), required a recipient who might benefit from it.[3] Whatever the origins of the dogma,[4] there is a certain logic in this refutation of it, from which it could be inferred that the acts of God (including speech) could not be temporally (or spatially) limited. That inference is of course substantiated by the dogma of 'acquisition' (*kasb/iktisāb*) which guaranteed the continuous presence of God in the affairs of men, and, unlike the doctrine of a created Qur'ān, was accepted as 'orthodox'.[5] Utterance of the divine will, whether in speech or in act, could be regarded either as quite arbitrary or expressive of some purpose. Theoretically, the choice was between an irrational hence ahistorical concept of deity and a rational hence historical one. In reality, there could never have been such a choice: the emergence of one or more such concepts as dominant was the product of several variables, not all of them theological.

A dialectic of theology and history is hardly attested in Islamic literature.[6] References in polemic to the community record disclose, however, some consciousness of history as the proving ground for the claims made by revelation. From there to the acknowledgement of history as revelation

[1] Kindī, *Risāla*, 42–6, 91–5 (trans. *Apology*, 44–9, 84–8).

[2] Yaḥyā b. ʿAdī, 'Fī ithbāt ṣidq al-injīl', in P. Sbath, *Vingt Traités philosophiques et apologétiques*, Cairo, 1929, 168–71.

[3] J. Peters, *God's Created Speech: a Study in the Speculative Theology of the Muʿtazili . . . ʿAbd al-Jabbār*, Leiden, 1976, esp. 95–104, 285: *al-qur'ān wa-sā'ir kalām allāh* (*sic*), 385–402; cf. *BSOAS* xl (1977) 613–15.

[4] *QS*, 77–84.

[5] L. Gardet, *EI* s.v. Kasb; but cf. also Bravmann, *Spiritual Background*, 107–13; M. Schwarz, '"Acquisition" (*Kasb*) in early Kalām', in *Essays . . . Walzer*, 355–87; Wolfson, *Kalam*, 663–719.

[6] Cf. Berger, *Social Reality*, 50; I need hardly add that my category '*nomos*' is not derived from Berger's employment of that term pp. 28 ff., though undoubtedly influenced by it.

it is, indeed, a major step. A sense of community membership may certainly produce a corresponding sense of ontological continuity, which itself may be interpreted as somehow 'historical'.[1] Such is more likely to occur where the community is more or less co-extensive with society, as in Islam, medieval Christendom, and pre-exilic Israel. Where the community is structurally sectarian, whether the consequence of 'institutional specialization' or of tardy or incomplete development, that likelihood is diminished, as for example in medieval Judaism.[2] On the other hand, the notion of historical process might easily be the product of an initial isolated theophany, in which the deity was seen to act not cosmically but at a particular time and place.[3] In brief, both '*ecclesia*' and '*nomos*' may generate a notion of history as revelation, but neither need do so. The literary deposit of that notion is, of course, 'salvation history', and it seems to me possible, from analysis of that type, to determine just how the underlying theophany was interpreted: as 'event' or as 'process'.

It could here be useful to recall that the circumstances of literary production include a number of social, political, and economic factors conducive to the creation of leisure and literacy. That these factors were operative in the appearance of Islamic literature in Mesopotamia at the end of the second/eighth century can hardly be contested. In common with other literary forms historiography presupposes and expresses, however obliquely, a degree of social stability, of political order, and of economic security. These might take the specific and direct form of patronage, or the general and indirect forms of aesthetic appreciation and intellectual stimulation. Underlying them all is a sense of achievement which serves as external referent: the shared experience of writer and reader, to be merely depicted, possibly affirmed, criticized or modified, but in any case acknowledged as the datum of literary expression. Salvation history is just such an expression, and its function in Muslim society was to formulate the experience of the community in appropriately ecclesial terms. Its datum, seen from the period and place of its earliest articulation, was the 'fact' of 'Abbāsid society. That fact required, or at least invited, not merely description but also analysis and justification.

A summary of my arguments for the content and composition of Islamic salvation history might be as follows. The literary type is interpretative hence mythic (Jolles: *Wahrsage, Deutung*). The substance of the myth is the polemical *topos*, its form the midrashic pericope generated by a keyword, its purpose the articulation of doctrine as event. The process is one of reification, and might be described as 'symbolic literalism'.[4]

[1] Berger, op. cit. 68 ff.: 'plausibility structures'.

[2] Ibid. 128–9, 138–42.

[3] Ibid. 121–5.

[4] Z. Werblowsky, *Beyond Tradition and Modernity: Changing Religions in a Changing World*, London, 1976, 107–9: in my opinion an especially felicitous modification of

The epithet 'midrashic' is proposed, since it was by means of that process that the referential style of Muslim scripture was provided with a plausible external referent. Of the various styles isolated in the literary type I suggested (1) 'dynamic' as the production of scripture that could be read historically, and (2) 'ornamental' as the production of history that could be read scripturally, both witness to the impingement of a theophany, expressed as foundation event, upon the community record. Reckoned also as midrashic styles were (3) 'parabolic' as narrative derived from sub-canonical scripture, and (4) 'exegetical' as narrative appended as complement to canonical scripture. In the former the theophany is implicit, in the latter explicit; the two styles may thus be evidence of a chronological development, but that cannot be demonstrated. For the non-midrashic styles (or, more appropriately, structures) I employed the term (5) 'documentary' as the production of materials designed to supply paradigms, prescriptions, in brief, normative patterns of conduct for the community whose genesis was being depicted. The amalgam of these ingredients may be characterized as a *praeparatio evangelica*: nomothetic, because it conformed to the literary laws of Biblical salvation history; prognostic, because it adapted the types of Biblical salvation history to the seventh century Ḥijāz; cumulative, because it adopted and extended the covenantal dispensation of Biblical salvation history. The absence of messianic elements might be thought to support my hypothesis that Islamic salvation history was composed in and for a community whose political future was more or less assured.

Of the two primary concepts of authority exhibited in this literature, 'scriptural' and 'apostolic', the former is polemical the latter paradigmatic. In the exegetical tradition a composite was achieved by interpreting both as of revealed status (*waḥy*) and by designating both exemplum (*imām*). For salvation history the link between the two was a product of the midrashic pericope: in *sīra* prescription was causally related to event, in *sunna* prescription was formulated as event. Collections of *exempla* are preserved in a style (owing to topical divisions, halakhic rubrics, and chains of tradents) both fragmented and 'static'. That impression is, however, relieved or indeed neutralized by the inclusion of secondary literary forms (*scil.* dispute and abrogation) attesting a sense of development. The principle of authority is articulated by means of halakhic symbols: community (*umma*) is related to leader (*imām*), and consensus (*ijmā'*) to infallibility (*'iṣma*). These relations seem to me to depend upon the conscious extension of theophany: from a single historical act into a continuing historical process. Similarly, the symbolic value of such basic concepts as *irshād/hudā* (guidance), *fitna* (disintegration) and *tawātur*

Bellah's 'symbolic realism'; cf. G. Scholem, *Major Trends in Jewish Mysticism*, New York, 1974, 349–50: Baal Shem and the transmission of symbols.

(succession) indicate a preoccupation with continuity and survival. It is thus the community record to which the criterion of success was applied. That the results were transmitted as salvation history was the consequence of a linguistic and typological legacy: as I have observed, it is difficult to see how they could have been differently formulated. Naturally, the 'literature of protest' (polemic) exhibits the same language.

Now if that interpretation of the evidence has any merit at all, it may be supposed that 'revelation' in Islam refers not only to its foundation event but also to its historical continuity. Such is of course acknowledged in modern Muslim writing, where it is often expressed as a dilemma: the immutable utterance of God v. the empirical data of historical change.[1] Solutions tend to fall into one or more of three categories: (1) retroflexive historiography, (2) prognostic exegesis, (3) distinction between metaphysical verity and historical veracity. It is not my intention here to attempt an evaluation of these propositions. For each considerable documentation can be found in Islamic tradition as well as numerous and articulate advocates in the contemporary world of Islam. I should like, rather, to ask whether revelation as an epistemological mode has been, or must be, confined to scripture, *ḥadīth qudsī*, and other instances of divine communication to the prophet. In the *Ḥadīth al-ifk* 'Ā'isha enumerated *qur'ān*, *ru'ya*, and *khabar*; and the use of *waḥy ghayr matluw* in reference to the prophetical Sunna is well known. A retrojective dimension, definitively truncated by the dogma identifying Muhammad as 'seal of the prophets', was supplied by allusion to earlier revelation in the form of Jewish and Christian 'scripture', itself occasion for the polemical charge of falsification (*taḥrīf*, etc.). 'Revelation' in the mystical lexicon (e.g. *kashf*, *ishrāq*) is of course witness to the continued presence and accessibility of God, though not in fact to His intervention in the linear progression of time. It is in Ṣūfī terminology that scriptural exegesis (e.g. *istinbāṭ*) may itself be regarded as 'revelation', comparable in most respects with the 'illuminational exegesis' practised in Qumran and Karaism.[2] For Qumran at least, the object of exegesis could be scripture or the course of history (*qadmōniōt*, *raz nihyah*), which served as well to document the actions of God.[3] The notion of continuity and progressive modification as divinely corroborated is, it may be added, reflected in the Rabbinic *bat qōl*.[4] In Sunnī Islam the corresponding principle of halakhic emendation (*naskh*) was retrospectively limited to the lifetime of the prophet, but applied in

[1] Cf. Wielandt. *Offenbarung und Geschichte*, *passim*; Grunebaum, *Modern Islam*, 97–127; cf. L. Gardet, *La Cité musulmane: vie sociale et politique*, Paris, 1961, 193–267 (*la communauté*).

[2] The phrase is Wieder's: *Judean Scrolls*, 81–94; cf. also Betz, *Offenbarung und Schriftforschung*, 36–7, 41–60; Schiffman, *Halakhah at Qumran*, 22–76, and esp. 76 n. 347.

[3] Betz, op. cit. 80–8.

[4] Bacher, *Terminologie* ii, 206–7.

practice for centuries after his death. In Shīʿī Islam the concept of divine corroboration in perpetuity rested upon the vicarious authority of the *imām*. While all these devices are only roughly approximate, they do exhibit a common concern for the functional continuity of revelation, itself depicted as a unique event. That concern may attest a sense of history, or possibly nothing more than nostalgia. The difference, I submit, is crucial.

An an object of nostalgia the monotheist theophany, particularly in its Jewish and Muslim forms, is not inappropriate. As the 'word of God' literally rather than figuratively (as in Christianity), revelation generated the concept of *lingua sacra*, which had a remarkable effect upon the development of such disciplines as philology and rhetoric in both Hebrew and Arabic, and even in literary sectors which might have been thought profane.[1] One consequence was that the collective memory of the theophany exhibits a strong linguistic/literary bias. For specifically exegetical works that fact is well known, but the phenomenon is much more extensive and also more profound than might be apparent from the simple equation theophany : scripture. This has been demonstrated by M. Arkoun in his penetrating analysis of an epistemological treatise composed in the fourth/tenth century.[2] Starting from the structuralist premiss 'clôture logocentrique' (Derrida, Barthes), he explains the operation of affective language as a lexical, cultural, and cognitive system, its dependence upon 'le style collectif' (*écriture*) and upon a semantic foundation derived not from etymology but from cultural context.[3] The persuasive thoroughness with which the 'system' operates is revealed by a statistical analysis of the lexical stock in any given work to show the facility with which neutral, even antithetical, terminology can be pressed into its service. The conviction, which has been my argument throughout these studies, that one is confronted (even in the most prosaic of technical texts) with a literary system is nicely put by Arkoun: 'C'est ici que l'expression "rêverie intellectuelle" prend tout son sens: le discours philosophico-religieux fonctionne comme le discours poétique à cela près qu'il substitue le concept à la métaphore, la dialectique à l'évocation, la lenteur de l'explication à la spontanéité du cri de douleur ou de ravissement. Le philosophe-théologien, le théologien fondamentaliste (*uṣūliyy*), comme le poète, cèdent à la pression lyrique d'un univers de significations concentrées dans un lexique et une grammaire qui perpétuent la substitution d'un monde *rêvé*, mais *cohérent*, au monde réel.'[4] The employment of enumeration, aphorism, taxonomic diagram, and dialectic is of course

[1] *QS*, 85–118.

[2] M. Arkoun, 'Logocentrisme et vérité religieuse dans la pensée islamique: d'après *al-Iʿlām bi-manāqib al-Islām* d'al-ʿĀmirī', *Studia Islamica* xxxv (1972) 5–51.

[3] Cf. Culler, *Structuralist Poetics*, 96–109, 131–60.

[4] Arkoun, art. cit. 24.

to be interpreted as evidence of stylistic concern, but also as witness to the ineluctability of the 'clôture logocentrique'.[1] From such source materials as these (and there are no exceptions) the historical portrait which emerges is itself a literary construct, designated by Arkoun 'l'histoire *vraie*', to a degree dependent upon but in essence (*logocentrique*) opposed to 'l'histoire réelle'. Though he does not put it in quite these terms, the distinction between 'true history' and 'actual history' is *heilsgeschichtlich*, derived from the unquestioned acceptance of 'un message divin *déjà lié à une réalisation historique*'.[2]

Now, it is precisely the concept of history which is here at stake: implicit reference to the criterion of 'success' (*des réussites temporelles*), subsumption of empirical data (*déjà vécue*), recourse to 'verifiable' interpretation (*déjà éprouvé*), all exhibit an epistemological stance most accurately described as nostalgic.[3] That is to accept the distinction between 'l'histoire vraie' and 'l'histoire réelle': that all historiography is exegesis aimed at interpreting an empirically available external referent. So regarded, every historiography must contain an element of imposture, and thus not so far distant from the self-deceptions of nostalgia, however unconscious these might be. Salvation history may indeed be so read, and commonly is by the uncommitted and the hostile, who acquiesce in the availability of an external referent but insist upon another interpretation. Within the 'clôture logocentrique' salvation history represents one of several interpretative systems, each designed as an exercise in legitimation. But the system itself (*écriture*) acquires by its very existence a kind of 'monumentality' which can be deciphered only by relating it to an external referent.[4] The problem must in fact be formulated as a circle in order that equal justice be done to the complementary processes of writing and reading. What, then, is 'l'histoire réelle'?

For the analysis of Islamic literature there is a related, but distinct, problem, commonly formulated as theological dogma and which can be stated as 'the suspension of linguistic analogy' (*tanzīh* : *bilā kayfa*).[5] Its precise context is ontological (divine attributes) but is also employed in eschatological doctrine (e.g. beatific vision), and seems to me to permit a rather special interpretation of 'logocentrisme', namely, that the notion of external referent is intrusive, at best optional. As a factor in the composition of salvation history, and this could hardly be contested, the 'suspension

[1] Arkoun, art. cit. 26–7, 29, 39: 'Ainsi, l'effort qui vise à faire de la religion une science transforme la science en religion.'

[2] Ibid. 41–2, 48–9.

[3] Ibid. 50: 'La raison affirme ainsi une suprématie méthodologique, mais c'est pour la mettre au service d'un *credo*. De là, l'arbitraire dont elle use à l'égard des religions irréductibles à l'Islam.'

[4] For all this cf. Culler, op. cit. 133–8: 'vraisemblablisation'.

[5] Wolfson, *Kalam*, 205–34.

of analogy' would justify the most arbitrary interpretation of 'events', including even negation. The end product may well be 'l'histoire vraie', but from an epistemological point of view it is nostalgia. Salvation history may thus be envisaged not only as an exercise in legitimation, but as an experiment in language foundation: 'the isolation of a semiological space' into which may be inserted a selection of themes and symbols intended to recall the event of revelation.[1] Pre-selection of the historiographical register is itself determined by the concept of 'event': its literary expression is thus subject to the normal methods of historical analysis. Clearly, these must include both linguistic and literary criteria: like any other genre historiography can be identified by its lexicon and style(s). It would, I suppose, be unwise to labour this point any further, but the recording of theophany as history requires some attention to the mode of transmission.

Knowledge of the community record (collective memory) depends after all upon a marginal literary precipitate. Of the types I have adduced (*sīra/maghāzī/sunna/ikhtilāf*) none can claim the disinterested or neutral character of archaeological and archival material. Each was composed, as it were, for the record: in theological terms they constitute a creed. For salvation history the credal component is conceptual only, but it is of some interest to note that in the credal format (*ʿaqīda*), as it has been preserved, concrete 'historical' references are not lacking, e.g. to Muhammad's successors, his companions, his wives, and his children, to the sectarian Jahmiyya, Qadariyya, Murji'a, and, Muʿtazila.[2] As an element in the profession of faith, 'event' attests concern for the historical image of the community, which could be something more than nostalgia. As cognitive category, '*ecclesia*' is significant when its referent (*umma*) may be defined in terms not only of its historicity but also of its vitality. But neither characteristic precludes an essentially ahistorical view of the past. Indeed, it can be, and has been, argued that there is here a kind of antithesis: that such conceptual and literary devices as myth, midrash, and *mise en scène* designed to create vitality and to ensure historicity are often, if not invariably, anachronistic.[3] That has many times been shown in analyses of the prophetical Sunna, and cannot be unexpected in the *sīra–maghāzī* literature. The impulse is exegetical: interpretation of the record to 'make it relevant'. The means to that end are multiple

[1] Culler, op. cit. 104: 'logothete' *re* Barthes on Ignatius Loyola.

[2] Wensinck, *Creed*, 104, 109–10, 119–21 (Fiqh Akbar, i, paras. 5, 10); 151–2, 183–4 (Waṣiyyat Abī Ḥanīfa, paras. 10, 26); 207–10, 218, 221–2, 239–42 (Fiqh Akbar, ii, paras. 4, 10, 14, 27); 269 (Fiqh Akbar iii, paras. 29, 31).

[3] J. Goldin, 'Of change and adaptation in Judaism', *History of Religions* iv (1964–5) 269–94, esp. 276, 282, 286–7; cf. J. Neusner, 'The religious uses of history: Judaism in first century AD Palestine and second century Babylonia', *History and Theory* v (1966) 153–71; Urbach, 'Halakhah and History', esp. 112–16.

and none need attest an interest in the linear progression of history or in accurate reportage. For the study of salvation history the question can become acute, since, as I have suggested, the 'history' may be merely commemorative, cultic in origin, and with little or no reference to future resolution or even to further progression.

In Muslim theology the theophany is ontologically defined as 'word of God' (*kalām allāh*) and exegetically treated as 'book of God' (*kitāb allāh*). From neither designation does the exact nature of the theophany emerge very clearly. In the light of extensive current discussion of this question in respect of the Judaeo-Christian tradition,[1] it might be thought pertinent to consider the Islamic data. The Arabic terms for 'revelation' (*waḥy*, *nuzūl*) are commonly interpreted as involving angelic agency (*irsāl*), while the semantically related 'inspiration' (*ilhām*) can designate unmediated communication.[2] It is the object of communication which is here of interest: whether disclosure of the divine essence or announcement of the divine will. Quranic usage attests only the latter, and I have discussed elsewhere the standard (apodictic *et al.*) formulae.[3] Such 'disclosure' formulae as can be found, e.g. Q. 7: 172 (Am I not your Lord?) and 20: 14 (Verily, I am God, there is no god but Me!) are presentative only, and occur in proclamation contexts. There is in any case no explicit self-disclosure, but rather, a kind of nominal demarcation. Ineffability of the deity is after all a cardinal dogma of Muslim theology and the source of the *tanzīh* doctrine. Revelation as 'word of God' is paraenesis, promise, admonition, and paradigm.[4] It is always a matter of what Pannenberg designates 'indirect communication', however immediate the form of address, namely of acts, signs, events.[5] These (e.g. retribution pericope, covenant) constitute the Quranic proclamation and presuppose a historical matrix: they have taken place in time past and are (thus) relevant to the present. References to future time are, on the other hand, generally indefinite: linguistically documented (imperfect tense) but conceptually open-ended. The underlying temporal framework is that of Biblical salvation history: the fresh dispensation is a further marker towards the eschaton. Muslim scripture can, in other words, provide a 'theology of the Word' only in the above sense: 'utterance' (*qawl*, *kalima*, *amr*) is always a reference to 'action' or 'event'.

Now, in the corpus of Islamic salvation history, of which scripture is only a part, the quality of 'revelation' remains unchanged. Indeed, emphasis upon its historicity is achieved by the various devices of reification described in my first chapter. The past (genesis: *mubtada'*), constructed

[1] W. Pannenberg *et al.*, *Revelation as History*, London, 1969.
[2] *QS*, 33–8, 75–7.
[3] *QS*, 12–20.
[4] Pannenberg, op. cit. 152–5 (Thesis 7).
[5] Ibid. 3–21.

round Biblical and South Arabian genealogies, is there retailed as *praeparatio evangelica*; the present (exodus: *mab'ath*) as fulfilment of the prognosis. The future is hardly mentioned. Imminence of the eschaton, not the least important of scriptural *topoi*, is confined to perfunctory polemic about the 'fact' of corporeal resurrection, as in the story of Ubayy b. Khalaf or the account of the deaths in battle of Yazid b. Ḥāṭib and Quzmān. Nor is the imagery employed to depict the advent and departure (death) of the prophet in any special way eschatological (e.g. *Sīra* i, 15–18, 69–70: *muhājar*; 157–8, 232–3, 356: symbolic value of the name 'Muḥammad'; *Sīra* ii, 642, 651–2: God's option to a prophet—the 'keys' of the terrestrial and celestial kingdoms). An exception might be 'Umar's insistence (*Sīra* ii, 655) that Muhammad had not died, but would, like Moses from Sinai (*sic*), 'return to his people', a motif which seems incidentally to exhibit some confusion between Moses' reception of the Law and his later ascension.[1] In fact, the death-bed scenes in the *Sīra* (ii, 649–61) are constructed primarily round the problem of succession (e.g. Abū Bakr and 'Umar respectively as leader of the congregational prayer, the affair of the *saqīfa* of B. Sā'ida: Anṣār v. Muhājirūn).

The utility of the Pannenberg formulation lies in its stress upon the proleptic and teleological character of revelation.[2] The argument there is indeed Christocentric, but relevant none the less to every analysis of salvation history, which, in order to be 'salvific' must also be 'historical', that is, composed with a view to its eventual resolution in time. In the Judaeo-Christian tradition the 'once for all time' revelation of the Law was transposed by the prophetic and apocalyptic acknowledgement of change into a concept of linear progression towards a stated (for Christianity already 'revealed') end. The past is proleptically interpreted as simultaneous promise and fulfilment. Whether the entire process may be understood not merely as 'history' but also as 'revelation' is precisely Pannenberg's argument. On the basis of the Biblical documentation I regard his/their thesis pretty well demonstrated, and am therefore inclined to extend it to the Islamic version of salvation history. There is, however, one obstacle: namely, that which I have repeatedly referred to as the referential or reductive style of the Islamic version. The exegetical/typological relation obtaining between Hebrew and Christian scriptures, as also between Israel and the early Church, cannot be established between either and/or both of those traditions and the Muslim one.[3] The extent to which that fact confirms or at least supports the view of an exclusively Arabian origin

[1] Cf. Meeks, *Prophet-King*, esp. 176–215; and the 'Muhammadan evangelium', *QS*, 63–75.

[2] U. Wilckens, 'The understanding of Revelation within the history of primitive Christianity', *apud* Pannenberg, op. cit., esp. 59–66, 70–7, 87–8, 110–15; and Pannenberg's own observations, 131–5 (Thesis 2), 185–206 (Postscript).

[3] *QS*, 33 *sub*, 'Composition'.

for Islam is not easily decided. I have here, under the intentionally flexible rubric 'sectarian milieu', engaged a number of issues selected to describe if not to explain that referential/reductive style. Morphologically and thematically the Muslim version exhibits a reflex of the Biblical tradition; conceptually it represents a dislocation of that tradition by positing its protagonist as 'seal of the prophets'.[1] From the standard exegesis of that locution, whatever its etymology may have been, it could be supposed that theophoric movement in history had reached its resolution. It may be recalled that the final theme of the *Sīra* turned upon selection of an *imām* to succeed Muhammad. The character of the community was thus not eschatological in the apocalyptic sense, nor was the portrait of its founder messianic in any sense. In the ongoing history of the community 'revelation' (*scil.* scripture) was crystallized as a credential of prophethood, and thus reverted to the 'once for all time' status of the Law.

That the revealed Law (*waḥy: sunna* and *qur'ān*) admitted of some modification I have noted. Though in reality legislative modification was extensive, it was theoretically bound to prophetical precedent, and hardly qualifies as witness to a concept of 'revelation as history'. It is rather, much closer to the Rabbinic concept of Torah. And that concept, it seems to me, may be characterized not as historical but as nostalgic. My explanation of this would be that the cognitive category '*nomos*' must be seen as having intercepted the notion of development implicit in the category '*ecclesia*', that is, in terms of my typology. Transposed into historical description: the theological definition of Islam was posterior to the fact of a socio-political community. The interpretation implied is one of recasting: a process of conscious 'exemplification' in terms of which the origins of the community were adapted to the circumstances of the 'sectarian milieu'. That interpretation is admittedly the product of literary criticism and nothing more, but may be thought to some extent corroborated by the date at which this literature made its first appearance.

. . . . .

The chronology of the literary process here suggested is reflected in the development of the creed (*'aqīda*). Though the oath of witness (*tashahhud shahādat al-ḥaqq*) did occasionally figure among the standard conversion formulae, at least in the record of individual converts, it was not an element in the early credal format.[2] This was, rather, derived from the catalogue of ritual prescription (*umūr/arkān al-islām*) such as was articulated in the presence of the Ethiopian Najāshī or appeared in the several treaties concluded between Muhammad and the Arabian tribes.[3] The eventual

[1] *QS*, 64–5.
[2] Wensinck, *Creed*, 17–35, 170–4.
[3] *QS*, 38–43; Sperber, 'Die Schreiben Muhammads', 1–93.

incorporation of the *shahāda* might be understood to signal an altered emphasis in the 'pattern of assent': from submission to authority (*islām*) to attestation of inner conviction (*imān*), from association (*ecclesia*) based on law (*nomos*) to solidarity based on faith (*numen*). The role of Ghazālī (d. 505/1111) in that process was indicated by Wensinck, whose exemplary analysis of the Muslim creed stressed the formative role of epistemological principles (*uṣūl al-dīn*): their adaptation from Aristotelian models, subtle elaboration, and final rejection in favour of a modified *gnosis*.[1] To depict the development merely as a progressive substitution of concepts would of course be a simplification: Ghazālī's epistemology was itself a very sophisticated structure.[2] It seems none the less clear that in the literature of dogmatic theology, as in that of salvation history, the initial cognitive category was '*ecclesia*'.

To association by the act of conversion correspond the modalities of disassociation exemplified in the terms 'hypocrisy' (*nifāq*) and 'rejection' (*ridda/kufr*) and documented in the *sīra–maghāzī* literature as acts of deceit and treachery (e.g. ʿAbdallāh b. Ubayy). The impression created is that of communal solidarity: cemented or fragmented according to the particular act. Intervention of the deity is limited largely to succour in the field of battle and the promise of celestial reward to martyrs. Elsewhere God's presence is attested by utterance (*waḥy/nuzūl/irsāl*) adduced as *post facto* corroboration (e.g. in the expulsion of B. Naḍīr from Medina and the declaration of ʿĀ'isha's innocence in the expedition v. B. Muṣṭaliq). The circumstances (on both those occasions at least) are, again, expressive of a concern for communal cohesion, depicted as threatened by the presence of alien interests (symbolized in both instances by the activity of Ibn Ubayy). My purpose in recalling these examples is to ask whether Islamic salvation history might not more accurately be described as 'election history'. The absence of an eschatological concern, indeed, of any preoccupation with the future course and resolution of historical time, could be accommodated to such a description. Moreover, the truncated and reductive (referential) character, to which I have several times alluded, may be thought to confirm the notion of present as opposed to future resolution. And yet, the concept of 'realized eschatology' is not quite appropriate, perhaps owing in part to its employment in current discussions of Christian theology, but also and rather more significantly, to the absence of a causal connection between the eschaton (whether 'present' or imminent) and the contemporary history of the community. The underlying motive (*Geistesbeschäftigung*) of Islamic salvation history, or 'election' history, might be formulated not as 'eschatology' but as 'protology': a reaffirmation and restoration of original purity. The course

[1] Wensinck, *Creed*, 248–75.

[2] Cf. H. Lazarus-Yafeh, *Studies in Al-Ghazzali*, Jerusalem, 1975, esp. 349–411.

of Biblical salvation history, essentially proleptic and teleological, was thus reversed to produce a *restitutio principii.*[1]

Dislocation of the Biblical paradigm, or rather, of the exegetical tradition fashioned from it, can also be deduced from the essential optimism of the Islamic version. It would perhaps be unwise to insist upon the absence of pessimism as a historiographical factor in the entire Muslim tradition, but the contrary of that proposition is not so easily documented.[2] The notion of decline from an ideal state is seldom accompanied by a conviction that reversal is impossible: attested by *inter alia* every movement to which the epithet 'salafiyya' has been attached. The object of my concern is, however, not the later tradition but rather, the ideal portrait depicted there as worthy of restoration. Nostalgia and optimism are not, after all, mutually exclusive, nor must either be even remotely conditioned by eschatological expectations. As I have indicated, the environment of apocalyptic, to which Rabbinic Judaism and Roman Catholicism represented more or less diametrically opposed reactions, is hardly attested in the *sīra–maghāzī* literature. It was the criterion of secular success, not of failure, which was adduced in confessional polemic. On the other hand, the contingent nature of success was never concealed, at least not for long, noted by L. Gardet as follows: 'Il est peut-être de la nature de l'Islam de garder intactes ses grandes notions de base, sans jamais les réaliser dans le concret autrement qu'à travers telle ou telle forme politique inspirée des contingences de l'histoire.'[3] As a summary of the entire historiographical tradition that observation is quite adequate, but in the *sīra–maghāzī* literature there is no note of despair, even of resignation. For that phenomenon (*scil. umma*) Gardet recommended different tags, e.g. 'idéal historique concret', 'théocratie laïque et égalitaire', 'nomocratie'.[4] It seems to me that the paradoxical quality of the first two rests upon a false analogy between historical and literary imagery: the 'ideal' was realized only in literature, and 'theocracy' was never more than an eschatological image. With 'nomocracy' I have clearly, in the light of all the foregoing, no quarrel whatever. Tension generated by the nomocratic ideal found expression in *fiqh* and *tafsīr*, as well as in later reference to *sīra*, not, however, in its actual composition.

There, on the contrary, ideal and reality coincide. In my discussion of its several styles, I proposed a distinction between 'mythic' and 'normative' tendencies, directed respectively towards interpretation and prescription. The manner in which these were combined is the achievement of the genre: to offer a historical reading of theology. It may be, and I have

[1] Cf. Aune, *Cultic Setting*, 1–28.

[2] Cf. Rosenthal, 'Influence of the Biblical tradition', 38–9.

[3] Gardet, *Cité Musulmane*, 327.

[4] Gardet, op. cit. 12, 325 (Maritain); 23, 31–68, and *passim* (Massignon); 27–8 n. 2, 119.

conceded as much, that for the *maghāzī* proper the converse is more likely: namely, a theological reading of history. In either case the motive was interpretation: on the one hand, of the monotheist tradition in terms of Arabian data, on the other, of the Arabian data in terms of the monotheist tradition. These operations were complementary, not identical. Their products were respectively a scriptural dispensation (*nomos*) and a community record (*ecclesia*). Whatever tension may have persisted between them is hardly evident in the corpus of salvation history itself, though it eventually became the object of considerable dispute. Its counterpart in the Judaeo-Christian tradition is formulated as an antithesis: Law v. History, and applied to the problem of soteriological modes.[1]

In that tradition, as well as in Islam, it was a question of defining dispensation. In my discussion of soteriology (second chapter) I proposed isolating the initial Muslim dispensation as an amalgam of three literary types: history, scripture, and paradigm; and its later theological expression as an extension of those types respectively as: eschatology, prognosis, and messianism. The aim of my distinction between 'initial' and 'later' was to stress the absence from the original Islamic kerygma of a futurist orientation (*scil.* eschatological, apocalyptic, messianic). The concept of salvation/redemption was in fact one of election: a matter of community membership and cohesion. Now, thus presented it must seem that particular significance is attached to the structure of the community, to the concept and source of authority operative there, and to their translation from principle into practice. Theoretically, these preoccupations may be subsumed under my rubric '*nomos*' to produce such descriptive epithets as 'nomothetic', 'nomocratic', 'covenantal nomism', etc. The model of a community illustrating these epithets *kat' exochen* is of course Rabbinic Judaism, often adduced as diametrically opposed to associations derived from sacerdotal (sacramental/sacrificial), eschatological (apocalyptic/messianic), or gnostic (mysticism/mystery cults) principles. The historical and social reality is naturally much more complex: veneration of the Law is accompanied by identifying it with a celestial archetype or with 'Wisdom', by regarding its study as a cultic and sacral activity, by interpreting it as symbolic of primordial and cosmological processes. Each of these extensions of '*nomos*' involves a historical factor, implies some notion of spatial and temporal circumstances, and thus dilutes, if it does not entirely demolish, the antithesis Law v. History.

To the corresponding Islamic phenomena the same reservations must be applied: as archetypal and symbolic of celestial truth as the Law undoubtedly is, its implementation was a pragmatic and terrestrial matter.

[1] e.g. D. Rössler, *Gesetz und Geschichte*, Neukirchen, 1962; but cf. Sanders, 'Covenant as soteriological category', 19 n. 21; and Maier, *Geschichte*, 19–30, esp. 21 n. 3; also Nötscher, 'Himmlische Bücher und Schicksalsglaube', 405–11.

The relation between Law and History is not so much antithetical as aetiological: in terms of the monotheist (covenantal) dispensation neither can be justified, even explained, without reference to the other, as must have become clear from analysis of the midrashic styles in the *sīra–maghāzī* literature. The aetiology may, on the one hand, be nothing more than a literary construct, but must, on the other, be seen at least to serve some purpose. That purpose can in this context be identified as the mechanism of transmission, by means of which the Law developed from a unique epiphany into the permanent property of a confessional community. The 'historicization' of the theodicy might, in other words, be thought to include not merely a plausible *mise en scène* for revelation, but also a chronological dimension into which it could be projected and thus preserved. The concept is *traditio/paradosis*: the after-life of an event perpetuated by constant reinterpretation. It is of course in that way that 'event' may be reformulated as 'process'. Concern for the validity (uninterrupted) of transmission and for the probity (unimpugned) of tradents is a feature of most communal religious expression, certainly for those evolved in the articulation of monotheism, e.g. the sayings of the fathers/houses, apostolic succession, and the sound chain of authority. These figured not only in doctrinal decisions but also in confessional dispute.

In his *K. Tamhīd*, the Ashʿarite theologian Abū Bakr Bāqillānī (d. 403/1013) devoted several chapters to analysis of the epistemological basis of transmission, appropriately framed as a refutation of the Jewish denial of abrogation. Here the term (*naskh*) is a reference not of course to halakhic hermeneutics but to supersession and the renewal of divine dispensation, as was characteristic of Judaeo-Muslim polemic. Bāqillānī's primary concern is to formulate a convincing reply to the question 'how do we know?', and to that end adduces the following arguments:[1]

1. Some Jews accept the logical possibility (*min ṭarīq al-ʿaql*) that the Mosaic Law might be abrogated (*scil.* superseded by a later prophet) but deny that God willed such, while others deny both that and the logical possibility. All save one party agree that *naskh* prior to the event is tantamount to cancellation (*badā'*) and absurd; and that one party permits the cancellation of ritual by way of punishment.

2. While the Samaritans acknowledge besides Moses only Aaron and Joshua, the rest acknowledge all the (Biblical) prophets after Moses, but neither Muhammad nor Jesus, the exception being the ʿĪsawiyya, who acknowledge both but deny that they were sent to abrogate the Mosaic Law.

3. Despite allegations to the contrary, evidence (*aʿlām*) for the prophethood of Moses has been challenged by many (e.g. Barāhima, Majūs), so that the Jewish transmission can hardly be binding.

[1] Bāqillānī, *Kitāb al-Tamhīd*, ed. R. McCarthy, Beirut, 1957, 160–90 (being chs. XII–XV: paras. 272–324; cf. also the appendix on 'authority' (*imāma*) 378–86 (paras. 632–45).

4. If the transmitted report is consistent and attested, it ought despite challenges be acceptable. In that respect the credentials of Moses and Muhammad are equally valid.

5. However few in number the original witnesses may have been, both Jews and Muslims today constitute a proof (*ḥujja*) derived from an eye-witness account of their respective claims.

6. If the tradition (*naql*) of the Muslims is invalid then so must be that of all other confessional communities, an assumption which strikes at the very foundation of all transmitted knowledge.

7. If the Jews insist that their knowledge is non-contingent (*ḍarūra*) they must be reminded that it is not universally agreed; if they admit that it is contingent (inferred: *istidlāl*) then it is no different from that of others.

8. If the Jews assert that the prophethood of Moses is attested also by Christians and Muslims, then remind them that others (e.g. Barāhima, Majūs) do not attest it, and that argument by the testimony of others is thus not sound.

9. The testimony of others may not always be regarded as independent witness; if it were the Jews would be compelled to accept Christian arguments for Jesus as messiah.

10. The Jewish charge of irrationality levelled at the trinitarian doctrine does not invalidate the claim that Jesus was messiah, which happens (in adoptionist form) to be shared by others, e.g. Muslims and ʿĪsawiyya.

11. The Jewish tradition might similarly be charged as irrational, in view of its anthropomorphic concept of the deity (*tashbīh wa-tajsīm*).

12. If the claim of the Jews for the Mosaic Law is not prior to Christian and Muslim witness, it is invalid; if it is prior then it is no more valid than the Muslim claim for Muhammad's dispensation.

13. If Christian and Muslim acknowledgement of Moses is derived only from a Jewish source, they are no more valid than it; if derived from God, the prophethood of Jesus and Muhammad must be admitted. The Jewish argument from a position of humility and tributary status (i.e. non-coercive) is no more valid than the corresponding Christian argument, which they do not acknowledge.

14. Corroboration by independent witness must be weighed against the possibility/likelihood of derivation from a single source.

15. Approximately as preceding (14).

16. The Jewish argument from non-coercion is not distinctive: no one was compelled (*bil-sayf*) to become Muslim.

17. If the death penalty among Jews for apostasy does not signify spread of the original faith by coercion, that charge cannot be levelled at Muslims.

18. Nor were the ʿĪsawiyya compelled to acknowledge either Jesus or Muhammad.

19. Approximately as preceding (16).

20. Establishment of the original confession had in every case to be voluntary.

21. If the Jews argue from unanimous tradition (*tawātur*) and insist upon regarding opposition (e.g. Barāhima, Majūs) as deceitful, then Muslims may employ the same argument.

22. If the Jews argue that their opponents acknowledge Moses but regard his miracles as fraudulent, then Jewish opposition to Muhammad may be interpreted in the same way.

23. The conditions for unanimous tradition include according to the Jews: number and dispersion to the extent that collusion is precluded, absence of coercion and of mystification, and a situation of humility; and they alone meet these requirements.

24. But those conditions (23) are gratuitous, being implicit in the designation *ahl al-tawātur*.

25. The Judaeo-Christian tradition on the crucifixion is derived from only four witnesses (the evangelists), but identification of the victim is not sufficiently certain to preclude a doubt (*shubha*).

26. Similarly for the credentials of Zoroaster: they are either derived from a single source or due to later distortion, as, indeed, is the Christian trinitarian doctrine.

27. Cross-reference to the author's postscript on *tawātur* and *imāma* (edition pp. 378–86).

28. Jewish arguments against abrogation, with reference not to reason (*'aql*) but to authority (*sam'*), namely, the express declaration of Moses to that effect, are neither certain nor unambiguous.

29. The prescriptions of the Mosaic Law cannot be literally 'eternal' but rather, are subject to such conditions as existence, ability, etc. (*scil.* for their execution).

30. The Jews assert that the report of Moses' declaration about the eternity of the Law is derived from an eye-witness account.

31. But if that account were really the product of *tawātur* it would constitute primary knowledge, and we should have to acknowledge it as we acknowledge (willingly) the existence of Moses. But since we do not, it cannot be so.

32. But, the Jews assert, if it is not so, their entire tradition is a lie and the basis of *tawātur* destroyed.

33. But similarly, if the Muslim rejection (*scil.* of the Mosaic claim) is a lie, the basis of *tawātur* is also destroyed.

34. The Jewish assertion can thus not be a necessary truth (i.e. primary knowledge), but contingent only and subject to interpretation.

35. Neither the exhortation to obedience nor the fact of disobedience can be used to reject the possibility of the Law being abrogated.

36. The Mosaic declaration has been too often translated (*sic*) and interpreted to be considered authentic.

37. Muhammad's dictum, on the other hand, that 'there shall be no further prophets', is authentic and unconditional.

38–40. The differences between the two dicta are three: Muhammad's is verbatim, neither translated nor interpreted; Muhammad's is derived from God's designation of him as 'seal of the prophets', while Moses was succeeded in Biblical tradition by several prophets; the very fact of Muhammad's mission, attested by signs and revelation, proves that that of Moses was not final.

41. Muhammad's mission is as well attested as that of Moses.

42. Jewish rejection of Muhammad's dictum is absurd, since it was derived from the scriptural locution 'seal of the prophets' and thus *mutawātir*.

43. Jewish arguments against abrogation with reference to reason turn upon the axiom that what God decrees must be good (*ṣalāḥ*), that what He prohibits must be bad (*fasād*), and that rescission would be tantamount to contradiction.

44. The argument from contradiction is spurious, since the fact of sequence (temporal) has been omitted: what is good at one time may be the opposite at another.

45. This distinction is pertinent to all prescribed ritual (e.g. *'ibādāt sam'iyyāt*: fasting, prayer, *qibla*, etc.); obedience and disobedience are relative concepts.

46. A related argument of theirs is that the divine decree implies desire (*murād*) while the divine prohibition implies antipathy (*karh*): exchange would be contradiction and thus impossible. This is equally spurious and for the same reason.

47. If, further, they argue from avoidance of *badā'* (cancellation owing to altered circumstances), that is unnecessary, since the fact of a temporal sequence is itself proof that there is no contradiction in God's design.

48. If, indeed, we permit *naskh* prior to realization of the act, that does not entail *badā'*, since its contingency is already known and taken into account.

49. That contingency is implicit in all the processes of existence, e.g. life/death, health/illness, joy/grief, which may not be interpreted as reward and/or retribution entailing *badā'*.

50–51. Indeed, no alteration (*taghayyur*) need/may be ascribed to *badā'* in the deity, but to the fact of contingency *in tempora*.

52. To acceptance by the 'Īsawiyya of Jesus and Muhammad but their rejection of Christianity and Islam (*ummatān*), let it be said that this is inconsistent and a repudiation of the basis of all tradition.

53. As for those who postulate (*scil.* Khuramdāniyya) a continuous succession of prophets, including Muhammad, let it be said that such is inconsistent with the utterance of the prophet himself ('there shall be no further prophets') and thus with the substance of prophetical tradition.

Now, while this summary does not quite do justice to Bāqillānī's thesis this much must be clear: the dominant concept of certitude is that derived from the authority of *traditio/paradosis* (*tawātur*).[1] The view is

[1] Cf. R. Brunschvig, 'L'argumentation d'un théologien musulman du xe siècle contre le judaïsme', in *Homenaje a Millás-Vallicrosa* i (Barcelona, 1954) 225–41; A. Abel, 'Le Chapitre sur l'Imāmat dans le *Tamhīd* d'al-Bāqillānī', in *Le Shī'isme imāmite*, Paris, 1970, 55–67.

of course retrospective, but presupposes concomitantly the notion of historical projection, that is, transfer across time. That emerges principally from the discussion of authoritative transmission, but also from reference to abrogation as requiring temporal and spatial sequence. According to Bāqillānī's argument, continuity is itself aetiological: the fact of preservation by unimpeachable authority (*ahl al-tawātur*) constitutes certainty, of which the fundamental criterion is widespread attestation (i.e. in terms of number, dispersion, absence of collusion and of coercion). Such authority compels acknowledgement and may thus be subsumed under the epistemological rubric 'primary/necessary'. Evidence (paras. 36–42) for the superiority of Muhammad over Moses is, after all, not *ratio* but *traditio*, and its context the fact of historical preservation (*naql mutawātir*). Similarly, the arguments from reason in favour of *naskh* make quite explicit the fact of development, or at least, of fluctuating circumstance. In another discussion of *naskh*, adduced in my third chapter, it was recourse to the notion of contingency which distinguished the position of Naẓẓām from that of Jesse. The difference may be thought to turn upon an acknowledgement of historical change.

But neither Naẓẓām nor Bāqillānī was concerned with the composition of salvation history. Their cognitive categories were exclusively theological, but reveal none the less a distinctive preoccupation with '*ecclesia*': tradition as community property. A corresponding diminution of '*nomos*', symbolized here by the Mosaic Law, is achieved by (or merely results from?) stressing both custody and contingency. The primary value of the Law is its evidentiary character (*'alam*) for the community, understood as the historical vehicle of divine dispensation. This bias could be interpreted as the conscious neutralization of '*nomos*' in salvation history, where it represents not continuity but truncation, even reversal of linear time. Here we are confronted by a phenomenon of some significance in the literary elaboration of Islam which I have elsewhere posited as a conflict between centripetal and centrifugal tendencies.[1] There, discussion was of linguistic phenomena and the tendencies seen as exhibiting respectively expansion and contraction; here, it is a matter of epistemology and the concept of history. But there is a discernible parallel: to establish a linguistic/literary standard (*scil.* Classical Arabic) was an authoritarian gesture, however ineffective it may in practice have remained, not very different from an assertion that the normative life of the community must be derived from a unique, eternal, hence immutable 'scripture'. Common to both is a distinctly static notion of authority, according to which change must signify corruption and conformity betoken nostalgic satisfaction. The tension thus generated has been a constant feature of Islamic tradition, at once debilitating and fruitful.

[1] *QS*, 89–90.

INDEX

RES IPSA LOQUITUR: HISTORY AND MIMESIS

When in London Albert Einstein, following upon the Royal Society's successful expedition to photograph a solar eclipse, described the movement of bodies as contingent on a 'system of co-ordinates',[1] he observed an ancient and general principle in the organization of all experience: namely, that empirical data were of use only insofar as they could be related to a field of perception already plotted. The principle was of course analogy, and the system of co-ordinates an essential framework for making what is strange and unruly into the familiar and orderly: in other words, an exercise in intellectual domestication.

In these days of intense speculation on why and how we think what we think, analogy is so much taken for granted that all mystery must seem to be accounted for, and all data in jeopardy of becoming 'obvious' (to employ a current catchword) or self-evident. Hence my selection of title for this important occasion, in which I am hardly qualified to participate, but nonetheless sensitive to the great honour of your President's invitation to do so. Naturally, it is not all that difficult to discover some point of contact between my interests and those of Einstein, whose thought and activities comprehended most of the human condition (Terentius: *Homo sum, humani nil a me alienum puto*). My subject this evening is (and for a very long time has been) the nature of historical discourse and its apparently endless proliferation of literary expression.

Acknowledgement of historiography as literature is, though somewhat grudging, now fairly widespread. This may be nothing more than recoil from attempts to make of history a fully fledged science (recently dubbed 'Cliometrics'), but 'literature' here seems to imply little more than the fact that history is usually written in narrative prose, with, as one historian put it, 'the added constraint of factuality'.[2] On both counts, of narrative style and of factuality, the assertion may be thought just a little ingenuous, as any serious student of 'literature' is bound to observe. It is well known that Aristotle reckoned history amongst his literary genres, but with the significant observation that its proper domain is the particular descriptive statement from which nothing relevant

1. In response to an invitation from the *Times*, 28 November 1919.
2. Cf. J. Barzun, *Clio and the Doctors*, Chicago 1974, esp. pp. 54–59, 116–118.

might be omitted.[3] That was in contrast to poetry, characterized by the universal truth of a general statement. Two remarks seem pertinent: (1) Aristotle's distinction between the two genres turns upon the implicit (!) role of *referent* in historiography, about which he is somewhat naïve; (2) his definitions are embedded in a discussion of *mimesis*, about which I will in due course have something more to say.

At least the scene was set, some twenty-five hundred years ago, for an analysis of what the historian ought to be about. In the view of Aristotle, it might seem, his task was to depict in the most minute detail the events of the past. There are some, even today, who suppose their task to be 'discovery of a pre-existing true state of affairs'.[4] Most, however, recognize that they must settle for something less than that, namely, a selectivity that in turn not merely imposes upon them choice of topic but also a corresponding stylistic constraint. What exactly, in other words, is a sentence?

With that question I am admittedly compelled to trespass upon the domains of the linguist, the philosopher and the literary critic, as well, of course, as that of the novelist. In a typically provocative essay, Clifford Geertz has shown how the traditional disciplinary lines of demarcation have been dissolved. In an impressive parade of names from Steiner and Lévi-Strauss to Doctorow, Borges and Nabokov, the intentional blurring of genres is demonstrated, to an extent that must obliterate the ancient and time-honoured distinction between history and fiction.[5] Now, whatever one might think of this development, it is clearly here to stay and must cause some unease among historians who had staked a claim on their special ability to tell us 'what really happened' (*wie es eigentlich gewesen*). Thus, the 'language game' has got to be played, and, moreover, from the premise that *text* is the primary datum of human experience. Further requisites are a literate public, a concept of 'reading' as productive, and curiosity about 'writing' as not merely interpretative but creative in the ontological sense (*Gestaltung*).

One consequence will be the need for historians to explain, in *post*-Aristotelian terms (!), how what they do is different from writing novels. Both those ancient parameters, 'referent' and 'mimesis', will undoubtedly benefit from further scrutiny. It is no longer enough to be assured that the 'sources' tell us this or that. The very prose in which the assurance is expressed has become suspect. To adduce many instances would not be so difficult but certainly distracting. What I propose here is examination of two such, actually quite dissimilar, but which

3. *Poetics*, 1451 and 1459; cf. G. Grube, *The Greek and Roman Critics*, London 1965, pp. 83–85; R. Humphreys, 'The Historian, His Documents, and the Elementary Modes of Historical Thought', *History and Theory*, XIX (1980), pp. 1–20.

4. E.H. Carr, *What is History?*, London 1961, esp. pp. 85–102; cf. J. Price, review of Carr, in *History and Theory*, III (1964), pp. 136–145.

5. C. Geertz, 'Blurred Genres—The Refiguration of Social Thought', *The American Scholar*, XLIX (1979–1980), pp. 165–179.

for methodological reasons appear to have attracted a very similar if not quite identical treatment.

My first example is the commentary generated by a *significant* (!) portion of Arabia in the seventh century CE. Of that there exists a good deal, in a more or less continuous stream from then until now. 'Stream' is perhaps not the right word: 'torrent' might be more appropriate to the volume of literature provoked by the uninterrupted effort to depict the origins of Islam. And that is the first point I should like to make. The very quantity of the corpus must figure in its critical assessment. Like the Mongol conquest, the discovery of the New World, and the French Revolution, that remote Arabic 'event' now constitutes a major preoccupation of the historians' guild. From this position it has undoubtedly profited, and that is my second point. Quantity not merely produces but determines quality: very few are the exegetical methods that have not been, in the course of this long and arduous confrontation with the past, exploited in an attempt to understand that literature. I see these as falling into one of the three following categories: (a) Islam as the re-casting of pre-Islamic Arabia; (b) Islam as the product of minority (external) historiography; (c) Islam as the response to interconfessional (Judaeo-Christian) polemic, what I have elsewhere essayed to describe as the 'sectarian milieu'.[6] Now, it is not my intention this evening to burden you with what I have offered historians by way of exegesis. The passage of time involves a significant intellectual therapy, and while I have not moved in any of the directions so ardently advocated by my many critics, I have managed to move, and this must be a token of some residual vitality. The process is standard and thus familiar: comparison throws up as many antitheses as it does analogies, and it was by juxtaposition of this first example with my second—a *not so significant* (!) portion of Syria in the fourteenth century BCE—that I was impressed by the enduring obstinacy of historical method.

But let us consider for a moment that remote portion of Arabia. Bereft of archaeological witness and hardly attested in pre-Islamic Arabic or external sources, the seventh-century Hijaz owes its historiographical existence almost entirely to the creative endeavour of Muslim and Orientalist scholarship. Though I am obliged to add that these have seldom been found in collusion, there is an impressive unanimity in their assent to the historical 'fact'. Since the evidence, or its absence, is common to both traditions, it might be thought that they share certain methodological presuppositions. These could be set out in the following ways:

(a) as 'paradigm' = the general hypothesis according to which empirical and other data are perceived;[7]

6. J.E. Wansbrough, *The Sectarian Milieu—Content and Composition of Islamic Salvation History*, Oxford 1978, passim, but esp. pp. 32–49 and 114–119.

7. S.C. Pepper, *World Hypothesis—A Study in Evidence*, Berkeley–Los Angeles 1966, esp. pp. 115–137; T.S. Kuhn, *The Structure of Scientific Revolutions*, Chicago 1970, esp. pp. 43–51.

(b) as 'structure' = the system of co-ordinates by which analogy and internal consistency are established;[8]
(c) as 'linguistic closure' = the syntactic and semantic constraints imposed by selection of a vocabulary to depict events in language.[9]

Now, together these rubrics are meant to comprehend the sum of techniques available to the historian in his exegetical task. They also happen to describe the means available to any writer, or, for that matter, speaker, whose intention it is to convey an impression (and it can be no more than that) of his own or someone else's experience. Appeal to 'common sense' is merely recourse to a (one hopes) shared paradigm; explanation can only be insistence upon an intelligible choice of structure; and style must inevitably reveal a personal decision about the adequacy of language to the task of description. This is not to say that historical or any other literature can persist (at least for very long) in a condition of solipsism. All expression is constrained—indeed imprisoned—by the grammar of a sentence.

And what has all that got to do with the seventh-century Hijaz? I would say approximately this: the sources for that historical event are exclusively literary, predominantly exegetical, and incarcerated in a grammar designed to stress the immediate equivalence of word and world. Or, I might be inclined to add: all we know is what we have been told. With neither artifact nor archive, the student of Islamic origins could quite easily become victim of a literary and linguistic conspiracy. He is, of course, mostly convinced that he is not. Reason for that must be confidence in his ability to extrapolate from the literary version(s) what is likely to have happened. The confidence is certainly manifest; the methodological premises that ought to support, or, at least, accompany it, are less so. One can only suspect the existence somewhere of a tacitly shared paradigm, that is, an assumption that the literature in question has documentary value. Such it has, indeed, though not quite in the sense here supposed. However that may be, the assumption itself might seem to be corroborated by a further curious circumstance: I mean the near absence of Islamic data from comparative studies of religion. The material from which relevant data could so easily be culled has come to be regarded as sui generis, as though of value only for the unique historical phenomenon it purports to depict. Now, while all historical phenomena are admittedly unique, the means of describing them are severely limited. I refer to linguistic constraints: whether these entail, or merely reflect, conceptual ones, is a problem I am unable to solve. In any case, the constraints themselves permit

8. R. Barthes, 'Historical Discourse', in *Structuralism—A Reader*, London 1970, pp. 145–155; J. Culler, *Structuralist Poetics*, London 1975, passim, but esp. pp. 96–109.

9. Wansbrough (above, n. 6), pp. 141–142 ad M. Arkoun, 'Logocentrisme et vérité religieuse dans la pensée islamique', *Studia Islamica*, XXXV (1972), pp. 5–51.

erection of a 'system of co-ordinates', and thus discovery of the analogies indispensable to description. Of course the procedure can be exaggerated, and we have had warnings enough about the dangers of 'parallelomania', at least when defined as historical diffusion. But that definition is neither complete, nor, for that matter, necessary.

Reading literature as history is a common if controversial pastime. While I am often tempted to respond by reading history as literature (and have frequently been accused of this impropriety), there is surely some more practical mode for making the transfer from unique event to general proposition. In order to deal with the reports of seventh-century Arabia, I divided the field into constants and variables: the former representing the 'basic categories' common to most descriptions of monotheism; the latter representing 'local components' that give each version its special character. Recourse to this simple taxonomy seemed to facilitate a discussion of Islamic origins in terms that would make sense to any student of religion, in short, to make of the unfamiliar an intelligible unit of study. The constants were prophet, scripture, and sacred language; the variables were the specifically Arabian features of these, together with such traces of local usage as could be inferred from its later abrogation by the new faith (e.g. in ritual practice and civil law). In this scheme of things, the problem of diffusion need not, but inevitably does, arise. The obvious, and certainly easier, alternative is to calculate the factor of polygenesis: that is, prophets are the agents of divine revelation which, once recorded, must contain the sacred language of God's word. That calculus does not, of course, yield a specifically Mosaic exemplar for Muhammad or a Davidic genealogy for Jesus. But those are variables and of only marginal interest to the structural study of religious phenomena. However, my proposals have found favour with neither Muslims nor Orientalists, and that, I suspect, for the very reason that historians regard their task as the elucidation not of constants but of variables. The paradigm, I have suggested, is Aristotelian and just possibly in need of revision. The two points at which such might be undertaken are the concepts of referent and mimesis.

Though mostly employed as an existential, hence empirical, concept, 'referent' requires for all but the contemporary chronicler an act of faith. The act is of course not quite arbitrary: it is sanctioned by guild membership. One reads the works of one's colleagues, and, sooner or later, something like a consensus emerges. In most cases that will have been underpinned by the 'hard', if often mute and impenetrable, evidence of archaeology and/or archive. But not always. And I have referred repeatedly to the literary and exegetical character of the sources for the seventh-century Hijaz. The implicit caveat is heard but seldom heeded. The notion of literary 'convention' must be in some way found abhorrent, for there is a perennial urge to substitute for it historical 'reality'. (I am here reminded of the recurrent question asked by my children, when many, many years ago I used to read aloud to them in that last hour before bedtime such classics as *Oliver Twist* and *David Copperfield*: 'Is it true?' they would ask. They meant of course, 'Did it happen?', and while I could hardly assure them of that, I was able to say that it was very true indeed.) In other words, 'referent' may also function as a literary convention, as that attractive (because reassuring) link between experience as reader and experience in life. But if 'referent' is a psychological necessity, its historicity is not thereby confirmed. Now, Aristotle told us that the purpose of history, as a literary genre (!), was to retail the event in all (not merely its significant!) detail. He took into account neither the fallibility of the eye-witness nor the constraints of the medium (= language) available to him for that task. I have already intimated that his assessment was ingenuous. Unfortunately, he uttered no further word on that particular subject, and one must suppose that those otherwise precious powers of analysis were in this instance satisfied with what everyone knows to be 'common sense'.

In respect of mimesis Aristotle had rather more to say. Much of it is widely familiar as an analysis of representation, and in particular of mimicry and imitation.[10] The context is tragedy and the examples theatrical. Of epic mimesis he thought rather less, and found only Homer to be an unqualified success. It was this treatment of the subject, defined as 'the reproductions of reality', that generated the now classical monograph of Erich Auerbach.[11] But elsewhere, Aristotle employed the term 'mimesis' to describe the relation of numbers to geometric figures, and thus introduced, as it were, a new dimension into the argument.[12] That was the condition that the mimetic process involved transfer to a different medium, a postulate not so easily derived from his analysis of tragedy. Epic poetry might have provoked this *apercu*, as would have history, but in the event did not. It is of course the notion of a new (or different) medium that requires a definition of mimesis not as 'reproduction' but as 'production of reality'. And that provides a rationale for the creative licence to which so few historians are inclined to lay claim. Grounds for this modesty must be manifold, and I would not dream of trying to identify them. What must, however, be said is that historiography, like every other kind of literature, does employ a new medium. That medium is language, which involves willy-nilly its own set of constraints. For example, nothing can be linguistically depicted except as linear and sequential. That very meaning of 'syntax' = order generates in narrative prose a capsular consistency that, in the context of historical discourse, takes on an uncanny resemblance to logic and causality. Language is also constrained by semantic association: every unit evokes not merely itself, but also its antithesis and a

10. *Poetics*, 1447–1462.

11. E. Auerbach, *Mimesis—Dargestellte Wirklichkeit in der abendländischen Literatur*, Bern 1946, passim, but e.g. p. 183 ad Dante.

12. *Metaphysics*, V, 14; cf. V. Zuckerkandl, 'Mimesis', *Merkur*, XII (1958), pp. 225–240; J.E. Wansbrough, *Bulletin of the School of Oriental and African Studies*, XXXIX (1976), pp. 443–445.

penumbra of metaphorical and metonymical reference. Employment of such simple and apparently unambiguous epithets as 'regalian', 'sacral', 'urban', 'mercantile' etc. must entail for every reader and, more important, every writer a concatenation of acquired imagery that can hardly be presupposed or, more important, pre-controlled.

Now, my purpose in adducing these homespun truths is to remind you of this simple and quite straightforward precept: the historical record consists of nothing more or less than human utterance and ought to be assessed by reference to all the criteria now assembled for this very rewarding task. If I have managed (and this is all but certain) to persuade you that what we know of the seventh-century Hijaz is the product of intense literary activity, then that record has got to be interpreted in accordance with what we know of literary criticism. My own experiment, in terms of structural features and formulaic phraseology, was never intended to be more than that: an experiment. Reactions to it provoke the impression that to historians the factor of ambiguity is not especially welcome. What seems to be required is some kind of certainty that what is alleged to have happened actually did. I doubt very much whether, for this particular segment of the story, we can attain to that certainty: the requisite material is not to hand. And that is the purpose of my second example of historical mimesis. Here, scholarship basks in an almost unique condition of liberty: the sources are exclusively archaeological and the record innocent of any contextual analogy to standard models. That these basic conditions have not deterred historians from erecting a 'system of co-ordinates' and from 'discovery of a pre-existing true state of affairs' must tell us something about the dedication to 'fact' of that professional guild.

About the second example: the phrase 'a *not so significant* portion of Syria in the fourteenth century BCE' is merely intended to convey the absence of an exegetical factor in the extant record from the Bronze Age settlement at Ras Shamra known to us as Ugarit. Its traces are severely and literally 'objective': these include a remarkably heterogeneous range of artifacts, several collections of cuneiform tablets exhibiting at least six languages, evidence of municipal, religious, funerary and domestic architecture, distributed in an urban plan containing carefully executed portions of enclosed and open space, on a site so far estimated to be an area of fifty acres, to which may be added the nearly adjacent coastal sites of Minet el-Beida and Ras Ibn Hani. Even without external support, all this had to be capable of yielding some sort of image for a toponym virtually unknown to Orientalist scholarship until the discovery of the Amarna correspondence.[13] Circumstantial evidence, subsequently perceived, has been only mar-

13. I.e. 1887: J.A. Knudtzon, *Die El-Amarna Tafeln*, Leipzig 1906–1915, esp. pp. 308–318 and (O. Weber) 1016–1017, 1097–1102; cf. C. Kühne, *Die Chronologie der internationalen Korrespondenz von El-Amarna* (Alter Orient und Altes Testament), Neukirchen–Vluyn 1973; J.G. Heintz, *Index documentaire des texts d'El-Amarna*, Wiesbaden 1982.

ginally helpful: e.g. random attestation in cuneiform (Ebla, Mari, Alalakh, Palestine) and Egyptian (Karnak, Memphis) sources. The full chronology of Ugarit is almost entirely notional: 'fourteenth century BCE', based on Amarna, is symbolic of a possible millennium 2200–1200.

'Significance', in other words, has had to be read into, not out of, the traces. The process might be described as one of metamorphosis: from discrete and antiquarian remnants towards a legible pattern of meaningful experience. That this could be achieved at all required a good deal of imagination and the application of several techniques in essence and fact quite different from those of the literary critic. Here we have no commentary for analysis, which is all we had for the seventh-century Hijaz, but rather, an abundance of hard and mute 'fact'.

So confronted, the historian of the ancient Near East has been compelled to adopt at least one—often more—of a number of strategies for expression of these data. In theory his choice might appear to be unlimited; in practice it has been unexpectedly restricted. Reason for this must lie somewhere in the acceptance of a paradigm for assessing discrete and random witness (archaeology is after all notoriously unpredictable): i.e. it can only be read in terms of a prefigured system of co-ordinates. Selection of the system will in turn depend on what is already available. For Ugarit the choice comprehended several (vaguely) contemporary models (themselves hardly certain in their political and Socio-economic contours): e.g. Hittite, Aegean, Cypriot, Canaanite, and Egyptian. The manner in which Ugaritic data have been slotted into these unstable structures inspires only qualified confidence. For example, the site has been described both as a 'maritime metropolis' and as a 'territorial state'. One might be excused for supposing that it was none of the above-mentioned contemporary contexts, but rather Venice, that supplied this particular model. The maritime dimensions of Ugarit are traced from the Aegean via the coast of Hittite Asia Minor and Cyprus to Egypt (on the basis of some very ambiguous documentation); its territorial dimensions are estimated to include some sixty kilometers of coastline by about forty kilometers of hinterland = 2400 sq km of political hegemony, containing 195 named localities with a population of around 25,000.[14] Evidence for that reconstruction has been derived from the occurrence of toponyms in Ugaritic chancery records, none of which provides unequivocal witness to the political entity so depicted. But that was only the beginning. Once the general situation of Ugarit had been staked out in the interstices of surrounding archaeology, it seemed easy enough to fill the gaps by recourse to a series of case studies, each the product of a separate comparison with materials quite disparate in time and space.

14. A panoply of this exegesis may be found apud M. Liverani, *Storia di Ugarit nell'età degli archivi politici*, Rome 1962; M. Astour, 'Ugarit and the Great Powers', in *Ugarit in Retrospect*, Winona Lake (Indiana) 1981, pp. 3–29; M. Heltzer, *The Internal Organization of the Kingdom of Ugarit*, Wiesbaden 1982 (with reference to earlier studies).

Perhaps the most remarkable, and certainly the best known, have been those adduced to support a reconstruction of culture in Ugarit: its language is described as Proto-West Semitic (mostly via Classical Arabic), its literature is deemed Canaanite epic (mostly via Biblical Hebrew), and its religion interpreted as a version of ancient Near Eastern mythology (via tenuous correspondence with the theophoric nomenclature of a Semitic pantheon).[15] While none of these postulates is entirely without substance, the first two might be thought to suffer from a kind of diachronic disability, and the third from a generous proportion of unaccounted for onomastic. At least two characteristics of the procedure inherent in this exercise are salient: (1) the easy metamorphosis of the philologist's hypothesis into the historian's 'fact'; and (2) the reconstruction of Ugarit as a source or vehicle of subsequent evolution. The methodological significance of both is enormous. Together they constitute the paradigm of historical explanation. One works, after all, from established fact towards a linear sequence of development. Nothing is more welcome than that which can be seen to herald the later circumstance, even or perhaps especially when its intrinsic ambiguity has been interpreted precisely to that end. The circularity of this logic has of course been noticed, but seldom taken fully into account in the actual calculation of results. To this day the Ugaritic language, even its alphabet, is something of an enigma, its literature only barely elucidated (and certainly not in a linear development that could have produced the Hebrew Bible), and its religious expression remains incarcerated in a plethora of as yet unexplained god-names and rituals.[16] But that is not to say that the reconstruction so far generated is without value. Every configuration of data has got to be of some use, if only to remind us of its methodological limits. But the sum of such lucubration is less important than the means by which it was delivered.

Less well developed, but gathering gradually in substance, are the 'case studies' concerned with the political entity called Ugarit. Here all available data have been assimilated to a model of monarchic authority: not merely monarchic, but autocratic in expression and dynastic in transmission. Once adopted, this interpretation has dictated the course of further description, e.g.,

(a) internal administration: the 'king' as initiator and final arbiter of executive decisions;
(b) external relations: the 'king' as sole respondent in negotiation, whether in tributary or autonomous status;
(c) military organization: the 'king' as sole donor of rank and authority;

15. E.g. S. Segert, *A Basic Grammar of the Ugaritic Language*, Berkeley–Los Angeles 1984; J.C.L. Gibson, *Canaanite Myths and Legends*, Edinburgh 1977; J.C. de Moor, 'The Semitic Pantheon of Ugarit', *Ugaritforschungen*, II (1970), pp. 187–228.

16. Cf. J.E. Wansbrough, 'Antonomasia—The Case for Semitic 'ṯm', in *Figurative Language in the Ancient Near East*, London 1987 (forthcoming).

(d) naval organization: the 'king' as disposer of fleet movement and allocation;
(e) economic activity: the 'king' as source and exclusive principal of commercial transactions.

Evidence for this remarkable versatility has been found in chancery records, admittedly plentiful but also notably lacunal in their coverage of the transactional apparatus. But once linked to a familiar model, the gaps could be filled by resort to imaginative reconstruction. Like all such, the 'regalian' model exhibits an a priori decision about the relevance of archaeological/archival data. It is here not a matter of selectivity, but of a hermeneutic grid by means of which all the available material could be processed. The result was thus predetermined. The method is admittedly a standard one and hardly without precedent. Its point of departure, however, is nothing more than a reading of the West Semitic term 'm.l.k.' as unambiguous reference to 'kingship', a meaning it did eventually acquire, but rather later than the period in question. Without that gratuitously adduced ingredient, the chancery records of Ugarit attest to the indisputable activity of a merchant oligarchy exhibiting the normal gain-motivated behaviour of businessmen.[17]

In this very context of source analysis a further point could be made. The polyglot chancery of Ugarit, to which I have already referred, has been traditionally aligned with the practice of contemporary and landlocked models served by Akkadian as *lingua franca*. While the abundance of tablets in that very language must attest to its widespread use, that can hardly be adduced as witness to its exclusive employment for international relations. One needs little more than the material pertinent to contact between Cyprus and Ugarit to suppose that in the Levantine context the Ugaritic language enjoyed intelligibility far beyond the confines of the metropolis. This surmise might also benefit from an historian's analogy: if the later Phoenician commercial expansion did not depend on, it almost certainly profited from, the concomitant spread of its local idiom. But even without this, one could guess from the Ugaritic finds beyond Ugarit that communication might occasionally take place outside the strictures of a complex and arduous school tradition (which is the only way that Akkadian can be described). Moreover, the respective distribution in the chancery records of Ugaritic and Akkadian scarcely shows demarcation along the lines of internal and external business—that is, Akkadian is abundantly exhibited in both spheres. It is tempting to suppose that selection is directly related to scribal training and a certain degree of experiment. The creation of a chancery rhetoric is the product of several variables, of which only the most obvious is communication. With a single exception, itself merely a paraphrase, we have no instance of a document

17. Cf. J.E. Wansbrough, 'Ugarit—Bronze Age Hansa?' in *Asian Trade Routes*, London 1987 (forthcoming).

in both Ugaritic and Akkadian versions. A provisional conclusion would have to be that the chancery scribe wrote the language he knew best. On the other hand, it would not be amiss to acknowledge the fragmentary character of archaeological data.[18]

In what, then, does the 'significance' of Ugarit consist? Its 'factuality' can hardly be disputed; its meaning, however, is a methodological construct. While this ought to provoke no particular surprise, it may be worth mentioning a recent application of the data. In his study of economic structures in the ancient Near East, Morris Silver made liberal use of the Ugaritic material to demonstrate the existence of a market economy in the second millennium BCE. As must be well known, the argument is addressed to the thesis of Karl Polanyi which asserted the opposite, namely, that economic transactions in the Bronze Age were initiated and implemented from a regalian centre, what is, in other words, professionally defined as a 'palace economy'.[19] While in my view Silver's interpretation of the data is emphatically sounder than Polanyi's, it must be said that both are economists, and thus dependent upon the exegesis made available by historians. To have achieved such diametrically opposed readings, each must have started from an independently adopted 'system of co-ordinates'. Like most of the random and discrete findings of ancient Near Eastern archaeology, the material from Ugarit is obstinately mute. Its organization demands a self-conscious commitment to a style of historical discourse that equates causality with continuity. But it is precisely the absence of continuity in these data that attracts attention to the stylistic exercise. Prosopography is exiguous, localities are elusive, institutions evanescent, and the actual transactions of daily life a matter of deduction from 'common sense'. That despite these disabilities a coherent account of Ugarit could have been produced attests to an admirable and perennial mimetic talent. For the archaeologist Aristotle's 'referent' is supplied; its 'context' = significance has got to be found, and that is the reason for my juxtaposition of two such markedly different specimens of historical inquiry.

And yet, their treatment has not been so very different. It must by now have become clear that my expectations of historical method are seldom fulfilled. I should have supposed that two such contrasting sets of data must generate dis-

18. Cf. J.E. Wansbrough, 'Ugaritic in Chancery Practice', in *Cuneiform Archives and Libraries—Papers Read at the 30th Rencontre Assyriologique Internationale, Leiden, 1983* (Publications de l'Institut historique et archéologique néerlandais de Stamboul, LVII), Istanbul 1986, pp. 205–209. Further observations on these matters are set out in my forthcoming study entitled *Chancery Practice and the Problem of* Lingua Franca.

19. M. Silver, *Economic Structures of the Ancient Near East*, London 1985, esp. pp. 71–144 ad theses of K. Polanyi finally expressed in the posthumous edition of H. Pearson, *The Livelihood of Man*, New York 1981; but cf. already K.R. Veenhof, *Aspects of Old Assyrian Trade and Its Terminology*, Leiden 1972, esp. pp. 345–357; R. Adams, 'Anthropological Perspectives on Ancient Trade', *Current Anthropology*, XV (1974), pp. 239–258; J. Gledhill & M. Larsen, 'The Polanyi Paradigm and a Dynamic Analysis of Archaic States', in *Theory and Explanation in Archaeology*, New York 1982, pp. 197–229.

tinctive modes of analysis. Instead, a mildly interesting convergence of method is discernible: while the artifacts of Ugarit have been translated into a narrative pattern of events, the literary account of the Hijaz has gradually assumed the status of an archaeological site. The element common to both is stratigraphic analysis. Its purpose is identification of something tangible that can in turn be called 'fact'. On a dig, this imagery is naturally persuasive; in a chronicle it is in danger of missing the point. But it does indicate selection of a paradigm that generates not merely the appropriate question but also the type of answer expected. Once uttered that expectation is rarely disappointed. It is after all in the nature of things that it should not be. And that is what one might, perhaps uncharitably, call the 'tyranny of history'.

Now, in recent years a great deal (even, perhaps, too much) has been written about the nature of 'historical understanding', identified by such tags as 'metahistory',[20] 'dialectic',[21] and 'hermeneutics'.[22] But no amount of conceptual theorizing has been able to dispel the apparently deep-seated conviction that 'history' is essentially historiography. Whatever acts of collection and collocation might precede the composition, its expression is narrative. I am also inclined to believe that its perception too is narrative: that is to say, follows a 'story-line', has something like a 'plot', is linear (exhibits causal nexus) and cumulative (everything counts). It is according to these parameters that one can understand the seductive power of sentence structure. Attempts to escape this force are made from time to time, e.g. in 'structuralism'[23] by dismissing the concept of 'referent'; in 'deconstruction'[24] by denying 'syntactic' continuity in experience. Neither has found, or is likely to find, universal assent. The reason for that lies probably in some vague but enduring conviction that the record has got to be readable. And this will be as much a matter of epistemology as of literature. There is, however, another factor in this process, a kind of safety-valve, as it were, that at the occasional expense of readability makes the record manageable: by reducing the cumulative burden and punctuating severely its linearity—

> there is no exercise of the intellect which is not, in the final analysis, useless. A philosophical doctrine begins as a plausible description of the universe; with

20. H. White, *Metahistory—The Historical Imagination in Nineteenth-Century Europe*, Baltimore 1973, esp. pp. 1–42.

21. F. Jameson, *Marxism and Form—Twentieth-Century Dialectical Theories of Literature*, Princeton 1971, esp. pp. 306–416.

22. R. Palmer, *Hermeneutics*, Evanston 1969, esp. pp. 3–71; E. McKnight, *Meaning in Texts—The Historical Shaping of a Narrative Hermeneutics*, Philadelphia 1978, esp. pp. 91–204.

23. See references above, in notes 8 and 22.

24. M. Foucault, *The Order of Things—An Archaeology of the Human Sciences*, London 1970; cf. H. White, 'Foucault Decoded—Notes from Underground', *History and Theory*, XII (1973), pp. 23–54.

> the passage of the years it becomes a mere chapter—if not a paragraph or a name—in the history of philosophy In literature, this eventual caducity is even more notorious.[25]

That statement, from one of the greatest contemporary observers of the human condition, can be differently expressed as 'textbook simplification', i.e. the summary of evidence in the form of detachable conclusions, or the relegation of earlier argument to condensed footnote references. These techniques, by which enormous effort and vast erudition are reduced to manageable proportion, might be described as perennial features, hence constants of the historical record.[26] They are particularly noticeable in the two works I mentioned a moment ago in the context of Ugarit. No one at all familiar with the sources (!) for Bronze Age history could suppress a gasp of astonishment at the occasional genius but persistent audacity of Polanyi and Silver in their recomposition of those laconic materials.

The 'detachable conclusion' is of course a recurrent feature in histories of science. There, apparently, the context of problem-solving matters less than the solution itself as component of an abstract process more or less independent of its historical circumstances. The average reader's knowledge of Einstein's contributions to a general theory of relativity, for example, are seldom conditioned by any acquaintance with his development as a musician, philosopher or Zionist. Despite some recent, and occasionally polemical, contributions the same may be said about historians of the Near and Middle East.[27] This would matter less for the ancient segment of that history, for which we have only archaeological evidence (and its modern exegetes are well known), than for the mediaeval period, for which we have only literary evidence.

But with that complaint we (or at least I) have now come full circle. My intention was to ask: 'what is obvious, or self-evident?' The answer, you must by now have guessed, is: 'nothing, nothing at all.' No record is unambiguous, and each demands an informed approach. In a recent and typical assault on this problem, Moses Finley declared a vested interest in the value of historical documentation over archaeological artifact.[28] With that assertion he must have wished to announce a preference for the authorial presence of the chronicler to the inarticulate existence of a chance discovery. To that I can only say that it may seem easier, but is in fact the more difficult alternative. Neither kind of witness can of course be properly interrogated. Nor can the circumstances of either be properly

25. J.L. Borges, 'Pierre Menard, Author of the Quixote', *Labyrinths*, London 1970, pp. 69–70.
26. Cf. Kuhn (above, n. 7), pp. 136–143; L. Mink, 'The Autonomy of Historical Understanding', *History and Theory*, V (1966), pp. 24–47.
27. E.g. E.W. Said, *Orientalism*, London 1978; R.C. Martin (ed.), *Approaches to Islam in Religious Studies*, Tucson (Arizona) 1985.
28. M. Finley, *The Use and Abuse of History*, London 1975, esp. pp. 87–101.

reconstructed. Each utterance requires a special sort of exegesis that ought to take the place of a candid but naïve appeal to 'common sense'.[29]

In conclusion I should like to repeat a story that is in this company very familiar, but which nonetheless is so stunningly relevant to the caducity of literary transmission that I could not resist:

> When the Baal Shem had a difficult task before him, he would go to a certain place in the woods, light a fire and meditate in prayer—and what he had set out to perform was done. When a generation later the 'Maggid' of Meseritz was faced with the same task he would go to the same place in the woods and say: We can no longer light the fire, but we can still speak the prayers—and what he wanted done became reality. Again a generation later Rabbi Moshe Leib of Sassov had to perform this task. And he too went into the woods and said: We can no longer light a fire, nor do we know the secret meditations belonging to the prayer, but we do know the place in the woods to which it all belongs—and that must be sufficient; and sufficient it was. But when another generation had passed and Rabbi Israel of Rishin was called upon to perform the task, he sat down on his golden chair in his castle and said: We cannot light the fire, we cannot speak the prayers, we do not know the place, but we can tell the story of how it was done. And the story which he told had the same effect as the actions of the other three.[30]

Now, could there be more eloquent testimony to the imaginative reconstruction of the past? Every author creates not merely his own precursors, but the very record of their activity, and I should not like to see historians exempted from this responsibility.

Read 16 March 1986

29. Valuable correctives in *Biblical Archaeology Today—Proceedings of the International Congress on Biblical Archaeology*, Jerusalem, April 1984, Jerusalem 1985, esp. F.M. Cross (pp. 9–15), B. Mazar (pp. 16–20), Y. Yadin (pp. 21–27), H. Tadmor (pp. 260–268), and E.E. Urbach (pp. 502–509).

30. S.J. Agnon, in G. Scholem, *Major Trends in Jewish Mysticism*, New York 1961, pp. 349–350.

THE SECTARIAN MILIEU: ANNOTATIONS AND GLOSSARY

In compiling these notes and glosses for the reprint of *The Sectarian Milieu*, I have tried to keep in mind the needs of a variety of types of readers. The original text does not pose the same problems as does *Quranic Studies* since in this work Wansbrough does not use Arabic script, and he frequently provides his own translations for the Arabic words and phrases that he transliterates. I have, therefore, only provided literal translations of Arabic when to do so seems to make the argument more comprehensible or more interesting. I have concentrated instead on explaining some of the allusions and references that various readers might find puzzling, many of which I did not understand when I first read the book, and some words or names that may be common to those familiar with the study of Islam but puzzling to those who are not. In view of the large number of mentions of individuals and events occurring in traditional Islamic sources, however, it is not possible here to provide commentary on, or identification of, most of them. Most readers of his book will have at least a general idea of the person or event in question, and more precise knowledge about them is not usually important for understanding the author's arguments.

I have tried to treat in the annotations those items that relate mainly to the specific page on which they occur, and in the glossary terms that are of a more general significance—expressions in Latin, Greek and other European languages, terms of rhetoric, terms commonly used in Biblical, Judaic and Christian (and occasionally Islamic) studies, etc.

I am grateful for help given by David Eisenberg, Andrew Rippin, and Stefan Sperl, but I am responsible for any imperfections and inaccuracies that remain.

ANNOTATIONS

Page x	
Nun weiss man doch . . .	Now we know then how that all really happened.
Page 2	
the *Sīra* of Ibn Isḥāq . . .	W. here refers to the titles of two of the earliest and most important collections of reports about events in the life of Muhammad; in the following discussion, as in scholarship generally, *sīra* and *maghāzī* are sometimes used to refer to genres of traditional Muslim biographical material pertaining to Muhammad's life; in common usage *maghāzī* focuses on his life, especially the military aspects of it, in Medina; *sīra* on his life more generally
Page 3	
exegical	read: exegetical
Page 4	
shayāṭīn	daemons
man istaraqa ʾl-samʿ	whoever hears by stealth [what takes place in the heavenly court]
Page 5	
Anṣār	those Medinese who supported the Prophet
ḥamalat al-ʿarsh	literally, the bearers of God's throne
ʿaqr wa-nahr	wounding and slaughtering
shiʿb	gorge, ravine
wa-ṣṭafāhu wa-ṭahhara . . .	and He chose him and purified his heart and inside
muḥājar	the site of the [Prophet's] mission
nahr	read: *naḥr*

Page 6

qiyāma	[day of] resurrection/judgment
ba'th	the resurrection of the dead
ḥisāb	the [final] reckoning
mizān	the scales [of the day of judgment]
janna	paradise
nār	hell
tannur	oven
ṣalāt al-khams	the five [daily] prayers
arḍ bayna ḥarratayn	literally, a region situated between two lava beds

Page 8

al-ḥuṭama	a term that occurs twice in the Qur'ān (104:4, 5) apparently as a name for hell; it is usually understood to mean "that which smashes"
wa-narithuhu mā yaqūl	We (God) shall inherit from him what he says

Page 9

Muṭallib	read: Muṭṭalib

Page 10

mā kānū bihi yastahzi'ūn	that at which they used to mock

Page 12

aḥzāb	literally, parties or confederates, the title of sura 33 of the Qur'ān, and understood to refer to the coalition of Muhammad's opponents that attacked him at the battle of the trench (al-khandaq) in year 5AH

Page 14

parashah	sections of the Torah read as part of the Jewish liturgy
paraenasis	read: paraenesis

Page 15

ay	that is to say, namely, i.e.
basmala	the formula "in the name of God, the Merciful, the Compassionate" (*bi-smi llāhi l-raḥmāni l-raḥīm*)

Page 16

Quranic sigla	the problematic single letters that occur at the beginning of several suras

mutashābihāt	Q. 3:7 says that the Book contains some *āyas* that are *muḥkam* and others that are *mutashābih*; the Muslim exegetical tradition provides various interpretations of what this means; a common understanding is that *muḥkam* means clear or plain, and *mutashābih* ambiguous or obscure
ahl al-kitāb	literally, people of the book; commonly used to refer to Jews, Christians, and other monotheists whose religions were tolerated under Islamic law

Page 17

mā ʿalayhi abāʾunā	that which our fathers followed

Page 18

bet ha-midrash	(Jewish) house of study

Page 19

Buʿāth	a fight, according to Islamic tradition, between Aws and Khazraj, the two Arab tribes of Yathrib/Medina, each supported by allies from among the Jews of the town
aḥzāb	see note to p. 12
yuʾminūn bil-jibt . . .	they believe in the *jibt* and the *ṭāghūt* [two relatively obscure words that relate to idols]

Page 20

and declared that Ezra	read: and not declared that Ezra

Page 21

mimmā tushrikūna	literally, from what you associate [as an object of worship with God]
al-sāʿa	literally, the Hour [of the end of the world]
lā narāhu muttasiqan...	we do not think it is as well-ordered as the Torah
taḥaddī	referring to verses in the Qurʾān that challenge the opponents to produce anything comparable to it

Page 23

baʿd al-mawt	literally, after death, *postmortem*
ḥammālat al-ḥaṭab	literally, the [female] carrier of firewood
mā qaddamat yadāhu	literally, what his hands have sent forth, i.e., his deeds

bayna yadayhi	literally, in front of him
kunya	the part of the traditional Arabic name, signalled by the presence of Abū (father of) or Umm (mother of) that indicates that a person is the progenitor of a named descendant; sometimes it is used conventionally or metaphorically as a sort of nickname (as Abū Lahab, father of flame)
Märchen	fables, fairy tales
Abū Ḥakam	literally, the father of a man of judgment/discretion, contrasted with Abū Jahl, the father of ignorance

Page 24

Najrān martyrs	Christians of Najrān in the Yemen, reportedly killed for their refusal to submit to the demands of the Jewish king that they accept Judaism; in the exegetical tradition the "men of the trench" (*aṣḥāb al-ukhdūd*) of Q 85:4 are frequently identified as the martyrs of Najrān

Page 25

ayyām al-ʿarab	literally, days of the Arabs; narrative accounts of battles and feuds between Arab tribes in pre-Islamic Arabia

Page 26

ghazwa	raid
the caravan or the army	according to the tradition, the battle of Badr occurred as a result of a raid made by the Muslims of Yathrib/Medina against a caravan of the pagan Meccans; when the Meccans learned of the raiding party they sent an army to protect the caravan

Page 27

ayyām Allāh	days/battles of God (cf., *ayyām al-ʿarab*)
maghāzī . . . mabʿath	see note to p. 2 above; *mabʿath* refers to the traditions about the comissioning of Muhammad as a prophet in contrast to those about his military exploits; in broad terms *mabʿath* refers to the Meccan period of Muhammad's life, *maghāzī* to the Medinan

Page 28

fa-laqad dhālika ʿibratan — that was an example/premonition

fa-kāna hādhā bayyinan — this was a clear sign/proof

qawl al-ʿarab — what the Arabs would say; their opinion

iḥdā al-ṭāʾifatayn — one of the two parties (see p. 26)

alleviation (*takhfīf*) — a reference to the expression *khaffafa llāhu ʿankum* (God has lightened your burden) at the opening of Q.8:66; the verse goes on to assure the believers that they could overcome enemies twice their number, and commentators commonly understood this to mean that, because of the as yet lack of development of the Muslim community, God did not yet impose on it the duty of fighting against much larger odds

yaʿnī and *yaqūl* — [God] means, and [God] says

Page 29

the Islamic 'fifth' — the portion of the booty to be set aside for the state/Imām according to the Islamic law of war

Page 30

umm al-kitāb — literally, the mother of the book

malḥama — trial; in the Bible the Hebrew *milḥomōt* (literally, battles, plural of *milḥomā*) is used in connection with the wars of God; in Arabic *malāḥim* (plural of *malḥama*) commonly has an eschatological connotation, referring to the trials that will precede the world's end

Page 34

mubtadaʾ (genesis) — the category of *sīra* material concerned with the history of Arabia and the prophet's ancestors before his birth

Hijra calendar — the Islamic era, beginning with the lunar year in which Muhammad's move (*hijra*) to Yathrib/Medina occurred (corresponds to 622–623 CE); the calendar is said to have been adopted by the nascent Muslim polity in 16/637

Page 35

'Constitution' or Umma document	a document, preserved in Ibn Isḥāq's *Sīra* and elsewhere, apparently regulating the relationship between the prophet, the Arab tribes, and the Jews in Medina
Muṭallib	read: Muṭṭalib

Page 37

dīwān	the state records, concerned primarily with the payments due to the fighters and their dependants

Page 41

Ebionites	the name given to a group of Jewish Christians (Jews who maintained observance of the Law but honoured Jesus as a prophet)
Pentateuch	the first five books of the Bible
Marcionite	associated with the second-century Christian, later regarded as heretical, Marcion
khilāfa	caliphate
Samaritan schism	the split between the Samaritans and the rest of ancient Judaism, symbolised by Samaritan rejection of the Jerusalem temple

Page 42

Biblical prophets	referring to those prophets whose histories are recounted or whose books are included in the section of the Hebrew Bible referred to as "the Prophets"

Page 43

Jesus and Ezra	Q. 9:30. The Jews say that ʿUzayr is the son of God, the Christians that the Messiah is the son of God. . . .
ʿĀshūrāʾ	the tenth day of the [first] month; the day of Atonement
elōhē abōtēnū	the God of our fathers

Page 44

Dieu a besoin des hommes	God needs mankind
gillūlīm	literally, pieces of filth or dung; figuratively, idols

Page 46

Najāshī	The name (= Negus?) given a Christian Ethiopian

	ruler or governor who is said to have secretly accepted Islam when he learned of it from the Muslim exiles who took refuge in his territory
qarana fil-ḥibāl	he linked together in the ropes
rabaṭa/kattafa	he tied, bound, fettered, shackled

Page 47

ḥurma, muhājar, ḥajj	sanctity/inviolability, place of exile/mission, festival/pilgrimage

Page 48

dalā'il al-nubuwwa	signs/proofs of prophethood; an important topic of *sīra* reports and the focus of a distinct genre of Islamic literature

Page 51

Qumran	the sectarian Jewish community, existing around the beginning of the Christian era, associated with the Dead Sea Scrolls; adjective is Qumranic
malḥama, etc.	the list exemplifies religious vocabulary widely understood as adaptations into Arabic from other languages: *malḥama*: battle, eschatological tribulation (cf. Hebrew *milḥomā*); *rāhib*: Christian monk, literally [God-]fearer (cf. Pahlavi *tarsāk*, Christian); *dajjāl*: deceiver, anti-Christ (cf. Syriac *daggālā*); *aḥbār*: learned, usually Jewish, scholars, religious elite (cf. Hebrew *ḥabērīm*); *ummī*: gentile, religiously unlearned, illiterate (cf. Hebrew *'ammē hā-aretz*); *iblīs*: a name of the Devil (cf. Greek *diabolos*)

Page 52

adoptionist Christology	the belief that Jesus was fully human but was chosen by God as His son (or, for Islam, His messenger)
quarrel about Qumran and the Karaites	W. here refers to the academic debate about whether, on the basis of some similar doctrines, the Karaite movement in medieval Judaism should be seen as a historical development of the Qumran community, or whether Karaism should be understood as having independently reinvented some of the ideas of Qumran

Page 54

Damascus Document	first known from medieval mss, discovered in Cairo in the late nineteenth century, the provenance of the document inspired much academic debate; when the Dead Sea Scrolls began to be recovered in the mid-twentieth century, extensive fragments of it were found among them and it is now accepted as a product of the Qumran community
moreh ha-ṣedeq	The Teacher of Righteousness; in the scrolls the title accorded the leader of the Qumran community, and its privileged interpreter of scripture

Page 61

wujūh/naẓā'ir/mushtabihāt	meaning/equivalence/ambiguities (in words or phrases)

Page 62

kāna	He/it is
la'alla	perhaps, haply

Page 68

tabāraka, subḥān, al-ḥamd	all expressing praise of God
mulk, mā fil-samawāt wal-arḍ	referring to God's power and majesty over "everything in the heavens and on earth"

Page 69

shōṭerīm	a word that occurs in some biblical passages, apparently referring to an officer or official, but the precise significance is debated; the root seems to point to an association with writing and documents
mesōrōt (anshē ha-ṣerekh)	two expressions that occur in connection with military matters in the Qumran scrolls; various interpretations have been proposed; both the roots *m-s-r* and *ṣ-r-k* seem to be associated with the idea of tying or fastening

Page 70

waḥy matluw	revelation existing in a text that is recited/read aloud
waḥy ghayr matluw	revelation not existing in recited texts

Page 71

waṣiyya/naṣṣ	the designation of the legitimate Shī'ī Imam by his predecessor

Page 74

majūsī	usually refers to Zoroastrians

Page 75

al-nusuk wal-ḍaḥāyā	W.'s interpretation—"propitiatory and ritual sacrifice"—is open to question
ka-dhālika	like that, just so

Page 76

ḥadīth al-ifk	literally, the account of the lie (about 'Ā'isha)

Page 79

muḥāribūn	those who fight (against God and His prophet)
asmakhtā	support; a biblical text used to support a regulation not yet envisaged in the Bible

Page 80

miqrā and *mishnah*	written and oral Torah; i.e., scripture in general (and especially the Pentateuch, the first five books of the Bible), and rulings claimed to have been revealed to Moses at the same time as the written Torah but transmitted orally until committed to writing in the Mishnah

Page 81

'ilm al-rijāl	the science of 'men', i.e., tradents
ṭabaqāt	literally, classes; the arrangement of the reports on tradents according to generations, places of habitation, and other principles
jarḥ wa-ta'dīl	literally, wounding and putting in order; the classification of tradents as reliable, weak, etc.
taḥammul al-'ilm	literally, the bearing/carrying of knowledge

Page 84

genos epideiktikon	a laudatory speech
Quintilian	first-century CE scholar of Latin rhetoric

Page 86

consensus doctorum	the agreement of the scholarly elite
communis opinio	the general view of the community
tawātur	the transmission of a report or text by several independent lines of tradents
ahl al-ʿilm	literally, those with knowledge: the scholarly elite, those who collect and transmit tradition

Page 87

ikhtilāf al-fuqahāʾ	differences of opinion among the legal scholars

Page 90

fī sabīl allāh	on the path of God
dalāʾil al-nubuwwa	signs of/proofs of prophethood

Page 92

mujāhid	someone who carries out holy war

Page 94

fifth (*khums*)	in Islamic law that part of the booty reserved as the share of the imam

Page 95

rajul ṣallā laka sajda wāḥida	literally, a man who has performed a single prostration to you in prayer
wafāt bi-balad rasūlika	literally, death in the land of your apostle
ʿan ahl al-ʿilm	on the authority of the transmitters of tradition

Page 96

fayʾ	technically, immovable spoils that became the property of the whole community not merely of those who had fought for it
taḍmīn	Arabic term for the literary device *inclusio*

page 97

targhīb fīl-jihād	literally, arousing a desire for (fighting in) the holy war
codex/*muṣḥaf*	i.e., a written text in the form of a volume

Page 98

historia ecclesiastica	ecclesiastical/Church history; a genre of Christian literature used here to refer also to Jewish, Islamic and other similar types of works
ecclesia	Church

Page 99

Grosskirche	literally, great Church; a broad, inclusive group

Page 100

karūbiyyūn:muqarrabūn	the Arabic word, modelled upon the Hebrew, for a class of angels ("cherubs") is assimilated to an Arabic root with connotations of nearness (understood as those near to God's throne)
qiyāma:qāma	the Arabic word, modelled upon the Syriac, for resurrection is assimilated to an Arabic root connoting standing
umūr al-islām	the matters/contents of Islam

Page 101

bay'at al-nisā'	the women's pledge of allegiance
bay'at al-ḥarb	the pledge of allegiance expressing willingness to fight
fa-'araḍa 'l-islām	he set forth the requirements of Islam
fa-kallamahu bil-islām	he spoke to him about the requirements of Islam
wa-talā 'l-qur'ān	he recited the Qur'ān
wa-qara'a 'alayhi 'l-qur'ān	he recited the Qur'ān to him
ḥanīf	a word commonly seen as non-Arabic in origin; in Arabic it usually designates someone who has adopted monotheism but not a specific monotheist religious identity; often identified as a follower of the religion of Abraham
ṣābi'	another word commonly seen as of non-Arabic origin; it has been suggested that it relates to the Mandaean baptist sect of the Sabeans

Page 102

hādhā Muḥammad wal-ṣubāt ma'ahu	this Muḥammad and the *ṣābi'*s with him
arbor and *lumen*	tree and light

Page 103

ʿāqib, sayyid and *usquf*	the titles ascribed to the three leaders of the Christian delegation; the precise significance of the first two is unclear but they seem to refer to secular authority; *usquf* is Arabic for bishop
qibla	direction faced in prayer

Page 104

min turāb	from dust, from the earth

Page 105

ilayka ʾl-maṣīr	the journey leads to you
ʿalā ʾl-ʿarsh istawā	[God] settled on the throne
ʿalā kull shayʿ qadīr	[God has] power over everything
sharaḥa ṣadrahu	he cut open his heart
maʿādh allāh	God forbid!
fiʾl-hudā wa-dīniʾl-ḥaqq	following guidance and the religion of truth
in shāʾ allāh	if God wills it
wa-hum yastahzūna bihi	they were mocking him
fa-kallamahu ʾllāh taklīman	God addressed him in speech
fī kull umma wa-kull qawm	in every community and among every people
yawm al-qiyāma	the day of judgment/resurrection (see note to p. 100)
al-ḥamdu lillāhi ʾlladhī . . .	praise be to God who . . .
ʿadhāb alīm	a bitter punishment
fanẓur kayfa . . .	see/consider how . . .
ʿadhāb al-jaḥīm	the punishment of hell
ahlu baytihi	the people of his house
ahlu ʾl-kitāb	the people of the Book
aḥbār al-yahūd	the scholars of the Jews (see note to p. 51)
iblīs	a name of the Devil (see note to p. 51)
ḥawāriyyūn	apostles (of Jesus)
karūbiyyūn	cherubim (see note to p. 100)
ṣiddīq	truthful, righteous

Page 106

uqnūm	hypostasis, person of the Trinity
lāhūt	divinity, divine nature
nāsūt	human nature

Page 107

ab, ibn, rūḥ al-qudus	Father, Son and Holy Ghost

Page 109

wie es eigentlich gewesen	as it really was
takhṣīṣ	specification
tafsīr	interpretation
taḥwīl	modification

Page 111

taʿṭīl [*sic*]	*taʿṭīl* would normally mean something like nullification or abnegation

Page 112

middot	rules governing the interpretation of scripture
innamā hiya umma bi-sharāʾiʿihā	it is its laws alone that make it a community
ʿudhr	excuse, permission for something
rukhṣa	concession

Page 113

tawātur/ijmāʿ/ṣaḥāba	multiple transmission/the agreement of the community/the companions of the prophet (all used as arguments guaranteeing the integrity of scripture)

Page 114

ʿilla	cause, reason (the following locutions all express the idea of something happening or existing because of something else)

Page 116

nisba	a relative adjective formed from the name of a person, tribe, town, profession, etc. usually by the addition of a long "i" (*ī*); e.g., Mālik > Mālikī

Page 119

classical *fitna*	the period of warfare among the Arabs/Muslims between 656 and 661 CE; ʿAlī and Muʿāwiya were rival contenders for the caliphate

Page 120

dīn al-ʿarab	religion of the Arabs
ayyām al-ʿarab	tales of battles between tribes and clans
ʿarabiyya	Arabic language
Kulturnation . . . Staatsnation	a national identity based on a common culture, compared with one based on a state

Page 121

Interessengemeinschaft	a community based on common interests
Lebensgemeinschaft	a community with a common way of life
qawm, nās, ahl, jamāʿa	all words referring, often imprecisely, to people in groups (tribes, military or other groups, families, communities, etc.)

Page 122

nisba suffix	see note to p. 116
Essene, Therapeutes	names given to two religious tendencies (the former often described as cenobite and mystical, the latter as healing), commonly described as sects of the early Christian period
Benei Berit	Sons of the Covenant
Benai Qyama	Sons of the Resurrection
laikos/gentilis	not a member of a religious elite

Page 124

riwāya (*traditio*)	(knowledge acquired from the study of) tradition
dirāya (*ratio*)	(knowledge acquired by the use of) reason

Page 125

tawātur/ittiṣāl	wide attestation/continuity (of transmission)
Es ist ja eigentlich. . . .	It is indeed a curious quirk of history that western Rome was destined to begin to exert the determinative influence upon a religion which had its cradle in the Orient, so as to give it that form in which it was to achieve worldwide recognition. But as an otherworldly religion that despises this world and inflexibly orders life in accord with a superhuman standard that has descended from heaven, or as a complicated mystery cult for religious and intellectual connoisseurs, or as a tide of

fanatical enthusiasm that swells today and ebbs tomorrow, Christianity could never have achieved such recognition.

[W. Bauer, *Orthodoxy and Heresy in Earliest Christianity*, translated by a team from the Philadelphia Seminar on Christian Origins, edited by Robert A. Kraft and Gerhard Krodel, Philadelphia 1971, 240]

Page 126

dass die Geschichte eine legitimierende Kraft besitzt. . . .	that history possesses the power to legitimise, that the state follows its own interests, aiming to maintain and extend its strength, and that the ruling the authority is hardly to be distinguished from the state
Die politische Gemeinschaft des Islam . . .	The political community of Islam grew out of the religious community.

Page 129

zanādiqa, dahriyyūn falāsifa	terms used polemically to designate followers of religious or philosophical movements portrayed as atheistic or non-monotheist

Page 131

nomos, numen, ecclesia	law/regulation; divinity/spirituality; church/community of believers

Page 133

al-nāmūs al-akbar . . .	the great *nomos* that came to Moses

Page 136

an yakūn ākhir al-amr muwāfiqan li-awwalih	that a thing's end be consistent with its beginning

Page 137

legitimierende Kraft	the power to legitimise (see the quotation from Wellhausen on p. 126)
al-qur'ān wa-sā'ir kalām allāh (n. 3)	the Qur'ān and the rest/other forms of God's speech

Page 138

Wahrsage, Deutung	literally, oracle/prediction, interpretation/explanation

Page 140

qurʾān, ruʾyā, khabar	a (part of the) Qurʾān, a dream/vision, a report
kashf, ishrāq	two words, often both translated as illumination, referring to the experience of the divine attainable by a mystic
istinbāṭ	eliciting or revealing a hidden meaning
qadmōniōt, raz nihyah	former things, the secret of what has come to pass
bat qōl	the divine voice from heaven; a form of revelation below prophecy

Page 141

clôture logocentrique	literally, logocentric closure; the structuralist and post-modern critique of the idea that words designate real things and therefore have determinate meanings that can be fully understood
le style collectif (*écriture*)	the commonly accepted literary norms of a society
C'est ici que l'expression . . .	It is here that the expression "intellectual musing" takes on its full meaning: philosophical-religious discourse functions like poetical discourse except that it uses concept instead of metaphor, argumentation instead of recollection, and slowness of explanation instead of the spontaneity of the cry of grief or rapture. The philosopher-theologian and the fundamentalist (*uṣūliyy*) theologian, like the poet, surrender to the lyrical pressure of a universe of meanings concentrated in a vocabulary and grammar that perpetuate the substitution of an *imagined* but *coherent* world for a real one.

Page 142

n. 1 Ainsi, l'effort . . .	Thus the effort to make religion a science changes science into a religion.
l'histoire vraie	true history
l'histoire réelle	real/actual history
un message divin . . .	a divine message *already linked to a realization in history*
des réussites temporelles	temporal successes
déjà vécue	previously experienced
déjà éprouvé	previously tested
n. 3 La raison affirme . . .	Reason thus asserts a methodological supremacy,

	but in order to put it at the service of a creed. Thence arises the arbitrariness that reason uses regarding those religions that cannot be reduced to Islam.
tanzīh:bilā kayfa	the rejection of anthropomorphism: the refusal to apply reason to support a belief
beatific vision	the believer's vision of God after death

Page 144

qawl, kalima, amr	speech, word, command

Page 148

Il est peut-être de la nature . . .	Perhaps it is in the nature of Islam to preserve its fundamental major ideas intact without ever fundamental major ideas intact without ever making them real except through this or that political form inspired by historical contingencies.
idéal historique concret	a realized historical ideal
théocratie laïque et égalitaire	an egalitarian and non-elitist theocracy
nomocratie	governed by a system of law

Page 154

naql mutawātir	transmission that is continuous and widespread

GLOSSARY

ad	(literally, to) usually indicates that a phrase or passage in a text is a comment or gloss upon a passage of scripture (e.g., *ad* Q.2:85–6)
ad hoc	for a particular purpose and for a limited time
ad hominem	with reference to a named individual
aetiological	concerned with the origin of a thing; relating to a story purporting to explain why something is as it is
alliteration	using consecutive words that begin with the same or similar sounds
anagoge	raising something from a lower to a higher, more spiritual, level; interpreting a mundane event in a way that gives it religious significance
anaphora	the repetition of a word or phrase in successive clauses
antinomianism	going against the law; regarding the law as having no authority
antonomastic	relating to the use of a noun with a limited meaning (especially a proper name) to express a general idea, or to the use of an adjective or adjectival phrase as a personal or proper name
aphorism	definition; short maxim
apocalyptic	(commonly) referring to the dramatic events connected with the end of the world
apodictic	relating to a powerful, usually divine, command
apologia	an argument in defence of something
apophthegm	a terse and pithy saying
apud	in, contained in
aretalogy	narration of the wonderful deeds of a god or hero
autodidacticus	a self-taught person
B.	abbreviation of *banū* = sons (of), or tribe; b. = son of; bt. = daughter of
basileia	those parts of a prayer, homily or such expressing recognition of God's majesty and power
bona fides	tokens of good faith or sincerity
calque	words in one language modelled upon those of another; it may be applied also to such things as ideas and institutions

canonical	relating to a body of texts (canon) that a particular community accepts as especially authoritative, frequently implying that they cannot be altered in any way; non-canonical refers to texts excluded from the canon, sub-canonical to those possibly relating to the canon but existing in forms significantly different from the canonical versions
catechism	a list of beliefs, often set out in question and answer form
causa	cause
caveat	warning
centripetal	tending to force things from the periphery towards the centre
Christology	doctrines concerning the nature of Jesus
cognate	usually here indicates words in different languages that are related to one another because they have developed from a hypothetical common root word (e.g., Arabic *jalāʾ* and Hebrew *galūt*, both meaning exile)
contingent	something the existence of which depends on the existence of something else
coproscopy (Ar. *qiyāfa*)	divination from human or animal feces
de novo	from out of nothing, completely new
diachronic	relating to the development of things over time; assuming that two or more things represent different stages in an historical evolution (opposed to synchronic, refusing to make conclusions about an historical sequence)
dialogue devant le prince	debate staged in the presence of the ruler
docetic	relating to docetism—the doctrine that Christ's body was not of human substance (and therefore he could not have died on the cross)
doxology	a formulaic passage in a prayer, homily or such, expressing praise of God
dramatis personae	the characters of a drama; the participants in a series of events
dynamic	used here to refer to a narrative that has been generated by a scriptural passage (cf. exegetical, where the narrative attempts more explicitly to supply an interpretation of a scriptural passage)
e silentio	arguing from silence; deducing the non-existence

	of something from the fact that there is no historical record of it
ecclesial	related to a specifically *religious* community
einfache Formen	literally the "simple/basic forms" which, according to the influential work (1st ed., Halle, 1929) of the Dutch scholar, André Jolles, constitute the universally attested building blocks out of which individual and culturally specific literary works are made
elevatio	see *anagoge*
ellipsis	the omission of words or information necessary for complete understanding; the adjective is elliptic(al)
eponym	the name of the (claimed) founder or ancestor
eschaton	the last times, strictly the period between death and the last judgment, but commonly referring to the end of the world
etymon	a word from which another has been derived
eulogy	a speech of praise; that part of a prayer, homily, etc. concerned with the praise of God
exemplification	in W.'s usage here, the attachment of a passage of scripture to the report of a mundane event in order to imbue the latter with greater significance; cf. *anagoge* and *elevatio*
ex post facto	something that follows something else in time and is dependent on it, whereas it may seem to be prior to it
fait accompli	something already achieved or done
forensic	associated with public gatherings
gnosis	truth or knowledge made known to its recipient by revelation or inspiration and not available to mankind in general; gnosticism refers to a body of religious beliefs and attitudes centred around the concept of gnosis
haggadah	a term of Jewish scholarship (literally meaning "the remainder") referring to non-legal materials, including stories about biblical and other figures and events important in Jewish history and tradition
halakhah	a term of Jewish scholarship referring to discussions or literature primarily concerned with law; halakhot are legal regulations

Heilsgeschichte	*see* salvation history; the adjective is heilsgeschichtlich
heresiography	a literary genre concerned with listing and describing what are perceived as heresies that have arisen in the history of religion
heterodoxy	beliefs that differ from those claimed to be orthodox
heuristic	helping to account for something
histoire événementielle	history understood as a series of (generally unconnected) events; often used as a term of polemic by post-modernists against more traditional historians
imām	a word with multiple related meanings; the title of the supreme leader of the Islamic community (*umma*) but connoting also the idea of model or example to be imitated
incipit	start, beginning
inclusio	a literary device that creates a frame for a passage by grouping similar materials at the beginning and end of it; frequently used in the Bible
in foro externo	in a public setting
intercalation	interpolation of additional periods of time into a standard calendar year, forbidden in Islam and said to have been a feature of the pagan period in Arabia (*jāhiliyya*)
ipsissima verba	the precise words
isnād	a term of Islamic scholarship referring to the "chain" of people who have transmitted a report or item of literature over time
isokola	the use, for rhetorical effect, of clauses or periods of equal length
isometric	in poetry, words or phrases with the same metre (rhythm)
K	abbreviation of *Kitāb*, book
kat' exochen	above all, pre-eminently
kerygmatic	relating to the proclamation or assertion of a perceived truth; kerygma ("proclamation") is a term used in scholarship on early Christianity to refer to the content of early Christian preaching
liberum arbitrium	free will; the dispute about whether human acts result from a free choice or are in some way determined
lingua franca	a common language shared by different groups

lingua sacra	sacred language
litany	a series of short prayers/petitions within a religious service, led by a prayer leader and responded to by the congregation
loci probantes	proof texts; passages of a text selected to support a particular argument
masoretic	a term of Jewish scholarship relating to the field of study concerned with establishing and maintaining the correct text of scripture
messiology	doctrines concerning the messiah figure (in Islamic terminology, Mahdī)
metanoia	a change of mind
midrashic	a term of Jewish scholarship referring to the development and elaboration of scriptural passages and allusions, including narratives that concerned figures and events from the Bible
mise en scène	putting an event, saying, etc. into a particular setting
Mishnaic	referring to the Mishna, a third-century Jewish collection of primarily legal discussions, and an authoritative text of Rabbinical Judaism
morphological	relating to the study of form or the rules that govern changes in form (usually here of words, phrases, literary features, etc.)
Muhājirūn	those Meccan supporters of Muhammad who migrated to Yathrib/Medina to join him there
nomism	attachment to a law
nomothetic	relating to the giving of laws; a nomothete is a lawgiver
oneiromancy	divination by dreams
ontological	related to a concern with the essence of things
ornatus	a rhetorical flourish or decoration
pace	literally, peace; usually in a footnote, indicates that the argument of the author conflicts with that of the work referred to in the note
parabolic	metaphorical, of the nature of a parable
paradigmatic	relating to the following of a model or example
paradosis	tradition; the handing on of received material
paraenesis	exhortation
parallelism	expressing in consecutive verses or clauses the same or similar ideas in different words; a rhyme in concepts rather than sounds

paraphrastic	of the nature of a paraphrase (expressing the meaning of a word or phrase in other words)
parousia	the second coming of Christ at the end of time
passim	at various places throughout the work referred to
per antiphrasin	by the use of words in a sense opposite to their true meaning
pericope	a short passage, usually of scripture, used in worship or as the basis of a homily
periphrasis	the explanation of a word or phrase by a longer or more elaborate version of it
pesher	the technical term in the Qumran community for the interpretation of scripture, including the interpretation of Biblical prophecies as foretelling current events as part of the apocalyptic drama
phenomenological	existing as an abstract concept of something (an institution, practice, etc.) as distinct from specific historical instances of it
pluralis majestatis	the plural of majesty; the use of the royal "We" when God or an earthly ruler refers to himself
polemic	an assault in words
polygenesis	the independent generation by different social groups or individuals of the same or similar ideas, institutions, literary forms, etc.
polysemy	the phenomenon of single words with a multiplicity of meanings
praeparatio evangelica	a preparation for/harbingers of the prophetic mission
pro et contra	for and against
prognostic exegesis	interpreting a text as foretelling a future event
prolepsis	the anticipation of something that has not yet occurred, anachronism; adjective is proleptic
prophetical logia	a body of oral or literary materials that had acquired sanctity or special importance and from which the canonical scripture was drawn
protokollon	a stereotypical formula introducing a document or other literary unit such as a prayer or story
Psalter	the section of the Bible containing the psalms
pseudepigraphy	the fictitious attribution of a text to an author
qibla	an Islamic term referring to the direction to be faced in prayer and certain other matters of ritual
raison d'être	reason for existence
ratio	reason

reflex	the way in which one thing (such as a text, word or a story) reproduces important features or attributes of something else
reification	interpreting an idea or mental image as, and transforming it into, a real thing
restitutio principii	restitution of the beginnings
salvation history	a genre of writing that shares many features (such as narrative structure) with other forms of history but is primarily concerned with the assertion and substantiation of a religious message or truth; it is not always easy to distinguish from other types of history
scil.	*scilicet*; to wit, that is to say, namely
Sitz im Leben	setting in life; a concept of Biblical Form Criticism, referring to the social setting in which a given literary unit is likely to have been used
sondage	sounding, testing; judging the whole of something through the assessment of part of it
soteriology	the doctrine(s) concerning salvation
Sprachgebärden	literally "speech gestures/acts"; recurrent expressions in a given language that may mean more (or less) than is evident from the words used
Stoffgeschichte	in W.'s own words: "the isolation of such components as theme and motif" (rather than of morphological constants)
strophic	a composition each line or clause of which is sung/recited to the same tune or rhythm
sub specie aeternitatis	as seen from the viewpoint of God or eternity
sunna	Arabic for custom, tradition; predominantly refers to the exemplary behaviour, words and views of the prophet Muhammad as recorded in the thousands of reports (*ḥadīth*s) about them transmitted in Islam; Muhammad's *sunna* came to be understood as an expression of the divine will and thus a major source of Islamic law alongside the Qur'ān
synonymy	the phenomenon of different words with the same meaning
taxonomic	relating to the science of classification; classificatory
teleological	relating to the perception of design or purpose in a series of events

testimonia	evidence, proofs
thaumaturge	miracle worker
theios aner	divine man
theodicy	justification of belief in God, especially with regard to the imperfections of the world
theologoumena	disputed topics of theological debate
theophany	an appearance or manifestation of God to man
toponym	the name of a place
topos (pl. *topoi*)	a conventional word, expression, theme, or idea that recurs in different contexts
tradent	a transmitter of written or oral tradition
traditio	tradition; see *paradosis*
v.	*versus*, as contrasted with
vaticinatio post eventum/ex eventu	foretelling after the event; appearing to predict something but knowing that it has already occurred
Vorlage	model, prototype (plural Vorlagen)